ASIAN AMERICANS

RECONCEPTUALIZING CULTURE,
HISTORY, POLITICS

edited by
FRANKLIN NG
CALIFORNIA STATE UNIVERSITY,
FRESNO

A GARLAND SERIES

Asian Americans: Reconceptualizing Culture, History, Politics
Franklin Ng, series editor

The Political Participation of Asian Americans: Voting Behavior in Southern California
  Pei-te Lien

The Sikh Diaspora: Tradition and Change in an Immigrant Community
  Michael Angelo

Claiming Chinese Identity
  Elionne L.W. Belden

Transnational Aspects of Iu-Mien Refugee Identity
  Jeffery L. MacDonald

Caring for Cambodian Americans: A Multidisciplinary Resource for the Helping Professions
  Sharon K. Ratliff

Imagining the Filipino American Diaspora: Transnational Relations, Identities, and Communities
  Jonathan Y. Okamura

Mothering, Education, and Ethnicity: The Transformation of Japanese American Culture
  Susan Matoba Adler

MOTHERING, EDUCATION, AND ETHNICITY

THE TRANSFORMATION OF JAPANESE AMERICAN CULTURE

Founders Library
Solebury School
6832 Phillips Mill Rd.
New Hope, PA 18938-9682

SUSAN MATOBA ADLER

Routledge
Taylor & Francis Group
LONDON AND NEW YORK

First published 1998 by Garland Publishing, Inc.

2 Park Square, Milton Park, Abingdon, Oxfordshire OX14 4RN
52 Vanderbilt Avenue, New York, NY 10017

Routledge is an imprint of the Taylor & Francis Group, an informa business

First issued in paperback 2019

Copyright © 1998 Susan Matoba Adler

All rights reserved. No part of this book may be reprinted or reproduced or utilised in any form or by any electronic, mechanical, or other means, now known or hereafter invented, including photocopying and recording, or in any information storage or retrieval system, without permission in writing from the publishers.

Notice:
Product or corporate names may be trademarks or registered trademarks, and are used only for identification and explanation without intent to infringe.

Library of Congress Cataloging-in-Publication Data

Adler, Susan Matoba, 1947–.
　　Mothering, education, and ethnicity : the transformation of Japanese American culture / Susan Matoba Adler.
　　　p.　　cm. — (Asian Americans)
　　Includes bibliographical references and index.
　　ISBN 0-8153-3159-2 (alk. paper)
　　1. Japanese American women—Ethnic identity. 2. Japanese American women—Social life and customs. 3. Japanese American mothers. 4. Japanese American families. 5. Child rearing—United States. 6. Japanese Americans—Education. 7. Intergenerational relations—United States. I. Title. II. Series.
E184.J3A35 1998
305.48'8956073—dc21
　　　　　　　　　　　　　　　　　　　　　　　　　　　98-8583

ISBN 13: 978-0-8153-3159-9 (hbk)
ISBN 13: 978-1-138-97648-1 (pbk)

Contents

PREFACE vii

ACKNOWLEDGMENTS xi

GLOSSARY OF JAPANESE TERMS xiii

1. MY IDENTITY AS A SANSEI 1

2. CHANGE ACROSS THE GENERATIONS 17

3. REARING COMPETENT LEARNERS 41

4. HOW JAPANESE ARE WE? 65

5. THE WORK ETHIC: *DO YOUR BEST!* 107

6. THE TRANSFORMATION OF CULTURE 135

APPENDICES 165

BIBLIOGRAPHY 191

INDEX 201

Preface

Asian Americans in the United States have been visible minorities seen throughout history as "the yellow peril" or "Japs," on one end of the spectrum, and "the model minority" on the other end of the spectrum. Asian American women, including many of the Japanese American women in this study, have also been ascribed with gender related stereotypes such as the sexual "Suzy Wong," the evil "Dragon Lady," the subservient "Madam Butterfly," and as the G.I.'s foreign non-English speaking wife. Rarely are they recognized as the administrators, physicians, artists, teachers, professors, or engineers that define their real-life experiences as working professionals.

There is also an implicit assumption that motherhood and child rearing play key roles in their lives and in their self-identities. This assumption had its origins in the role Asian immigrant women played as "keeper of the household" in addition to that of domestic or farm laborer. These multiple roles helped supplement family income when Asian men, some well educated, were discriminated against in the job market. It also had roots in the Japanese value system that holds a strong tradition of honoring motherhood. The common saying, *Kodomo no tame ni*, meaning to sacrifice personal wants for the sake of the children, has been modeled by generations of Japanese American mothers. Like most immigrants, they worked hard so their children's lives could be better. A contemporary example of the role of totally supportive mother can be seen in the Japanese *kyöiku mama* who contribute to their children's education and well being with conviction and intensity, often defining their own self-worth in relation to their children's academic success (Simons, 1987).

This book, based upon a study of the beliefs of three generations of midwestern Japanese American women, examines the influences of race and ethnicity on beliefs about child rearing and education. It explores how individual Nisei (2nd generation), Sansei (3rd generation) and Yonsei (4th generation) women interpret Japanese cultural concepts brought to America by the Issei (first generation immigrants). It discusses how Japanese the women believe themselves to be, individually, generationally and collectively when reared or while rearing children in environments removed from strong ethnic communities. Through vignettes reflecting multigenerational group conversations about family cohesion, the work ethic, educational expectations and sense of racial and ethnic identity will be shared.

Chapter 1 situates the author as a member of the group being studied and places her within her family and cultural contexts. It tells her story of racial and ethnic identity, development as an educator and mother, and sense self as a scholar and researcher.

Chapter 2 examines the historical and socio-political contexts in which each generational group lived and reared children. The Nisei were reared, then interned as young adults on the west coast before settling in the midwest. The Sansei grew up in generally White middle-class neighborhoods during the 1940's-50's and reared their children during the era of the civil rights and women's movements. The Yonsei were reared in racially similar environments as their parents but during a time when contemporary Japanese influences and the emergence of ethnic studies created new socio-political awarenesses.

Chapter 3 shares both literature and data on the Japanese mother-child *amae* relationship, and questions whether this inter-dependency is perpetuated or transformed by Japanese American mothers. It examines the beliefs and practices of Japanese American mothers as they attempt to develop attributes such as independence and self-sufficiency in their children.

Chapter 4 opens the door on multiple interpretations of identity appropriated by study participants and discusses how they perceived and coped with ascribed stereotypes and racism. Stories are shared about how the women interpreted their "Japaneseness" and of their mixed feelings of affiliation with the Japanese American community. These data are contrasted with some of the perspectives on ethnic and racial identity portrayed in the writings of Japanese American women authors and poets.

Chapter 5 examines the Japanese concepts of *gaman* (to endure) and *gambare* (to persevere) in the context of education and schooling. The concept of role perfectionism illustrated by the often repeated saying, "Do your Best" is compared from Asian and western perspectives. It examines the relationship between effort and achievement and shares the cultural confusion and mixed messages communicated by some Japanese American parents.

Chapter 6 outlines the cultural themes that have emerged and draws conclusions about how Japanese culture has been transformed across the generations. The author identifies some of the influences that generated the construction of a midwestern Japanese American culture and compares the three generational groups in terms of their ethnicity, cultural integration, experience with racism, linguistic facility, knowledge and experience with internment and redress, placement in the historical contexts of the civil rights and women's movements, and educational attainment. This analysis of midwestern Japanese American women

Preface

demonstrates a qualitative difference from the culture that Japanese American women experience in places like California, Hawaii, New York, or where-ever there is a strong ethnic community.

The appendices at the end of the book provide specific information on the study design, theoretical orientation, participants, methodology and additional data tables.

This book attempts to share the voices of thirty-five women, author included, to paint a portrait of one unique subset of Japanese American women. In no way does it represent all midwestern Japanese American women, but rather it illustrates the reality of intra-group ethnic variability. There are many portraits to be shared and strands of commonality that weave its way through a gallery depicting Americans of Asian heritage. To those who don't know us, we are still that visible minority of foreign orientals, but for most of us, we see ourselves as *American with a Japanese face*. We may smile when we meet new immigrants from Japan (we are all *Nikkei*, an inclusive term for those who share Japanese heritage), or we may feel comfortable around other Asian Americans as we see them in mirror image and we face similar alienating discrimination. But most of us don't speak Japanese fluently, nor do we truly understand Asian customs any better than most mainstream European Americans.

So who are we as Japanese Americans in this multicultural, multiracial society? This book takes a gendered glimpse and is a product of my passion to study my family values, my ethnic heritage, and myself as a Japanese American woman, mother and scholar.

Acknowledgments

I would like to express my gratitude to my family, my mentors and colleagues, my readers and editors, and the Japanese American women who openly shared their beliefs and feelings with me, for without them, my study could not have become this book. The original study was funded in part, by the Japanese American Citizens League's 1994 Nisaburo Aibara Memorial Scholarship, for which I am grateful..

My father, Kishio Matoba, gave me the challenge and model to pursue a career in education; my mother, Chiyeko Hiraoka Matoba, gave me the personal strength to pursue my goals and provided tremendous support for my study of Japanese American women. My sister, Jeanne Lynett, and her family provided insight and reflection on our years growing up and on parenting. My brother, John Matoba, and his family, provided a cross-cultural view of child rearing in the 1990s, and an appreciation for the joy of family. My son, Michael Adler, who at 16 years old, is leading me on a *forever journey* through my growth and development as a mother. And, my loving husband, Robert Adler, without whom I could not have done this book, I am indebted for his technical assistance, his editing and layout, and his commitment to my success.

I thank my mentors at the University of Wisconsin-Madison, Stacey Lee, Marianne Bloch, Gary Price, Amy Ling and Carl Grant, for their tremendous knowledge, guidance and critique on the original study. My colleagues at the University of Michigan-Flint, Roy Hanashiro, who assisted on the glossary of Japanese terms, and Bob Barnett, who proofread the manuscript, have given me encouragement and support. I am grateful to Yonsei artist Julie Sittig for her creative contributions and to Gail Nomura and Barbara Kim, in Asian and Pacific American Studies at the University of Michigan-Ann Arbor, for their constructive feedback, and to my editors, Kristi Long and Rebecca Wipfler at Garland Publishing Company, I appreciate their patience and support.

Finally, to the 34 women in my study, I am deeply indebted to you for the conscientious telling of your stories and beliefs and for your caring friendships. Your lived experiences, as midwestern Japanese American women, mothers, grandmothers, Nisei, Sansei and Yonsei, can be shared with others, who strive to rear children who will understand and appreciate their cultural heritages, and develop strong racial and ethnic identities.

Glossary of Japanese Terms

akarui	bright-eyed, cheerful
amae	a dependency relationship primarily between a mother and her children, "indulgent love"
amaeru	to depend and presume upon another's benevolence, kindness, goodwill
amayakasu	to spoil a person
chu	loyalty, faithfulness
doryoku	effort
enryo	reserve, modesty, to withhold.
gaman	endurance, perseverance
gambare	effort, self-motivation
genki	active, spirited, energetic
giri	duty, obligation
ha zu ka shi	embarrassment or reticence
haji	shame
hakihaki	brisk, prompt, clear
hakushi	white sheet, new start, to make a fresh start
hana	Japanese card game
hansei suru	to reflect on one's actions, to think over
happa	half or part Japanese, mixed
hi-ge	another part of *enryo* is the devaluation and open denigration of self and family in public
honne	an individual's true feelings, usually kept private
ie	household, family
Issei	first generation to live in America, immigrants
isshokenmei	utmost self-exertion
ki	basic life force, the soul, see *kokoro*
Kibei	born in the U.S. but reared and educated in Japan for part of their lives
koden	gifts of money at funerals
Kodomo no tame ni	to sacrifice personal wants for the sake of the children
kokoro	the heart, soul, spirit, see *ki*
kuro	hardship
kyōiku mama	Japanese mothers who devote themselves to their children's education and well being with conviction and intensity, often defining their own self-worth in relation to their children's academic success
matsuri	festival

Meiji period	historic period, 1868 - 1912
minyo	folk dancing
Nikkei	an inclusive term for those who share Japanese heritage
ningen	human beings
ningen-rashii	human-like
ninjo	humane sensibility, humaness, warmheartedness
Nisei	second generation, born in America, thus citizens, children of the Issei
ojigi	to bow, to know one's place in the social structure
omiyage	gift
omote	front
on	ascribed obligation, indebtedness
origami	paper folding
oriko	obedient, smart
otonashi	mild, gentle
rikai saseru	to get a person to understand logically
Sansei	third generation Japanese Americans.
sensei	teacher
shikata-ga-nai	it can't be helped
shitsuke	upbringing, training and discipline
soto	public, outside
sunao	compliant, obedient, cooperative
taiko	drum
tatemae	words for public consumption
uchi	private, home
ura	behind, back
wakaraseru	to get a person to understand
Yonsei	fourth generation Japanese Americans

Mothering, Education, and Ethnicity

1. My Identity as a Sansei

Growing up as a third generation Japanese American in the midwest during the post World War II years, I knew little about and thought little about my race and ethnicity. In our family we never spoke about being Japanese American and of course, references to life in the internment camps were never made. I thought of myself as no different from my European American friends, neighbors and classmates. I went to Girl Scout meetings (my mother became a leader), took violin lessons, did my homework, ate spaghetti and teriyaki, wore party dresses with crinolines and rode my new bicycle. Grandma, who spoke "broken" English laced with Japanese words, lived with us and generally did housework and cooking while my mother worked as an executive secretary for the Boy Scouts. My father worked at an art store while attending the University of Wisconsin-Madison to become a teacher. He saw himself as an artist, philosopher and educator. My mother was the realist, the facilitator and voice of common sense in our family.

The effects of prejudice occasionally surfaced but were never directly discussed. We were lead to believe that any racist attitudes and acts of discrimination reflected the perpetrator's prejudices and were certainly not "truths." In family lore, there is one story of a day in the 1950's when I came home from elementary school and announced that I no longer wanted to be Japanese. No doubt I had reacted to some negative taunt like the "slanty" eye gesture depicting Asian features or the harassing comment, "Why don't you go back to where you came from?" My mother tells another family story of how my nephew, who is *happa* or half Japanese came home from school this past year with the same sentiment about his own biracial identity. Has the acceptance of ethnic and racial differences not changed that much in 40 years? Are we oversensitive to issues of race and ethnicity as some have implied? Indeed the political climate in the post World War II years for Japanese Americans might have lead to desires for assimilation, or the need to be "low key" and not stand out, as one participant described it. But in today's multicultural American society, the need for all parents and teachers to prepare children to understand differences and recognize similarities among diverse groups of Americans is vital and pervasive. It is the underpinning for the development of effective cross-cultural communication and mutual respect.

While growing up, there were few cultural artifacts reflecting our Japanese roots in our home and our contact with other Japanese American families was limited to occasional gatherings. The Issei grandparents enjoyed chatting in their native language as they played the Japanese card game *hana*, the Nisei parents socialized by reminiscing or comparing experiences, and the Sansei children just got to know each other. I remember those days as being enjoyable mainly because it gave me new playmates. We attended different schools throughout the community so we had few, if any, Asian American classmates.

I had not specifically thought about being Japanese American or being part of any ethnic community, nor had I experienced any direct racism. The realization that others would define me as Asian rather than American had not been consciously considered. But there began to be indications of change in my awareness. For example, in high school and college I found myself dating primarily White, middle class men, several of whom described me as their "oriental" girlfriend. I also found that some of the Asian male graduate students showed interest in me assuming that I felt some affinity for their foreign culture. And when I became a mother my world view changed from focus on myself as an individual to focus on myself as a nurturer and facilitator of family. Like my mother and grandmothers, child rearing became my new primary quest in life, relegating profession and self-fulfillment to secondary positions.

When I began teaching public school in Colorado, I was asked to serve on multicultural curriculum committees for the school district and encouraged to create an intensive unit on the Japanese culture for my elementary school. Later when I began teaching at the college level, it was assumed that I could teach multicultural education, being a person of color and of Asian ethnicity. On campus, I was invited to participate in politically controversial activities, like the development of an ethnic studies program and the recruitment of minority students. I soon discovered that I was being identified as one of a small group of professors of color, ethnic minorities assumed to be hired through affirmative action initiatives. I saw myself as an early childhood education professor and member of the teacher education department, not some racial pawn or socio-political activist.

Those professional experiences caused me to reflect upon the need and perhaps desire to begin an earnest study of my family's cultural history and of my own identity as a midwestern Japanese American woman, educator, and scholar. I asked my parents to come to class to discuss their experiences as internees at Manzanar. They were eager to help me professionally, but they were reluctant to share particulars about their personal life in camp. Their response to the gravity of what I had asked them to do opened my eyes to a socio-political period and family history that some prefer to keep buried. It is due to the Japanese American Citizen's League's Curriculum Project on Internment that those governmental policies and lived experiences depicting this part of American history are not forgotten.

I believe that one's search for identity is a complex and life-long process. Through my eyes while growing up, the world was White and I was one of them, an "All American Girl." But through the lens of those who didn't personally know me, I was an exotic, foreign oriental, and through the lens of my European American friends I was an assimilated Japanese American. Michael Thornton (1992) writes that identity is both ascribed (defined by others) and appropriated (self-definition). Identity encompasses a variety of areas including race, class, gender, ethnicity, age and religion, which intersect and hold differing priorities for individuals. Thornton (1992) best describes this complex term as follows:

> To have identity means to join with some people and depart from others; it is a dialectic between identification by others and self-identification, between objectively assigned and subjectively appropriated identities. Much of an individual's inner drama involves discovering the assigned identity, reacting to it and recognizing that certain groups are or are not significant (p. 173).

Maria Root (1992), in her study of biracial women, extends this explanation to include the need for people to change their self-reference label in order to adjust to different contexts. She writes: ". . . we can have a different contextual identity in different situations though our sense of self can remain stable . . . The labels Asian, Asian American, Amerasian, or Sansei can refer to a single person at different points in time and in different settings" (p. 183). Whether assigned or appropriated, ethnic identity may be manifested in the form of stereotypes, or generalizations made about a particular group based upon individual impressions. Thus, the model minority, the exotic oriental woman and the yellow peril stereotypes, most commonly associated with Asian Americans, may evolve from specific historical contexts and may be perpetuated without regard to the context, source or reference group.

As my research progressed, I began to understand cross-cultural differences and to appreciate both my race and ethnicity. I learned how value systems of families are constructed from individual and collective experiences, interpretations of ethnic heritage, and the role of race and gender in American society. I learned that Japanese concepts such as *amae*, *gambare*, and *gaman* have influenced my family's value system and the way I was reared. But in my attempt to make sense of these complex issues, I focused on particular concepts and chose to separate race from ethnicity in order to classify the concepts. The classifications are not static nor are they exclusive definitions of that category.

Racial and Ethnic Identities

In this study, "Asian-ness" refers to racial identity, Japaneseness refers to ethnic identity, and "American-ness" refers to one's nationality and citizenship. Racial identity is described from a purely physical perspective (Asian features), and the socio-political identification of Japanese Americans by others outside the race. For example, while living in Colorado Springs, Colorado, a largely military town in the early 1970's, some people assumed that I was either a Korean or Japanese "war bride" or a former Vietnamese "call girl." Even as a public school teacher, I was asked how I learned to speak English so well. Responses such as these continually reinforce the concept of foreignness or "other-ness" rather than Americanness, or citizenship. This challenge to the nationality of Asians, regardless of motive, was the basis for racist beliefs that lead to internment during World War II. Since Japanese Americans could not be distinguished from Japanese nationals (the enemy), assumptions were made about their affiliations.

Japaneseness has been defined in a variety of ways: as a cultural perspective of customs, dress, language and artifacts, as behavior patterns of stoicism and reserve, and as eastern philosophical beliefs based on Buddhism or Confucianism. Most of the women in this study had little contact with Japanese customs, language and dress and considered themselves more European American than Japanese. Japanese culture was not part of their daily lives, therefore, they did not consider Japanese identity as having particular relevance to their basic beliefs or behavior. Although it may have been silently inculcated, a strong Japanese value system had not been consciously identified. This is probably an apt description of how I felt and lived for many years, well into adulthood.

American-ness was a given and perhaps most relevant because most participants saw their Japaneseness embedded in their national identity. Allegiance to America and the strength of its citizenship was unquestioned. In her poem *Mirror, Mirror*, Mitsuye Yamada (1986) describes this concept to her Sansei son. American can mean looking oriental or Asian on the outside, but feeling a sense of belonging to your nation and belief in its fundamental values of life, liberty and the pursuit of happiness, on the inside.

She infers that the term "all American" includes the interpretation of Japanese cultural beliefs taught in Japanese American families. Individuals will integrate these beliefs and make them relevant and applicable to their daily lives in an American multicultural society.

Race and ethnicity are indeed closely related, perhaps inseparable parts of identity formation and depend upon self definition (Root, 1992: Thornton, 1992: Yanagisako, 1985). They can easily overlap. For example, some women in this study saw Japaneseness as a racial marker combining race and culture or they used the terms Japanese and Asian interchangeably. Some indicated that the term Japanese referred to their racial status while American described their cultural orientation. They felt that race was more salient to their identity than being culturally Japanese because they had been categorized as non-White or Asian more often by others than as Japanese or Japanese American. This may be more significant for midwestern Asians because the way in which people commonly make generalizations about others depends in part upon the kind of associations that are made within the community. In Los Angeles, Sansei may be defined as Japanese American because of their association with the JACL (Japanese American Citizen's League) or with a Japanese Buddhist church group. But where there is no strong ethnic community or even a pan-ethnic association, and a relatively small or scattered population of Asians, they may be defined more readily by race than by ethnicity.

Since there did not seem to be a consistency by which participants in the study defined each term, I chose to create the following flow chart which illustrates a logical separation between race and ethnicity and the concepts associated with each category. This study focuses on the women's perspectives on child rearing and education; therefore, I placed the mother-child *amae* relationship and the *gambare* effort aspect of achievement as concepts rooted in Japanese culture under the topic of Ethnic Identity. Since inter-marriage is relatively high for Japanese American women, and Yonsei in the midwest include many biracial women, I used the categories of stereotypes and biracial identity as topics relevant to Racial Identity.

Being an Insider

The ongoing process of articulating the interaction between myself, also a midwestern Japanese American woman, and my participants and of interpreting their words through my filters raises issues of the legitimacy of this kind of subjectivity. Alan Peshkin (1988) views the researcher's own subjectivity as a key contribution to the interpretation of the data because it combines personal perspectives with data collected from participants. "As with assumptions derived from the literature, subjectivities must be made explicit if they are to clarify, rather than obscure, research design and findings," write Howe and Eisenhart (1990, p. 7). Subjectivity operates throughout any research process explains Peshkin.

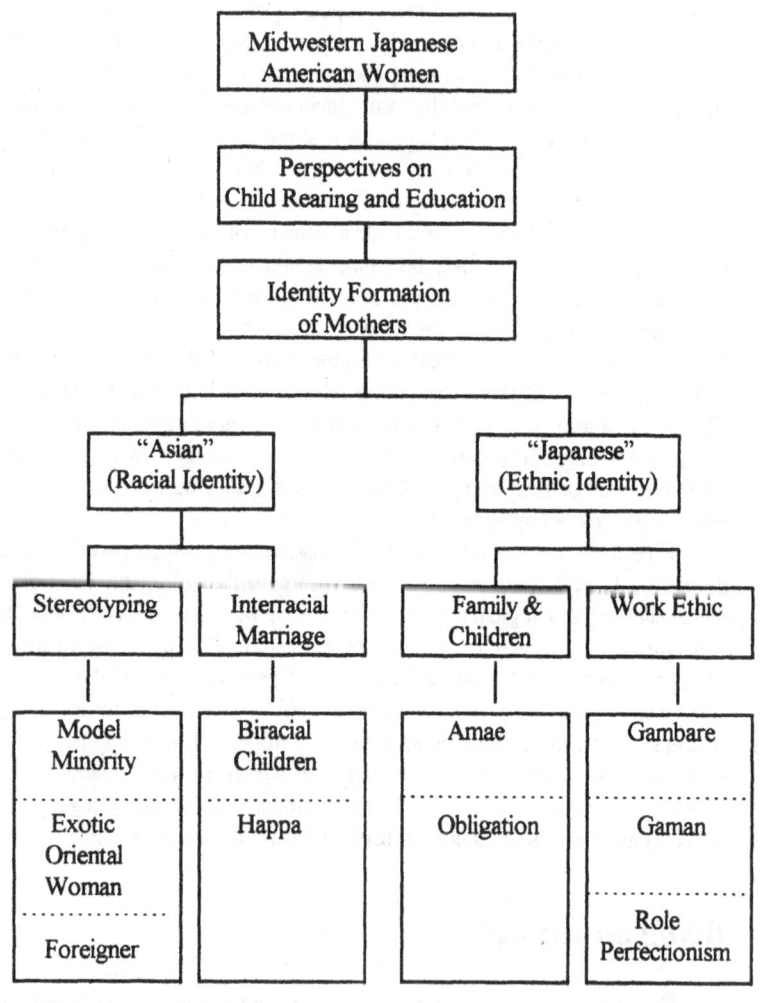

Amae: Mother-child inter-dependency
Gambare: "Keep going" effort, self-motivation
Gaman: "No pain, no gain" endurance, perseverance
Happa: Half or part Japanese
Role Perfectionism: "Do your Best," "Try your Best"

When researchers observe themselves in the focused way that I propose, they learn about the particular subset of personal qualities that contact with their research phenomenon has released. These qualities have the capacity to filter, skew, shape, block, transform, construe, and misconstrue what transpires from the outset of a research project to its culmination in a written statement. If researchers are informed about the qualities that have emerged during their research, they can at least disclose to their readers where self and subject became joined. (Peshkin, 1988, p. 17)

In Peshkin's personal subjectivity audit he includes the Ethnic-Maintenance I, the Community-Maintenance I, the E-Pluribus-Unum I, the Justice-Seeking I, the Pedagogical-Meliorist I and the Non-research Human I (p. 18). Each research site elicits a subset of personal I's according to Peshkin. This was an intriguing concept so I applied it to myself.

I see myself in terms of: the midwestern Japanese American I; the Ph.D. scholar/researcher I; the middle-class, middle-aged mother I; the Sansei daughter I; the ethnic-multicultural I; and the female feminist I. I anticipated the emergence of the Sansei daughter I during interviews with the Nisei women of my mother's generation. And when I shared thoughts with Sansei and Yonsei mothers who have intermarried, the ethnic-multicultural I empathized. I took great care to assure that the Ph.D. scholar/researcher I would not inhibit open discussion or prove intimidating to some participants. Finally, I attempted to keep the female feminist I in check or initially low key in order to avoid imposing my political perspectives without hearing the voice of others.

The work of Japanese American anthropologist Dorinne Kondo provided a model for "insider" subjectivity in the research process. Data for Kondo's (1990) ethnography of the Japanese workplace was gathered while she worked at a factory and lived with a Japanese family. She allowed her Japanese heritage to assist her in areas of access and to help facilitate communication. (She was fluent in Japanese and familiar with their interactional style.) The Japanese family accepted her initially as a typical Japanese woman and felt comfortable with her in their home as long as she "acted Japanese." "Most people preferred to treat me as a Japanese-sometimes an incomplete or unconventional Japanese, but a Japanese nonetheless," she wrote (p. 13). Kondo's acceptance by the Japanese as being racially one of them proved helpful initially, but their disappointment as she struggled with the language attempting to develop an acceptable degree of cultural competence eventually created dissonance and stress. Kondo also discovered that the Japanese in her study related to her in two contrasting ways; as a guest/daughter, and as a researcher. While conducting my research I attempted to emulate Kondo's openness as she documented and discussed her own shifting identities.

I was concerned that my study participants might react to me similarly due to the respect for higher education felt by many Japanese Americans and my position as a Sansei in this three generation study. Also, the high degree of acceptance accorded to me during my pilot study particularly by Nisei participants may have been the result of their friendship with my family. While some women were eager to share their views and even suggested other friends as possible participants, others expressed reluctance to be interviewed. I sensed a conflict between their desire to accommodate the daughter of their friend, and an unwillingness to talk about their experiences and views as Japanese Americans. In fact, I was told by a Sansei participant that a Nisei woman I had interviewed would probably not have consented if I hadn't been a Japanese American family friend who "understood" (which might also have meant, who could be trusted) her Japaneseness.

Akemi Kikumura (1981) described a similar reluctance with her mother's comment about *haji*, or shame; that one doesn't discuss private matters (such as personal feelings) with anyone but family. I have considered the personal nature of this research throughout the process and have attempted to be as sensitive as possible. I had some indepth conversations with participants who chose to participate in only certain parts of the study because they were not comfortable discussing family dynamics, personalities and the dysfunctional nature of family relationships. Asking Japanese American women to talk about their family members and personal feelings is in some ways like asking them to undress. Some expressed the need to talk but were reluctant, especially if certain family members were still alive.

It was my intent to bridge any generational or status gaps by utilizing a feminist interview model that is based upon the "feminist ethic of commitment and egalitarianism in contrast with the scientific ethic of detachment and role differentiation between researcher and subject" (Reinharz, 1992, p .27). This was a challenge because social hierarchy in Japanese culture is highly valued, placing educators and elders in relatively high positions. Thus, my emerging relationship with Nisei participants required my negotiating the roles of daughter or scholar as the topics of discussion dictated. On some topics (such as internment), I allowed the words of Nisei participants to speak for themselves, refraining from entering a researcher's interpretation, while at other times I participated in the mutual construction of knowledge, weaving my beliefs with the input of others. This occurred in group interviews where occasionally I actively participated and during individual interviews where I shared my own stories, either in response to theirs or to motivate conversation.

With the Sansei and Yonsei, I shared some common experiences and easily empathized with their views, which allowed me to build rapport more quickly. I tried to be sensitive to my own responses to their words in order not to make assumptions too quickly. I recall feeling a sense of understanding and affiliation when participants provided examples of stereotyping that I had previously struggled with. Based upon my own emotional response, it would have been easy for me to assume that they reacted as strongly as I did, but that was not necessarily correct. I therefore made every attempt to separate my responses from theirs to guard against imposing my perspective. I did this by probing deeper in order to abstract their meanings and by using "I" messages of ownership and "I wonder" types of open-ended queries.

Having a shared heritage with all participants may cause some to assume that the researcher also shares common perspectives and beliefs about race, Japanese culture, and ethnicity. This is not necessarily true, although some participants frequently used the phrase, "you know," referring to understanding and empathy rather than just as a colloquial figure of speech. When it was used frequently and accompanied by glances or body language of familiarity, I took it as an acknowledgement of closeness and positive comfort level. But I continued to probe for meaning.

I recall one time when Nisei M. Kana and I were discussing the Japanese concept of *enryo*. She explained, "The funny thing is that I've never considered . . . *enryo* yes, I *enryo* . . . you know what I mean . . . I think it's just my characteristic. I'm not as . . . I'm a little bit more hesitant when among Caucasian people, I think. I think it's just my make-up, you know what I mean, the oriental make-up of enryo . . . " She looked at me directly, so I responded with an affirmative nod. But I also indicated that I was trying to figure out whether these cultural traits were being transformed through the generations. Thinking back, the funny thing for me is that if she had asked me about *enryo* five or ten years ago, I would have been totally in the dark. I had not thought much about this Japanese interactional style, nor did I even recognize its existence until I began studying Japanese culture. Then, what was intellectual became familiar on the psychological level. Yes, I do *enryo* to some extent and I learned it from my family. In fact, this trait became more and more evident as the study progressed. I found myself holding back, not wanting to impose for a variety of reasons.

After initially sending out invitations to participate, I made some phone calls to those who did not respond. I was very reluctant to keep asking because I felt that I was imposing and that those who chose not to respond did so for personal reasons that I should respect. I realize now that I had been socialized to this more conciliatory approach rather than being direct and assertive, which may have had roots in both my gender and ethnicity. Some who chose not to respond were friends of my mother's, so I know they would have liked to support me, but they didn't feel comfortable participating in research. One Nisei woman indicated that she had very little to share and that if I wanted to learn about Japanese Americans, I really should talk with her husband. Gender and specified roles in the family were clearly articulated. It is a shame that this person did not feel comfortable participating, because she could have shared a lot of insight regarding gender as well as generational expectations.

Researcher subjectivity can also become a liability as Gehrie (1976) points out. The interpretation of data gathered in any type of research will reflect the researcher's world view and theoretical orientation. Even if the researcher is an "insider," or member of the group being studied, the interpretation may be considered biased because conclusions could be made which reflect the "inner definitions of self" rather than the specific data. Mark Gehrie (1976) provides a critique of Kitano's research in his study on Chicago Sansei that illustrates this point. He challenges the inferences made by Kitano:

> As a Nisei, it is understandable that Kitano (as a member of the parents' generation) might prefer to see the Sansei as adhering as nearly as possible to his own ideals. By interpreting his test results and measurements to indicate that Sansei are becoming "typically" American by virtue of becoming "completely acculturated," however, Kitano is not only making a questionable inference about the meaning of observable behavior, but also coming to conclusions about inner definitions of self which are at an even greater distance from his data. Such generalizations about the experience of Sansei are not supported by the data in his study. It is this kind of methodological error-the inference from measured behavior to evaluation of experience-that highlights the values of the researcher, and tends to interfere with the understanding of the meaning of observable group dynamics. (p. 256)

Gehrie attributes the methodological error to human values, or the beliefs of the researcher. Instead of focusing upon behavioral measures, Gehrie's (1987) study places emphasis on the ". . . understanding of the inner experience of members of a group" and uses the data about experience to discern the "continuity of feeling states" (p. 356). Gehrie's interview method was nondirective, using no agenda or questionnaires. Weekly hour-long interviews with ten informants were conducted over a ten week period. Gehrie's data are arranged and interpreted by the frequency of topics and ". . . according to the way in which emotions and feelings are handled or dealt with by various individuals" (p. 357). Racial identity, experience and adaptation were the main focal points of his study.

Ethnographers and anthropologists using interpretivist methodology have sought "to elicit the *native point of view* and to elucidate how different cultural constructions of reality affect social action" (Marcus & Fischer, 1986, p. 25). Referring to the metaphor of cultures as texts popularized by Clifford Geertz (1973), Marcus & Fischer point out that there is a vast difference between behavioral scientists and cultural interpreters, who "read" social activities for their meanings as they observe (p. 26). The orientation of this empirical study lies firmly with the cultural interpreters rather than the behavioral scientists.

Narayan (1993), in her discussion of insider or "native" anthropology, proposes that rather than focusing on the typical outsider/insider or observer/observed dichotomy, that the anthropologist consider herself in terms of "shifting identifications amid a field of interpenetrating communities and power relations" (p. 671). She continues:

> The loci along which we are aligned with or set apart from those whom we study are multiple and in flux. Factors such as education, gender, sexual orientation, class, race, or sheer duration of contacts may at different times outweigh the cultural identity we associate with insider or outsider status (pp. 671-672).

Like Kondo, Narayan is concerned about making the ethnographer's identity and location explicit and in confronting the issue of authenticity. In this postmodern feminist study I listen to my participants, trying to reflect their words in my writing and I also share my personal accounts, having experienced similar situations in my lifetime. The dilemma and solutions are clearly articulated by Narayan's comments:

> I write as someone who bears the label of native anthropologist and yet squirm uncomfortably under this essentializing tag. To highlight the personal and intellectual dilemmas invoked by the assumption that a "native" anthropologist can represent an unproblematic and authentic insider's perspective, I incorporate personal narrative into a wider discussion of anthropological scholarship. Tacking between situated narrative and more sweeping analysis, I argue for the *enactment of hybridity* in our texts; that is, writing that depicts authors as minimally bicultural in terms of belonging simultaneously to the world of engaged scholarship and the world of everyday life. (p. 672)

Constructing My Own Identity

On the homefront, cultural lessons were being inculcated from a Japanese American world view, sometimes from both parents, or from one parent, from grandparents, or from extended family. One participant whose family knew mine recalled our early gatherings when we were young. "I remember that your father was more traditionally Japanese," she told me. Although my mother had complained about his Japanese views, especially about the role of women, I had not thought about what she really meant. Thinking back I remember once in high school when I was a cheerleader and wanted to go to the football game with my friend who already had her drivers license. My parents made a big deal about driving me to her home rather than allowing her to go out of her way to pick me up. This made no sense at the time, but now I understand that this was *enryo*, a collective strategy of not inconveniencing others. I also recall that my father wasn't thrilled that I was a cheerleader who blatantly pranced around in public, essentially calling attention to herself. Apparently this was not a suitable role for his daughter.

The same Japanese American worldview became apparent when my mother gave me a beautiful wind chime, saying that she just loved listening to chimes and would come to my backyard to listen. She wouldn't consider putting it out on her apartment balcony because, as she explained, "not everyone else appreciates the sound." Why was she concerned about the feelings of others? Was she afraid that she would have to deal with conflict, an angry neighbor? Perhaps this might have been true during the postwar years when confrontation was regularly avoided, but I knew that she could diplomatically deal with just about anyone. Besides, I wondered, how could people not enjoy this musical instrument? It was concern for the whole community of apartment dwellers that prompted her not to assert her individuality. This cultural orientation had been quietly passed down through my family.

Toward the end of my data gathering, I had the opportunity to see the visiting Smithsonian exhibition entitled *Strength and Diversity: Japanese American Women 1885-1990* with my mother Chiyo, and my sister Anna. Here are my impressions, reflections, and feelings of belonging.

It was on a warm, springlike March Saturday (a relief from the snowstorm at the beginning of the week) that my sister Anna drove her car through bumper-to-bumper Chicago traffic to the Field Museum. It was a special day because it was *Matsuri* Festival Weekend, which is dedicated to honor mothers and grandmothers, and our mother Chiyo had consented to come with us (She doesn't like to travel long distances in the car). There would be *taiko* drum performances, a Japanese American singer-pianist, *Minyo* (folk dancing), an Asian American theatre company, hands on calligraphy, and crafts. In addition, Lani, a study participant, would be there as a storyteller. We planned to meet Connie, a close family friend who I had always called "Aunt," and her sister-in-law for coffee (or was it tea) between events. We had not all been together for years.

We arrived to the sound of the *taiko* drums resonating through the cavernous main hall, with enthusiastic, young, Yonsei or Gonsei (fifth generation) drummers. We headed for the Angel Island Theatre Company's performance about a young Nisei woman's arrival in Chicago after the war. "What camp are you from?" seemed to be the classic greeting of the Nisei. We moved downstairs where the outer foyer of the exhibit had photos and items assembled by the local Chicago Japanese American Historical Society. I wondered if my mother recognized anyone in the photos. After watching a short historical video which ended with my favorite poem by Mitsuye Yamada of her son's question about his own identity, the three of us went in, and on our individual ways.

I stopped first at the display labeled 1910-1930 depicting immigrant Issei women. The general description said:

> Issei fathers made decisions, but Issei mothers had a strong say in matters that affected her children. A mother taught her children Japanese values of hard work, responsibility, perseverance, cooperation and respect for elders. She reminded her children to never cause shame to themselves, their families, or community.

There were photos of women and their children with personal reflective words describing how these Issei mothers were remembered. Two were as follows:

> My mother was the source of my values. She was not the kind that hugged but I could see that she was strong, not overpowering, not dominant, but just an easy speaker. When she said something you just listened. She never hit or spanked me. If I was inattentive, she'd just shut the door.

> My mother taught me to be deferential, to be quiet, not make waves, not to talk back. I was taught the value of quietness *O-to-nashi*. When she said that about a person, they were praising her. So you assumed you should be *o-to-nashi*.

I wondered about my maternal grandmother, who I only knew from occasional visits to California. She was quiet, passive and very honest according to my mother, but she certainly didn't produce a deferential daughter. My mother was, by contrast, a tomboy and a risk-taker. My paternal grandmother was a "picture bride," like many other Issei women, but she was more outgoing, independent and had strong opinions.

It was very crowded at the museum. I knew there was a bus load of people coming from Milwaukee sponsored by the Japanese Citizens League, but I found that another JACL bus load from Dayton, Ohio had also arrived. I went off to greet Lani before she started her performance. She had previously told me how storytelling had liberated her and opened new vistas in her personal development. It was a delight to see her relate to the young children who were present. One little biracial girl reminded me of my niece when she was younger. Fortunately we were able to meet Connie for a short conversation during the folk dancing before we left. Connie's mother was from the same prefecture in Japan as my grandmother so the families became friends in camp. When we all moved to the midwest they became our extended family.

On the way home I thought of how my identity had been shaped throughout the years, sometimes with mixed messages about what it meant to be American. In contrast, it was hard to absorb so much "Japaneseness" in a few hours. My sister and mother seemed to have had a good time, although it is difficult to judge since neither openly expresses feelings. How did I feel? What did I learn about myself? Three observations illustrate my reaction. One was of a young interracial couple (White and Asian) who were leaning on each other, embracing, while intently reading about the internment. It reminded me that as I internalized the *haji* (shame) of my country and the victimization of my family, I have had support and understanding from my European American husband of 28 years.

Another impression was gathered when I gave my seat at the theater performance to an elderly woman who, as it turned out, happened to know some of our family friends from Madison. It reinforced the positive feeling of networking that connects people by ethnicity, by a larger community of Japanese Americans. I felt a sense of belonging, of group affiliation through a shared legacy and empathy for similar experiences. The third observation was of the contrast evident by seeing the many generations of Japanese Americans at the exhibition. School aged children (many biracial) were carrying fans and flowers they had made at the craft booth and were listening intently to Lani's folk tales. Elderly couples or multi-generational family groups were moving stoically through the gallery, occasionally greeting others. Young adults chatted openly about the displays; one Nisei girl said her parents came to America after internment. I guess I focused more on the people and events of the day than the content of the exhibition.

It was personally fulfilling to be with so many other Japanese Americans, mostly strangers but with a shared past. It was a full and memorable day of seeing friends, artifacts and photos of my roots, the

My Identity as a Sansei

legacy of Japanese American strength against adversity. I saw so much diversity within this ethnic group and felt that we as individuals and as a group have so much to offer our country. And the elegant historic quilt depicting immigration and internment made by strong persevering Issei women, silently spoke of our unique history. It chronicled how Japanese Americans are different from the Japanese even though we share a racial bond. Today, in this museum, we were all *Nikkei*.

Fisherman's Chronicles by Julie Sittig

Top: Author's family with paternal grandmother, 1949
Bottom: Author's sister and maternal grandmother, 1950

2. Change Across the Generations

Every culture has, according to Stanford Lyman (1994), a predominant time-person perspective which helps to organize temporal and personal categories with respect to past, present and future. For Japanese Americans, these are perceived in terms of generational distance from Japan. Lyman (1994) describes this situating of generational groups from the immigrant group and he raises the notion that each group holds identifiable personality characteristics. He writes:

> The Japanese (in America) do not merely distinguish native-born from foreign born but rather count geo-generationally forward or backward with each new generational grouping. Moreover, from the standpoint of any single living generational group, the others are imputed to have peculiar and distinctive personalities and attendant behavior patterns that are evaluated in positive and negative terms. Each generation removed from Japan is assumed to have its own characterological qualities, qualities that are derived at the outset from its spatio-temporal position, and are thus not subjective to voluntaristic adoption or rejection. Thus, each generation is living out a unique, temporally governed lifetime that shall not be seen again after it is gone (p. 287)

The immigrants who were born and reared in Meiji Era Japan referred to themselves as Issei or, literally, first generation to live in America. The children of at least one Issei parent who were born and reared in the United States are referred to as Nisei, or second generation. Kibei were born in the U.S. but reared and educated in Japan for part of their lives. Sansei are the third generation children of the Nisei or Kibei and grandchildren of the Issei. Yonsei are fourth generation and Gosei are fifth generation Japanese Americans. According to Lyman (1994), one is assigned to the generational group by virtue of birth, yet one can be informally considered a member of a different group by demonstrating behavior more associated with that group. He explains:

Older Nisei whose social and personal characteristics are similar to those of Issei are sometimes treated as if they were the latter. Sansei peers of Nisei are treated as the latter if they behave accordingly. But Nisei who appear to their fellow Nisei age peers as "too Japanesy" are sometimes associated in the minds of their more Americanized friends with Kibei, while those who are "too American" are associated with Sansei. Finally, the offspring of geo-generationally mixed parentage- for example, Issei-Nisei, Nisei-Sansei, Nisei-Yonsei, and so on- and of racially mixed parentage are not easily classifiable. In practice, they tend to demonstrate the sociological rule that status is as status does; that is, they enjoy the classification that social relations and personal behavior assign to them and that they assign to themselves. (p. 288)

The Japanese Culture of the Issei

The first Issei immigrant to the U.S. mainland was a young fisherman-castaway named Manjiro (later changed to John Mung by Captain Whitfield) in 1843. At sixteen years of age he became the first Japanese American schoolboy (Hosokawa, 1969, p. 21). Hosokawa (1969) traces Japanese immigration from 1886 to 1891 with 194 and 1,136 arrivals, respectively. But in 1898 there were 2,230 immigrants from Japan in the United States. Hosokawa (1969) explains: "The vast majority were male, unmarried, too young to be burdened with family responsibilities, and extraordinarily venturesome. Leaving hearth and home to make one's life in a foreign land was a wrenching experience, particularly for a people whose family ties were strong" (pp. 38-39). Kitano (1976) adds that the early Issei were a relatively homogeneous group of young male laborers with four to six years schooling from agricultural provinces (kens) of Hiroshima, Kumamoto, Wakayama, Fukuoka, and Yamaguchi (p. 11).

The 1908 Gentleman's Agreement between the United States and Japan limited immigration, but by 1913 wives, children and parents of early male immigrants were being allowed to come to America (Kitano, 1976, p.30). Second and third sons commonly immigrated since the traditional system of family inheritance and responsibility was passed down in linear fashion to the eldest son (Yanagisako, 1985). Young men without wives in Japan began to participate in the picture bride process where couples would be matched and become acquainted through an exchange of pictures and personal correspondence (Kitano, 1976).

Kiefer (1974) notes the short duration of original immigration from Japan (between 1885 and 1924) and adds that most of the women arrived between 1907 and 1924 (p. 96). Some of the women in this study, including my grandmother, arrived on the west coast during this period of time.

The majority of the Issei spent their developmental years during the Meiji Era between 1867 and 1912 and brought the culture of that period with them to America (Kitano & Kikumura, 1976, p. 44). Chie Nakane (1970) describes the Japanese social structure by which the Issei established their lifestyles. Major components include:

1. Japanese membership is by situation rather than qualification, therefore identification with family or company is more important than profession or peer group.
2. The *ie*, or household, which acts like a corporate residential group, is the most important frame for early socialization and upbringing.
3. The power of the group is one of its strongest elements in that the group control of behavior includes both ideas and behavior.
4. The Japanese system encourages loyalty to one "frame" or system.
5. Rank and status are determined primarily by age, sex, the order of entrance, and the period of service, rather than by competence, training or efficiency (Kitano, 1976, pp. 34-38).

In his discussion of the cultural roots of Asian (Japanese and Chinese) families, Suzuki (1980) lists the following Confucian concepts as being fundamental to the Japanese worldview: humanism, collectivity, self-discipline, order and hierarchy, wisdom of the elderly, moderation and harmony, and obligation (p. 79). Human nature is considered basically good and a man can become virtuous "through an individual's diligent and sincere efforts to conduct himself morally and to develop his full potentialities as a person" (p. 79).

Mutual dependence and kinship ties are emphasized in the concept of collectivity. Control over emotions (*gaman*) is considered necessary in order for a person to think logically and make objective judgments (p. 79). "A person is also expected to make every effort to utilize his own capabilities and resources to solve his personal problems and improve his life. Failure is attributed to either lack of resolve or the result of fate beyond an individual's control" (Suzuki, 1980, p. 80). In addition, the proper relationships between a Japanese man and all aspects of his life are clearly delineated. The cornerstone of these relationships is that between a child and his parents, therefore filial piety (homage and unquestioning obedience) is stressed. All of these relationships are expected to be mutually dependent, based upon two-way obligations; therefore, obligatory relations (*giri*) are extended to others through gift giving and mutual assistance. "As part of his obligation to his group, an individual is obligated not to bring dishonor or shame to his family by socially unacceptable behavior" (Suzuki, 1980, p. 80-81).

The pursuit of knowledge is stressed because in Confucianism, knowledge is considered essential for wisdom and goodness. The wise and experienced elders will therefore be held in high respect. In Suzuki's (1980) words: "These value orientations were reflected in the practice of ancestor worship, the high value placed on education, the respect given to tradition, and emphasis on the past rather than the future" (p. 80). For the Issei in America, conflicting orientations evolved due to the necessity of investing in their American children for future survival, while retaining a respect for Asian traditions and beliefs of the past.

The cultural values of moderation and harmony, have allowed Japanese Americans to easily acculturate into mainstream society without losing their Japaneseness or becoming an ethnic threat to Whites. A "flexible mode of thinking . . . that values relativity and gradualism and prohibits rigid absolutes" became the norm for Japanese Americans (Suzuki, 1980, p. 80). Issei and Nisei were able to incorporate the Christian religions with their Buddhist beliefs without conflict due to this relativistic ethic which professed that "specific cultural beliefs and practices could be altered so long as they strengthened the survival of the community" (O'Brien & Fugita, 1991, p. 42). This flexibility and receptivity to acculturation may have been passed along through the generations.

The necessity for maintaining harmony is also found in the Japanese interactional style of politeness, restraint and sensitivity to the position and feelings of others. Because open confrontation is avoided, "Asians appear to be humble, modest, nonaggressive, and unemotional to many westerners, who therefore, often mischaracterize them as inscrutable" (Suzuki, 1977, p. 80). "The typical Issei," writes Christie Kiefer (1974), "is required by his culture to accept responsibility for himself, his family, and his ethnic group; he is aided by traditions that place personal and social harmony above self-consciousness and which accept tragedy as a normal ingredient of human life" (p. 66). Yamamoto (1968) succinctly summarizes the cultural orientation of the Nisei in the following paragraph:

> The Japanese manners, celebrations, values, and attitudes were altered only with the incorporation of American Victorian and post-Victorian values. Japanese Americans learned to *Ojigi*, to know one's place in the social structure, to be patient *gah-man*, to be concerned about the family and groups rather than to be selfish *wah-gah-mah-mah*, to work hard and excel with the Japanese spirit *Yamato-Damashi*, and to be quite concerned about the reactions of family and peers that one would be laughed at, *minna-warau*. (Yamamoto, 1968, p. 134).

Kitano (1976) also refers to Japanese social norms defining them as shared meanings in a culture that serve to provide the background for communication. He lists these codified norms as: *on* (ascribed obligation), *giri* (contractual obligation), *chu* (loyalty to one's superior), *ninjo* (humane sensibility), and *enryo* (modesty in the presence of one's superior) (p. 123). These are particularly significant because they are the norms that were incorporated into the Meiji national school curriculum as ethical doctrine and brought to America by the Issei (Kitano, 1976, pp. 122-123). In describing the cultural relativism and adaptability previously discussed, Kitano (1976) writes:

> Rather than a stream making its own course, the stream follows the lines of least resistance-their norms emphasize duty and obligation; their values include conformity and obedience. Part of the "success" of Japanese adaptation to the United States was their ability to respond to the problems of lower status with those normative patterns learned in Japan. (Kitano, 1976, p. 123)

The *enryo syndrome*, as described by Kitano (1976) has been maintained through the generations but has changed from prescribed behavior of deference to superiors to a reticent response in a variety of contexts like, "how to behave toward the White man . . . what to do in ambiguous situations . . . how to cover moments of confusion, embarrassment, and anxiety" (p. 124). *Ha-zu-ka-shi*, observed as embarrassment and reticence, was emphasized through childhood discipline in terms of "others will laugh at you," or social control through shame (p. 125). *Hi-ge*, another part of *enryo* is the devaluation and open denigration of self and family in public, since boasting or praise is considered to be in poor taste. For the Nisei and Sansei, this *enryo syndrome* would be difficult to maintain because there would be little reciprocity from others for this behavior. When an Issei tells another Issei that his own son is not very clever, or that his own wife is a poor cook, proper behavior would elicit a contradictory response praising the son or wife. But Nisei and Sansei might internalize the negative comments from their own parents without understanding the context or the reciprocal Japanese communication system.

Some informants in the author's pilot study (Adler, 1992) recalled grandparents using *ha-zu-ka-shi* as a means of deterring misbehavior and gave examples of *enryo*. One Nisei informant defined *enryo* as "you think of others before yourself." Her example was when someone offers to take her home, she would reply, "Oh, no, that's too much bother . . . I don't want to be an imposition to anybody." Even though she may have wanted or needed a ride, she felt it necessary to politely refuse.

Takeo Doi (1991) known for his analysis of the mother-child personality relationship *amae*, writes about other Japanese concepts. *Tatemae*, originally an architectural term meaning "raising the ridgepole," refers to "conventions created by people on the basis of consensus" (Doi, 1991, p. 12-13). *Honne*, the mutually constitutive term for *tatemae*, refers to an individual's own motives and opinions. Thus, *tatemae* relates to the formal appearance while *honne* is the inner feeling which is kept private. "It is essential to note here that the individual is not always self-consciously aware of the distinction between *tatemae* and *honne*" writes Doi (p. 13). One's behavior reflects the consensus of group norms while personal opinions may in fact be at odds with this but since Japanese do not openly express personal or individual viewpoints, this is not considered hypocrisy.

Tobin (1991) points out that in addition to *tatemae* and *honne*, Japanese children learn other distinctions between *omote* and *ura* (front and rear) and *uchi* and *soto* (private and public) even as infants (Tobin, p. 17). The child learns to shift levels of intimacy and restraint as he moves from the inner circle of family relations as a toddler, to relationships with peers, teachers and neighbors in preschool and elementary school. Tobin (1991) explains the cultural difference:

> In Japan, unlike in the U.S., circumspection, circumlocution, formality, ceremony, ritual, and manners are viewed as vehicles for expressing as well as masking pleasure and for realizing rather than for binding the self . . . Less likely than Americans to view social conformity as a sign of weakness of character, joining the group as a betrayal of individuality, or ritualized public discourse as hypocrisy, the Japanese value the *omote*, the formal dimension of self, as much as *ura*, the spontaneous dimension. (Tobin, 1991, p. 18)

When the Issei emigrated to the United States, they brought with them, the group orientation of responsibility to the *ie*, or household in which members play clearly defined roles and "where subordination of each member to the will and interests of the group was taken for granted" (Kiefer, 1974, p. 123). In the traditional Japanese family, the person and the role he or she plays within the *ie* (household) are essentially identical. By the Sansei generation, the Western notion of the rights of the individual had been adopted. Kiefer (1974) defines individuation as "the acquisition of the American belief in the moral rightness of individual autonomy and self-expression" (p. 122).

Harumi Befu (1986), a Japanese American anthropologist, contrasts the American definition of individualism with the Japanese concept of personhood. This "peculiarly American" vision of individualism embraces the concepts of self-reliance, independence, freedom and free will so that the person becomes a decision-maker who is solely responsible for his or her actions (p. 22). Japanese personhood considers interpersonalism (or interconnectedness of people) as a dimension which includes three characteristics; particularism, mutuality of trust and interdependence (Befu, 1986, p. 23).

Particularism refers to the value component in a relationship meaning that "those who are connected have a commitment to one another, and this commitment varies, depending on the relationship that obtains between them" (p. 23). In Japanese society there is a well defined hierarchy which denotes a person's status. Mutual trust is extended to others in Japanese society to the degree that a person would assume responsibility for vouching for another's character. Interdependence is so strong that an obligation to assist others is implied in the relationship. Befu (1986) explains this implied obligation with the following example:

> When a person asks someone to do him or her a favor, the request is based on the assumption that it will be honored. To have a request refused means a loss of face. The favor-seeker should be able to divine what the other person is willing and able to do, given their particular degree of mutual commitment. (Befu, 1986, p. 23)

In contrast, individualism, allows a person to consider self-interest first and freely refuse a request without consequences. There is little consideration for the position or feelings of the other person by favor-seeker or receiver.

The change from collectivity to individualism, according to Kiefer (1974), occurred within two generations, a relatively short period of time. The increased contact with non-Japanese and Nisei child-rearing practices, which favored a warmer and more egalitarian relationship between parent and child rather than the rigid Issei approach, contributed to this change. Kiefer (1974) writes: "The practice of egalitarianism subtly communicates the idea to the child that he is important as a person, not merely as a member of the group. The lenient Nisei parent is often unwittingly undermining the very sense of familial responsibility that he is eager for his children to learn" (p. 124).

Associated with the identity of a person is the quality of self or character. Befu (1986) maintains that a person's character is shaped by a mental substance called *ki* or *kokoro* meaning basic life force or soul. According to Befu (1986), in order for a person to become self-disciplined, the *ki* or *kokoro* must experience hardship (*kuro*), endurance (*gaman, gambaru*), effort (*doryoku*) and utmost self-exertion (*isshokenmei*) (p. 24).

An associated term with *gambare* (perveverence and tenacity) is the concept of role perfectionism discussed by Befu (1986). It implies that doing well against all odds despite the lowly level of menial tasks, is still expected and that *gaman* (endurance) enables a person to overcome the feeling that the role is unworthy. This concept was reiterated in literature by Japanese American women and provides a concrete example of it. This quote, taken from Jeanne Wakatsuki Houston's (1985) *Beyond Manazanar: Views of Asian-American Womanhood*, describes the author's conversation with her Issei mother about hard work that might lead to death. Houston writes:

> When I told her my fears she only laughed and said, "I like to wash clothes. It gives me time to think of other things in my head." She tapped her forehead. "Besides, I'm not a washer-woman. This is just a chore. I'm your mother.". . . I did not then understand the weight of her explanation. Being mother was not only enough for her, it was a prized identity. It meant she had a family, and in her world--her peers and community almost exclusively of Japanese descent--the family was supreme. Thus, the chores and duties which she inherited as Japanese wife and mother were not her identity as such; they were just a means to accomplish the end, which was to keep her family intact, happy and well. She never confused her tasks with who she was. (Houston, 1985, pp. 8-9)

Cultural Comparisons, Japanese and "American"

I would like to caution readers to carefully consider comparative generalizations made between two different cultural and national groups, Japanese and "American." (I use quotes because these characteristics are based primarily upon European American perspectives, without consideration for the multicultural nature of American society.) Connor's 1977 study of tradition and change in three west coast generations of Japanese Americans (Issei, Nisei and Sansei) examined the degree to which various generations have retained distinctively Japanese characteristics or have replaced them with those that are distinctively "American." Connor (1977) makes such generalizations based upon research of identifiable psychological and behavioral characteristics confirmed by experts in the fields of psychology and sociology (p. 8). He is careful to note that the lists contain not only those characteristics that are clearly dominant in each of the cultures, but that they also omit those areas in which the two cultures share characteristics (p. 8). Connor's compilation of Japanese characteristics falls into five groups emphasizing collectivity, duty and obligation, hierarchy, deference, and dependence. The "American" characteristics fall under the major headings: individualism, equality, rights and privileges, self-reliance, and self-assertion. The following lists outline the 20 characteristics for each group:

JAPANESE
1. Reliance on the group.
2. Children trained to be docile, obedient, and dependent.
3. Mother-son bond.
4. Emphasis on hierarchy.
5. Emphasis on duty.
6. Dependency need.
7. Passivity (nonagressive).
8. Submissive attitude toward authority.
9. Emphasis on collaterality.
10. Achievement of goals set by others.
11. Emphasis on ascribed status.
12. Compulsive obedience to rules and controls.
13. Obligation to the family.
14. Emphasis on self-effacement.
15. Restriction of personal relations to a small group.
16. A sense of responsibility to others.
17. Deference and politeness to superiors at all times.
18. A sense of fatalism.

19. Success through self-discipline.
20. Emphasis on compromise, precise rules of conduct, and a situational ethic.

"AMERICAN"
1. Individualism.
2. Children trained to be independent.
3. Husband-wife bond.
4. Emphasis on equality.
5. Emphasis on rights.
6. Independence, fear of dependence.
7. Aggressiveness or active mastery.
8. Grudging acceptance of those in authority.
9. Emphasis on individual autonomy.
10. Achievement of individual goals.
11. Emphasis on achieved status.
12. Resentment and dislike of rules and controls.
13. Obligation to oneself.
14. Emphasis on self-assertiveness.
15. Openness and accessibility to others.
16. Responsibility to oneself.
17. Tendency to mask or play down the superiority of others.
18. A sense of optimism.
19. Success through pragmatism and the exploitation of opportunities.
20. Emphasis on moral righteousness, generalized rules of conduct, and a universal ethic.

Cross-cultural generalizations of this kind, which are created to establish a clear dichotomy, should, I believe, be critically viewed since they purport to represent a group of culturally similar individuals. It seems that a comparison between a homogeneous society like Japan, where individual diversity is minimized, although it exists, with that of a multicultural, multiracial society like the United States is somewhat misleading. Perhaps in 1977, the emphasis on Americanism and a common American creed (which still remains today in conservative right-winged politics) led to the assumption that all Americans ought to think and behave in ways founded upon White European perspectives. But when considering if and how Japanese cultural patterns and norms might be transformed by Japanese Americans across generations, I do not believe it is disingenuous to use Connor's list as a point of reference. Though the difference in historical periods of research (1977 and 1995, when data for this study was gathered) and the difference in geographical location (west coast and midwest) may present significant contextual differences, the participant groups essentially originated from the same Issei immigrants.

Midwestern Nisei, Sansei and Yonsei

Upon leaving World War II internment camps, the Nisei were given limited choices as to where they could settle. Those who left early before the end of the war were not allowed to return to the west coast. They had to go east beyond the militarized zone. In addition, the government attempted to control (or socially engineer) the resettlement so that enclaves of Japanese Americans did not settle in any one community. Historian Ronald Takaki (1989) explains how President Roosevelt, at a November 1944 press conference made it clear that the seventy thousand interned families should be scattered throughout the country so they would not discombobulate American society (p. 404). In 1940, less than 5% of the Japanese American population lived outside the west compared to 30% in 1970 (Albert, 1980, p. 100).

In the midwest, Chicago, Minneapolis, Detroit and Cleveland became gathering areas for former internees, including some Nisei in this study. Between 1940 and 1950 the Japanese American populations of these cities had grown; Chicago, from 340 to 11,233, Minneapolis-St. Paul, from 37 to 905, Detroit, from 84 to 959 and Cleveland, from 27 to 1,189 (Albert, 1980, p. 90). By moving to areas where there were WRA (War Relocation Authority) offices, these families were aided in their adjustment to mainstream society. Darrel Montero (1980) notes that this dispersal of Nisei after the war contributed to the rapid assimilation of Japanese Americans compared to other Asian American groups. The WRA, it seems, was instituting a "residential segregation and assimilation" policy (Albert, 1980, p. 174).

Generations of midwestern Japanese Americans who were geographically removed from their ethnic communities did not necessarily follow the patterns of acculturation, or cultural maintenance, that groups who have access to community events that reinforce ethnic group traditions follow. Simply due to dispersal and lack of affiliation, midwestern Japanese Americans may not display the social and personal characteristics of their generational group previously discussed by Lyman (1994). In other words, midwestern Sansei and Yonsei may be far more "Americanized" than their cousins who live in Los Angeles or San Francisco.

In fact, research indicates that most midwestern Sansei seldom participated in Japanese customs and generally did not learn the Japanese language (Albert, 1980). In some cases when Issei elders lived with their children, older Sansei learned to communicate in "broken" Japanese, but English was the main language spoken in most of the households. Albert (1980), describing Sansei in Chicago and the Twin Cities writes: "Most have acquired a smattering of words and phrases and many even studied Japanese for a time, but fluency in Japanese is irrelevant to most Sansei" (p. 319). Their lifestyles would probably be considered mainstream American while their beliefs and attitudes might reflect their Japanese American heritage. Mei Nakano (1990) believes that with the loss of the Japanese language, "many of the cultural values that inhere in it (are) bound to be lost" (p. 221). Oral and written language are symbolic representations of beliefs and worldviews; thus, the conceptualizations developed by children reflect family and societal values.

Nakano (1990) also attributes racism and the incarceration of Nisei during World War II to the desire for rapid assimilation of Japanese Americans. She writes:

> If the stigma attached to their race induced Nisei to strive to be "100% American," the searing experience of the concentration camp no doubt caused them to avoid even more assiduously their connection to things Japanese in the years directly following World War II. Thus, in their most formative years, their children were likely not to have been exposed to any great extent to features of their Japanese heritage. Nor were they likely to hear about their parents' imprisonment. This pattern of denial on the part of their parents up until the late sixties was certain to make its imprint. (p. 221)

Thus, for midwestern Nisei the stigma of internment along with their racial visibility as ethnic minorities in White midwestern communities, accelerated the assimilative process. Uchida (1982) describes the Nisei perspective and the differing cultural and historical contexts between their generation and that of the Sansei.

> In 1942 the word "ethnic" was yet unknown and ethnic consciousness not yet awakened. There had been no freedom marches, and the voice of Martin Luther King had not been heard. The majority of the American people, supporting their country in a war they considered just, refused to acknowledge the fact that their country was denying the civil rights of fellow Americans. They would not have supported any resistance to our forced removal had it arisen, and indeed such resistance might well have been met with violence as treasonous. (Uchida, 1982, p. 147)

In the epilogue of her book *Desert Exile*, Yoshiko Uchida (1982) suggests that the Sansei generation, who experienced the Vietnam War with its protest marches and civil rights movement, began to question why the Nisei did not fight for their civil rights during evacuation. The Sansei were beginning to re-examine and resist the assimilative forces. Uchida (1982) writes:

> They were right to ask these questions, for they made us (the Nisei) search for some obscured truths and come to a better understanding of ourselves and of those times. They are a generation for whom civil rights meant more than just words. They are the generation who taught us to celebrate our ethnicity and discover our ethnic pride. Their compassion and concern for the aging Issei resulted in many worthwhile programs for all Japanese Americans. (p. 147)

The Sansei and Yonsei generations began to seriously question the values of their home cultures in relation to the expectations of the dominant White society in which they lived, but were unable to easily separate them. The process lead to a transformation of Japanese American culture.

Referring to a survey of Sansei, Yonsei, fifth, and sixth generation Japanese American college students in the Los Angeles area, Kitano and Daniels (1988) note that they "still believed in such values as hard work, good education, family and community solidarity, and perseverance-values passed down from their Issei and Nisei heritage." They tended to voluntarily retain ethnic ties even though they "overwhelmingly believed in interracial dating and marriage" (p. 73). Suzuki (1980) also sees the Japanese American family as a "close-knit, cohesive social entity" still subscribing to traditional Asian cultural values such as group orientation and obligation to parents and family (p. 94). But in general, Kitano and Daniels (1988) view the dominant mainstream society, which offers employment, as the primary socializing force while the ethnic community and family provide "supportive frameworks" (p. 73). In their words:

> Sansei are more apt to reflect the ambience of their surrounding communities, rather than a strictly ethnic one. A Japanese American growing up in St. Louis will be more Missourian than Japanese, just as Sansei from Los Angeles, Honolulu, and New York will reflect the culture of these cities (p. 73).

The flexibility to adapt in a bicultural fashion can create problems for some Japanese Americans who feel disconnected from both worlds

(O'Brien and Fugita, 1991, p. 117). Gehrie's (1976) study of Sansei in Chicago uncovers a sense of loneliness felt by those who were removed from the support network provided by strong ethnic communities. But having a superficial sense of acceptance into mainstream culture, while lacking an ethnic peer group, some Chicago Sansei felt "a sense of being an outsider, and not belonging anywhere" (p. 367).

The women in this study indicated that they were influenced by three historic events (the internment of Japanese Americans during World War II, the civil rights movement and the women's movement) in decidedly different ways. For example, the internment experience for Nisei women contributed to their desire to make their children more independent and assimilated. The Sansei and Yonsei, on the other hand, knew very little about the camp experiences of their mothers and grandmothers, and became more cognizant of their American historical roots when the movement for reparations began. (See the Redress Bill or the Civil Liberties Act of 1988 in Nakano, 1990, pp.202-207). Internment was rarely a subject discussed at home.

Some of the well educated and professional Sansei women felt more in tune with the women's movement than the civil rights movement interpreting any discrimination as a result of gender rather than race. They had grown up removed from ethnic communities where issues of racial discrimination were shared and political action reinforced. Nisei women, had faced overt racism in most societal contacts on the west coast and were grateful to have jobs in the more accepting postwar midwest. Mei Nakano (1990) describes this tenuous position of Nisei women on "liberation":

> If women in the society-at-large had difficulty advancing their program of liberation, Nisei women found it doubly hard. Like their mothers, they had found a large measure of contentment in their roles of wife and mother. To a large extent, too, they had lived for, and through their children. Their children's successes or failures became their own. (p. 198)

Nakano (1990) continues noting that although home and family responsibilities were "sacred duties", Nisei women had a "duty to themselves":

> They lived in a different world than did their mothers, one in which, if they were to participate as equals, they needed to seek equality. They would continue to support their children in every way, but they also recognized the necessity to expand their horizons. (p. 198)

For some Sansei, instigated by the civil rights movement, the desire to seek their cultural roots lead to political activity regarding the internment of their parents and grandparents. Kiefer (1974) points out that in addition to concern for civil rights, Japan had risen to world eminence and the Sansei were increasingly exposed to situations where they were stereotyped by non-Japanese Americans. This description of west coast Sansei during the 60's and 70's might be applicable to midwestern Sansei ten years later since the third generation is younger in the midwest. Certainly the concern for Japan's world prominence hasn't changed. Christie Kiefer (1974) describes this process:

> But being fluent in non-Japanese language, well-versed in the local non-Japanese culture, and much closer to non-Japanese people than their parents had been, . . . the Sansei were strongly pressured to accept definitions of themselves offered by non-Japanese. In these intercultural contexts the Sansei were in effect told by their non-Japanese acquaintances: "You are not like other Americans. You are Japanese, Oriental, Asian, or Third World." This discrepancy between the messages in the two contexts (ethnic and mainstream)-a discrepancy that the Nisei had been able to tolerate-became unbearable for the Sansei because of the increased importance of intercultural contexts in their lives. Perhaps the only workable solution was to develop a healthy pride in their Japanese ancestry and culture. (pp. 106-107)

As the women sought their cultural roots, others continued to define them, classify them and relate to them as racially Asian, with an implied foreign status. This was easier for Nisei to understand, having experienced incarceration at the hands of the White majority. Awareness of race and ethnicity proved to be more complicated for the Sansei and Yonsei who desired acculturation rather than assimilation. The internment experience, with its wholesale incarceration of an entire ethnic group and the civil rights movement, with its emphasis on identification with one's racial group, reinforced a variety of stereotypes that may have influenced the racial and ethnic identities of the women in this study. Most of the participants in this study have experienced stereotypes of Asian Americans and Asian women at one time in their lives.

Americanized and Mixed Race Yonsei

This study demonstrates that ethnic identity can persist and ethnic culture can be transformed in spite of assimilative forces and without direct and frequent contact with ethnic communities. Ethnicity can be ascribed by others, self-selected and constructed. The Yonsei, for example, construct their racial and ethnic identities in response to a variety of influences: family models, the messages they receive from their peers, the home cultural environment, family surname, identifiable physical traits and experiences with racism (Stephan, 1992: Root, 1992). Biracial participants may choose to select one ethnic orientation over the other during a particular time in their lives.

In her article on mixed-heritage individuals, Cookie White Stephan (1992) writes: Ethnic identity has been shown to be both subjective and unstable . . . Individuals with the same biological heritage often have different ethnic identities" (p. 51). If Japanese American parents of biracial Yonsei provide exposure to Japanese customs, language, food, religion, and to other people of Japanese heritage, the children may identify with their Japanese ethnicity even while adopting a mainstream lifestyle. Or, by being perceived as racially Asian by others, without feeling culturally Japanese, the Yonsei may still become victims of prejudice and discrimination.

Fugita and O'Brien (1991) describe the emergent ethnic perspective as one in which the cultural content brought from a native country and the process by which it was shaped in the new world contribute to the persistence of ethnic identity and ethnic community. They write:

> A central theme of the emergent ethnicity perspective, then, is to turn away from the process of assimilation and focus on evolving adaptive responses and ethnic identifications whose specific cultural content will change as the ethnic group faces different structural exigencies. The concept of emergent ethnicity suggests that the reasons individuals have for maintaining ethnic identification and ethnic community involves change with each succeeding generation. Thus, persons of a later generation may no longer be compelled to participate in an ethnic community out of economic necessity yet they may find interaction with fellow ethnic group members satisfying because of the opportunity to share experiences with others within a mutually understood and preferred interaction style. (p. 21)

The reason for maintaining ethnic communities appears to change for each subsequent generation. The Issei may have maintained their Japanese identity due to imposed segregation resulting from their cultural differences, lack of facility with the English language and general racism fueled by nativist beliefs. The Nisei may have retained connections with their ethnic communities for economic reasons in the face of postwar discrimination. This reliance on the ethnic community was less prevalent in the midwest, according to Albert (1980), where opportunities for integration into the mainstream were enhanced by relocation efforts and geographic dispersion.

But why would Sansei and Yonsei choose to develop their ethnicity especially when they had been considered by some accounts to be assimilated (Kitano & Daniels, 1988: Montero, 1980)? The issue of whether Japanese Americans and other Asian Americans have been culturally and/or structurally assimilated is a continuing debate among Asian scholars. Some, like Michael Omi (1986), maintain that assimilation of racial minorities does not conform to ethnicity theory which assumes that those immigrants who are willing to adopt norms and values of the White society will eventually become accepted and therefore equal. In the case of racial minorities, write Omi & Winant (1986), "permanent racial difference and nonincorporation" are as plausible as acceptance and assimilation into mainstream society (pp. 22-23).

Japanese American Interactional Style

Japanese American interaction and communication styles as described by participants in this study can be characterized as being indirect, non-confrontational with differing amounts of verbalization ranging from no conversation to prolonged lectures. This is consistent with some of the literature on Japanese and Japanese American interaction styles (Lyman, 1994). Some participants mentioned the Japanese term *enryo*, meaning to hold back the expression of one's desires in order to show deference to superiors (those in authority), to prevent potential embarrassment (to oneself and others) in ambiguous situations or to not cause inconvenience to anyone. Lyman (1994) describes this interactional style: "Circumlocutions and indirect speech are regular features of Nisei conversations serving to mute one's own feelings and prevent the eruption of another's" (p. 293). The women in this study of all generations either recognized this behavior in themselves or in members of their families.

Several Sansei participants were articulate about the development of their own interactional style. For example, Lani spoke about how she developed as an expressive storyteller from a quiet, introverted and generally compliant personality. She valued this changed as a means for attaining liberation from the culture into which she had been socialized. In her words:

I get to be a storyteller which has become a huge and important and absolutely unexpected turn for me. It has been exceedingly affirming and healthy for me as a way to draw attention to myself and be in a position where you stand up and talk to a whole crowd of people, but you do it nicely, you do it well, you do it healthfully. And you rise above the Japanese cultural thing that says you should never draw attention to yourself. So I think of it as being something that really pushed me out of my culture.

Imoto articulated the Japanese interaction style of her Nisei mother but noted that she and her siblings (10 all together) run the gambit from assertive and direct to quiet and reserve styles, illustrating inter-family and intra-group differences. In describing her mother she said:

When she wants to ask me for something she doesn't come right out and ask me first, she wants to know what you're doing that day, or she asks it in a different way rather than . . . on Wednesday do you think you could, whatever. . . She'll try me out first. And I notice that I do that too. I go around things rather than go directly at them. And that's something that I struggle with and I think find annoying about myself. My (Caucasian) boyfriend has pointed it out to me also.

Kim perceived her mother as being more open and direct while she saw her father as having this indirect style. She also contrasts it with the style of some of her European American friends, reflecting a generalization about all Whites as being open and assertive. She described her perception of this cultural difference in the following way:

There's this way that, you just know what, you can anticipate what somebody needs and you get up and you give it to them. It's as simple as that but also I really ought to do this because I know my father expects it, for me to do it. It doesn't require any words. And I always loved and envied this ability of friends of mine, of White people to be able to just be really large with their needs and their emotions and just kind of let them all splatter out. It's really refreshing. . . It's really messier you know, it just spreads out on the floor but you know where they stand. You can choose to step around it and walk out the door or you can acknowledge it. .
Then you have the chance, it's your decision whether you

want to deal with it or not. And I really like that. And it's OK to not (deal with it). But that's not the way . . . I don't think, Japanese Americans do it.

And like the Sansei previously mentioned, Anna articulated the struggle she experienced between the indirect Asian interaction style of her family with what she perceived as the direct approach of mainstream American culture. In Anna's words:

My personality fits with the American culture, it conflicts with the Asian. I have always, since a small child, had my own opinions, believed in my own rights as an individual, was forthright and direct. The problem was that I lived in an Asian culture family. So I learned the Asian skills (to serve others, to deify the family) better than the American . . . but I never learned to know my place.

Interestingly, Anna's mother Nisei Chiyo expressed some of the same sentiments about herself and felt just as captive in that Asian culture family. Both were struggling to define themselves in their bicultural world.

All of these women, reared to blend in and not be the "nail that needs to be hammered down," found themselves negotiating a society that rewards directness and is stimulated by verbal confrontation. Some of the Nisei and Sansei women practiced the roles of conformity, compliance and harmony within the household while learning skills of forthright communication and earnest confrontation in order to negotiate the outside world. Others had models of resistance who mentored them, supported them and provided the freedom for them to acculturate without losing their identity.

The strong commitment to the growth and development of children was practiced with a low key style of indirect facilitation. Sansei Mimi described her mother's parenting style with this analogy:

I remember one time my brother got a little pet mouse so we (mother and 3 children) were all sitting on the floor and the mouse was just kind of scampering around. I guess now looking back on it, that's how my mother was with us, sort of there but not interfering too much and kind of letting us, you know, scamper around. And I think she kind of let us play in our own way while she was doing housework. I felt that we were pretty independent but that also we were well taken care of, you know, all of our needs were taken care of and then we were left to play. And my folks never, I don't think that they ever really had a babysitter even until we were two or so.

Several other participants including one Yonsei mentioned that they rarely had babysitters and when they needed to go out, they usually took their children. Some like myself, had grandmothers living in the home or, like Lani, aunts and uncles living in adjacent flats. For many, relatives were preferred babysitters over strangers. In fact, for the few divorced women with children in this study, one of the factors contributing to divorce that was mentioned was lack the of time and commitment their former spouses had for their children. As one put it, "He couldn't understand why I preferred being with my children over going out on the town with other couples."

Interactional styles, like other cultural elements, can be transformed across generations. Limited verbalization within the family may have resulted from a combination of language barriers, role expectations, *enryo* and the tension between rearing independent self-sufficient children and the closely monitored interdependence of *amae*. For example, when faced with racial slurs, most of the women in this study found ways to cope on an individual basis rather than involving their parents. There was a feeling of not wanting to upset or embarrass their parents, tied with an assumption that they ought to be able to deal with prejudice and discrimination on an individual basis. Reliance upon personal strength, which was modeled by Nisei and Sansei parents, was stronger than going to the family for assistance. Thus the family became the source of support and acceptance but not necessarily the source of active communication and problem solving. This may generally be true for most midwestern Japanese American women or unique to this group of fairly independent, highly educated women. Other midwestern Japanese American families, including examples in my own extended family, reared their children to be more psychologically dependent on parents. The *amae* interdependency characterized by many Issei was maintained in my uncle's bicultural family. Even though the children were biracial, with a European American mother, the Japanese influence of nurturing and dependency upon family advice and decisions flourished.

The transformation of interactional style, for this participant group was not as clearly identifiable because there may be a discrepancy between what participants believed about themselves and the behavior that they exhibit. Since observation was not a part of the study design, interactional style and modes of communication can only be assessed through self-reporting. In addition, the context and the degree of receptivity by others needs to be considered. For example, a participant may feel that she is being very direct and assertive but may, in fact, be perceived as being vague or hesitant by others in relation to their interpretation of assertiveness. But, based upon the perceptions of the participants about their own interactional style, it appeared that as a group, there was a move from an indirect, nonconfrontational style, especially within the family structure to a more direct and assertive style outside the home. Nisei were described by others as being more Japanese in their style while Sansei and Yonsei described themselves as being more mainstream "American." Interestingly, two of the biracial Yonsei were described as very assertive and even confrontational by themselves and their mothers, while two of the 100% Japanese Yonsei felt that they were not expressive and assertive enough, and continued to deal with their desire to become more extroverted. One Sansei woman described her personal transformation from a quiet, reserved personality to an expressive storyteller.

It was unclear and debatable whether the indirectness and less verbal approach in which they were being socialized was a reflection of their Japanese heritage or a reflection of being female in American society. Perhaps the intersection of gender and ethnicity reinforces a general pattern of behavior which is adjusted for communication within the home or in the public domain. Some of the literature on Asian Americans indicates that both men and women are rewarded for being non-confrontational, which may result from their status as ethnic minorities rather than specific cultural expectations (Kitano, 1976, Osajima, 1987). Differences between Asian ethnic groups in terms of interactional styles and gender roles are wide, though not generally apparent to westerners. For example, Korean American and Chinese American women have not been socialized with *enryo* and *gaman* in the same manner as Japanese American women. In specific realms, they tend to be more direct and vociferous than most Japanese women. The recognition of intra-group diversity in Asian American populations is critical. It has been predicted that the traditional Japanese interactional style will be transformed as Japanese Americans integrate into mainstream society (see Kitano & Daniels, 1988; Montero, 1980; Suzuki, 1980), and that issues of Asians as a racial group will become more salient than ethnic identity (see Omi & Winant, 1991).

Resisting Gender Expectations

For some women, especially those living in multi-generational households, family cohesion was marred by gender and culture conflict.

"Let me stress something," said Nisei Chiyo, "My biggest problem was (that) I fought for equality in our marriage. It's unJapanese and Grandma hated that part of it. I knew she felt that I should not be equal." This desire for equity was contradictory to the hierarchial assumptions of the Japanese culture ingrained in Issei lifestyle and may have led to the humorous "retraining" of Mona's husband in vignette A and the kind of facade, or the masking of true feelings, discussed in vignette B. But other Nisei women did not experience the conflict and constraints of gender roles dictated by cultural differences in the same way. Some, like Mariko, did not resist and felt comfortable in her primary role as parent, thereby supporting her husband in his business.

Others, like Nisei Mia and Chizu, had strong independent mothers who became role models for them. "My mentor was my mother," wrote Mia, explaining how her mother went off to continue her education at a Tokyo missionary school during a period when women rarely traveled alone in Japan. "She was a determined person . . . and she showed her independence all through her life," Mia continued. Mia saw a parallel with her own life comparing her mother leaving to pursue her education in the 1890's to her leaving camp after evacuation. Her brothers returned to Seattle but she "left home and never went back." She summarized her views by saying, "You see, I always viewed my mother as progressive . . . This is why I say she was my mentor. And so I had that same spirit, I think."

Nisei Chizu spoke of her mother as having sacrificed opportunities for marriage (she was a widower at a young age) because she chose to stay in America fulfilling a promise to her late husband to make certain that the children got a college education. She recalled how her mother used psychology to help her children cope with and endure the inequities of life. When Chizu complained about being too tall (for Japanese), her mother would say, "Gee, you should be happy. People look at you first." And when the family could not afford a new dress for Chizu, because her brother's schooling to become a dentist was a family priority, her mother would encourage her to *gaman* (endure). Chizu's mother would say, "I'll buy it for you later . . . Just think, it will be the latest (fashion), instead of right now." By using what Chizu referred to as "opposite psychology," her mother attempted to inculcate patience.

Yonsei Leia spoke with admiration about how her mother overcame cultural and gender expectations empowering her to believe that she could achieve anything she desired. "Probably the most prominent characteristic I've seen in her is her strength and her determination, her work ethic and her ability to just find a goal and design a solution and you know, to reach the other side," she explained. Leia shared that her grandfather (the prominent one previously mentioned) was thrilled when her mother married because he "wanted someone to take care of his daughter." But, according to Leia, "My mom didn't let those preconceptions of who she was limit her."

As a Sansei second daughter, I received the same messages of gender expectation while pressure was put on my younger brother to follow in his father's footsteps. My sister and I followed the gender role models of our mother and grandmother: inner strength and willingness to acknowledge and challenge inequities. But unlike them, we were not bound by intransigent Japanese traditionalism. Fortunately, like many of the self assured women in this study, I had support from some family members to define myself rather than let tradition define who I should become and to act upon opportunities to assert my independence.

Gender expectations seem to have been transformed across the generations due to the response of the Nisei women to gender expectations which, along with the economic constraints of the post war period, may have limited their opportunities for further education and career development. Nisei women in these groups indicated that they had been socialized to accept secondary female roles, although they did so with both protest and resolve. There wasn't as much pressure to accomplish in academics, as Nisei Chiyo explained, and although many of them went, a college education wasn't expected of Nisei women. Sansei and Yonsei women generally felt free to study whatever they wished in college, even though some received suggestions for embracing "female" careers like teaching and nursing (which, as M. Kana pointed out, excluded Japanese Americans during and after the war). There did appear to be a sense of gratitude for the mothers who were recognized as mentors of a woman's pursuit of education.

The transformation of family roles and relationships has moved from the traditional obligation in which the elder family members maintained positions of respect and authority to a focus on the nuclear family with shared responsibility for elders by all siblings, or in many cases by the female daughters (see Yanagisako, 1985 on kinship patterns). Some Nisei women experienced cultural conflict since they were socialized into the "Japanese way" but found the "American way" of identifying roles and developing family relations more suitable. Sansei and Yonsei retained a sense of responsibility for parents and for maintaining family cohesion, which was described as obligation or a desire based on family pride. There appeared to be a move from strictly defined roles within the family for the Issei and some Nisei to a focus on developing individual relationships between family members (parent-child and siblings).

Top: Author and mother, 1947
Bottom: Author's sister and mother, 1948

3. Rearing Competent Learners

Shitsuke, according to Hendry (1986) is a Japanese word with multiple translations meaning breeding, upbringing, child training, home instruction and discipline (p. 11). Japanese child-rearing philosophy coincides with Froebel's view that children are naturally good and that one must be concerned with both the body and the mind. Like Locke's "tabula rasa," the Japanese word *hakushi*, meaning white sheet, emphasizes the importance of environmental stimulation in order to promote learning (p. 17). Japanese children are considered to be a gift bestowed by god until age seven; thus, they are cherished. There is no equivalent for the western Christian concept of original sin or a rebellious spirit: Japanese children are thought of as inherently good (Hendry, 1986; Yamamura, 1986). Although the sanctification of children has diminished, the belief of essential goodness of children has not changed.

Even in post war Japan the overprotectiveness and indulgence observed in nuclear families had roots in these traditional ideas (Yamamura, 1986, p. 30). Yamamura (1986) notes that ". . . a strong sense of the child as a divine blessing has been preserved in the Japanese mentality until very recently. This conception has further reinforced the tendency for parents to take the task of child rearing seriously" (p. 32). Early childhood training is particularly valued by parents as reflected in the common saying; "The soul of a three year old lasts till 100" (Hendry, 1986, p. 17). Young children are nurtured and indulged, creating a more permissive atmosphere than one created by European American mothers. Japanese mothers are more often in the company of their infants and offer a more soothing and quieting approach with more carrying and rocking than European American mothers. By communicating in a physical rather than verbal manner, Japanese mothers desire to produce quiet, contented babies. European American mothers, on the other hand, want more vocal, active babies (Caudill & Weinstein, 1969).

Another divergent cultural behavior distinguishing Japanese child rearing from European American approaches is evident in sleeping arrangements. In Japan, children co-sleep with their parents; infants with their mothers and older children with their fathers or other relatives when a newborn arrives. A Japanese child can expect to co-sleep with an adult until approximately ten years of age, then with a sibling until approximately fifteen years (Caudill & Plath, 1974, p. 289). Hendry's (1984) study of Japanese kindergartens (ages 3 or 4 to 7 years) reports that of 176 families, 37 children slept in the same bed with their mothers, 118 slept in the same room with their parents, 20 slept in a separate room and 1 slept with a grandmother (p. 21).

In discussing the ramifications of Japanese sleeping arrangments, Caudill & Plath (1974) state: "Japanese place great emphasis on collaterality (group interrelatedness) not only in the family but in many spheres of activity. They also find much of their enjoyment in the simple physical pleasures of bathing, eating and sleeping in the company of others" (p. 305). In contrast, they write, "In western eyes, Japanese co-sleeping patterns may appear pathogenic, or at least to be taken as a denial of maturation and individuation" (p. 306). European American moral sentiment on subjects like incest may have deterred the perpetuation of this cultural pattern by Japanese Americans.

The Japanese Amae *Relationship*

The intense closeness of the parent-child relationship is evident in the indulgent treatment of children, family sleeping arrangements and a psychological and behavioral interdependency called *amae*. First described by Takeo Doi (1974) and Meredith (1966) *amae* refers to a dependency relationship primarily between a Japanese mother and her children. Doi (1974) defines *amae* (v. *amaeru*) to mean "to depend and presume upon another's benevolence" and describes a child's behavior toward his parents. (p. 145). It is an "all powerful drive" or a "fundamental emotional urge" of dependency needs (Hendry 1986, Doi, 1974). In relation to child development, Doi (1974) says:

> We do not say that an infant does *amaeru* until he is about one year old, thereby indicating that he is then conscious of his wish to amaeru, which in turn suggests the presence of a budding realization that his wish cannot always be gratified. Thus, from its inception, the wish to amaeru is accompanied by a secret fear that it may be frustrated. (p. 149)

In Japanese society, *amaeru* is acceptable because parental dependency is fostered and this behavior pattern is even instituted into its social structure. Husbands and wives do *amaeru* toward each other as do teachers and students, doctors and patients (Doi, 1974, p. 150). *Amaeru* is taken to mean that one can behave as one pleases without consideration for the other person, also translated to indicate a willfulness and self-indulgence presuming the good will of the person with whom one is familiar (Mass, 1986, p. 10)

Amy Iwasaki Mass (1986) has coined the term, "indulgent love" for *amae* since it assumes both desire to be indulged and loving behavior on the part of the person who gratifies the wish for *amae* (p. 9). Mass (1986) calls attention to another Japanese word, *amai* meaning sweet, indulgent and lenient, noting that amae refers to the sweet pleasurable feeling of being indulged (p. 188). When a mother and child have this *amae* relationship, the child feels a bond or oneness with his/her mother and therefore is free to behave as he/she wishes. When a mother *amayakasu* (another verb form of *amae*) she indulges, pampers and spoils her child (p. 188).

Amae, according to Mass (1986), is interpreted as the overall quality of nurturing, anticipating children's needs, and helping children achieve a high level of functioning (p. 183). Her study indicated that over a majority (61.4%) of Japanese Americans felt that *amae* was less important than other Japanese values and "because most Japanese-speaking respondents associated *amae* with indulgence and spoiling, there was a negative connotation to the word" (pp. 171-172). Mass also points out that non-Japanese speaking "Sansei who were not aware of the pejorative connotations to the word *amaeru* were more accepting of behaviors associated with *amae*" (p. 172).

Merry White (1987) discusses *amae* in relationship to motivation and learning. She writes, "... the assurance of security and unconditional love is a source of high human motivation" (p. 22). There are two types of goals for children in Japan: one that provides incentive and satisfaction in the child's relationship with his total social environment and one that affects his academic performance in school. Motivation to act in a particular manner holds differing interpretations when one considers the notion of freedom in a cultural context. To westerners, freedom to choose implies a degree of personal isolation and autonomy, while freedom to be indulged means "to do as one likes within the bounds of a permissive relationship" to the Japanese (White, pp. 23-24). European American concepts of child development stresses separation and individuation where Japanese *amae* stresses the permanence of human relationships, where indulgences can be freely given and received (White, p. 25).

In her research on families in Japan, Hendry (1986) notes that close neighbors of the family, who are classified in familial terms by young children, play a significant role guiding the integrating the young children into the world outside of the home. "... other mothers become 'aunts', fathers become 'uncles' and their children become 'big brothers' and 'big sisters', according to ages" (p. 58). These neighbors, along with the child's siblings play a major role in this socialization process. The sense of community responsibility for child rearing plays a more significant role in societies with a collective orientation. Children are both a reflection of their families and communities.

Children in Japan are taught at an early age, in preschool, to relate to the needs of their peers in order to act cooperatively, as a collective unit. Japanese teachers refrain from interfering in student conflicts (Tobin, Wu & Davidson, 1989). Japanese American mothers in the U.S. may be striving for the same kind of harmonious relationships for their children by preparing their children to become mediators or circumventors of problems. Confrontation, especially aggressive interactions, are discouraged in preference of problem solving.

Japanese American Child Rearing

The Issei immigrants brought a strongly patriarchial family orientation with them from Japan but even in that first generation the mother often assumed more authority on family matters than her counterpart in Asia (Suzuki, 1980, p. 85). By the Nisei generation, husbands and wives began to play complementary roles with joint decision making and more cooperation (Suzuki, 1980, p. 88). Since many Issei immigrants either worked on farms or ran family businesses, both parents were actively involved in the workforce. Nisei spent much of their childhood in "close, protective care and supervision of their parents" (Suzuki, 1980, p. 85). "Thus, except while they were in school, they were almost always in close contact with their parents," writes Suzuki (1980). He continues, "Even out in the Japanese community they could not escape scrutiny by relatives and family acquaintances" (p. 85). This cooperative concern for the welfare of the children reflected the Japanese *ie* or household system of joint responsibility, with patriarchial authority.

This picture changed drastically for the Sansei generation who were raised in postwar America removed from rural Japanese American communities. Supervision of the young Sansei was generally conducted by Nisei mothers, who made decisions on family matters, while their husbands attended college and/or worked full time. Nisei women typically remained at home until their children reached their teens or finished high school (Nakano, 1990). Johnson (1976) found that Nisei mothers were decision makers in areas like finances, social activities and child rearing.

Seventy percent of the Japanese American informants in Mei Nakano's (1990) study believed that child rearing was their primary responsibility. Although midwestern Nisei and Sansei women might agree, fullfilling this responsibility would be more difficult in an area where there was limited family contact and support. The extended family was becoming replaced by the nuclear family since many Issei parents and other relatives returned to California after internment rather than living with their Nisei children. Young couples and single college students headed east.

In midwestern Japanese American families during the postwar years many fathers were university students and mothers were primary homemakers but often both parents worked part or full-time in order to support their young children. Sometimes grandmothers or extended family members became caretakers while both parents worked. Many Nisei who relocated in the midwest came because, unlike the west coast, some universities were willing to accept Nisei students. Since the internment had interrupted studies of several thousand Nisei who were attending colleges, the Japanese American Student Relocation Council assisted these students after the war in transferring to universities in other parts of the country (Albert, 1980, p. 140). "By the academic year 1945-46, more Nisei students were enrolled in Twin Cities area institutions than in any other city except Chicago" writes Albert (1980) (p. 140).

As Nisei parents settled in the heartland of America, their beliefs about child rearing were evolving with input from both their Japanese families and their European American peer groups. Acculturation produced changes in values and perspectives of the Japanese American family so it came with some generational conflict. According to Kiefer (1974) it has also created some personal distress and confusion, but has had fortunately "remarkably little effect on family solidarity" (p. 115). Although ideal kinship relations in Japanese culture and American maintream culture may share some similarities (intimacy and long term cooperation), the manner in which they evolve differs tremendously. "The Japanese view conflict between role demands and inner feelings as a regrettable human characteristic that is to be corrected as much as possible by the suppression of any feelings that are disruptive" (Kiefer, 1974, p. 114). Independent behavior which might disrupt normal functioning of the family and cause conflict is discouraged and personal feelings that might challenge family peace and harmony is restrained and hidden. Within this structure, roles of family members are clearly defined and highly interdependent (Sue, 1973, p. 141). Mainstream European American families, on the other hand, prefer to air personal differences with active and ongoing verbal exchange. Family strife occurs in an open, overt manner, which would make Japanese Americans feel quite uncomfortable.

Few studies have been conducted specifically on Japanese American child rearing (Kitano 1961, Higa 1974, Connor 1974, Caudill & Frost 1974, Frost 1970). Suzuki (1980) maintains that despite rapid acculturation, many traditional Asian child-rearing practices appear to be continuing in contemporary Asian families (p. 89). He summarizes the general trends:

> The early years of childhood are still characterized by close, nurturant care by the mother, who tends to be more permissive with the young infant than her Anglo counterpart. Infants are seldom allowed to cry for prolonged periods before they are picked up by their mothers. Mothers tend to feed their infants on demand rather than by scheduling. On the average, weaning takes place at a later age than for Anglo infants. Toilet training is also more gradual. Parents often allow the young child to sleep with them, occasionally tolerating such behavior even after the child begins school. (pp. 89-90)

Kitano's 1961 study of Issei and Nisei examined the effects of education and acculturation on child-rearing attitudes. The Parental Attitude Research Inventory (PARI) was used to identify any differences between the generations. Findings indicate that the Issei differed significantly from the Nisei in their attitudes and that more education provided varied models for patterning attitudes and behavior. Those with less education became dependent on mothers and grandmothers, the "traditional carriers of culture" for their models (Kitano, 1961, p. 18). Kitano (1976) writes:

> The Issei view of child rearing is more "old fashion" children are viewed as dependent, quiet, unequal, and to be raised with strictness. In contrast, the Nisei view is more "modern" and more American-children are viewed as comrades with a subsequent sharing of experiences; they are encouraged to ask questions; and they are permitted a higher degree of sexual exploration." (p. 137)

Nisei mothers tended to take a more scientific approach gathering information on child rearing from literature (i.e. Dr. Spock, child development articles) and through professional sources (i.e. pediatricians, midwives, other experts). Issei mothers generally adopted habits and methods learned through social contacts in the ethnic community and modeling of her mother or grandmother. Kitano's (1964) second study, which compares child-rearing attitudes of younger and older Nisei with similar populations in Japan, suggest that age-sex groups across national boundaries have more similarities than age-generation groups within a country. Older Japanese, whether in Japan or America held similar beliefs as did the younger generations in both countries.

Caudill & Frost (1974) compared maternal care and infant behavior of Japanese American, European American and Japanese families. Using similar research methodology as Caudill & Weinstein (1969), Frost observed and recorded the behavior of Sansei mothers and their three to four month old babies in the Sacramento area. Findings indicate that Japanese American mothers have retained certain patterns of behavior from their Japanese heritage. They spend a greater amount of time playing with their babies which relates to the finding that Yonsei babies play less by themselves. Yonsei babies and Japanese babies are more alike in doing less nonnutritive sucking on their fingers or on pacifiers than American babies. And Sansei mothers are more like Japanese mothers in their amount of carrying and lulling their babies to sleep. But in general, Japanese American mothers and their infants are closer to European Americans than to the Japanese, especially in the amount of lively chatting they do which stimulates happy vocalization and physical activity in their infants (Caudill & Frost, 1974, p. 12). However, there has been criticism of the research methods used in these studies (Levine, 1980) casting a shadow on the validity of their findings.

Connor's (1974) study of Japanese American acculturation uncovers some Japanese personality traits in all three generations. The Issei had "marginal acculturation" due to their lack of fluency in English (p. 160). The bicultural Nisei believed that they were unique and midway between their parents and their children, therefore they could combine the "best of both cultures" (p. 163). The Issei and Nisei viewed the Sansei as "completely Americanized" and they rated themselves "being over 70 percent acculturated" (p. 163). Using the Edwards Personal Preference Schedule (EPPS), Connor (1974) found the Sansei to be (compared to European Americans) "more deferent, more abasive, less dominant, more affiliative, less aggressive (and had) a greater need for succorance and order" (p. 164). By taking his finding with those of Lois Frost (1970) on Japanese American child rearing, Connor concludes that there may be a continuation of dependency needs fostered in Japanese American families. Connor (1974) writes:

> While not so pronounced as in the Japanese mother, the Sansei mother has retained enough of the Japanese caretaking style so that we are already able to detect discernable differences in her child's behavior at the age of three or four months. Moreover, these differences are exactly the sort of differences we would expect if we were looking for evidence which would indicate the inculcation of dependency needs. (p. 164)

Masanori Higa (1974) also compares "Japanese" mothers' attitudes toward child rearing. His term "Japanese" denotes ethnicity rather than nationality categorizing his informants as American-Japanese, Immigrant Japanese (war brides) and Motherland Japanese (in Japan). His findings contradict the work done by Kitano (1964) in that American-Japanese mothers were found to be the most restrictive of their children and the Immigrant Japanese mothers were the least restrictive and conservative. Higa's (1974) interviews, with a Hawaiian sample, revealed that American-Japanese mothers were quite conscious of their Japanese ancestry which caused them to become "overzealous disciplinarians" expecting their children "not to disgrace their race" (p. 20). The American-Japanese mothers wanted their children to be "obedient to authority rather than independent and aggressive" (p. 20). Slogans like, "Be a good student" and "Be a good citizen" were designed to encourage their children to surpass the children of other ethnic groups (p. 20). Immigrant mothers, on the other hand, had a tendency toward "hyper-correction" or "hyper-adjustment" holding liberal and democratic attitudes that their children were American rather than Japanese. The motherland Japanese beliefs fell in between the other two groups.

Midwestern Japanese American Women

This study investigated the level of awareness on the part of midwestern Sansei and Yonsei of the Japanese concept, *amae*. Women of all three generations gathered to converse about themselves and their families. The following two vignettes depicts these gatherings.

Vignette A

It was a sunny July morning as eight women gathered in my small livingroom. Nisei Chiyo, Mona and M. Kana, and Shigeko, an older Sansei, knew each other from years of living in the same community. They all arrived about the same time and quickly got caught up in the "How have you been? I haven't seen you in so long" type of conversations. Bonnie, a Sansei arrived a bit early (before the ten o'clock "meeting" time) as she was in a nearby neighborhood. At first, Mona conversed with Bonnie as if Bonnie were her mother who Mona knew just after the war. Mona later expressed her confusion, commenting how much Bonnie and her mother resembled each other. Imoto, a Sansei who grew up in Milwaukee, brought her sister Mindy along who was visiting from Hawaii. Both women were very soft spoken, so I was concerned that the microphone, which was attached to the television, would pick up their voices. As people arrived they sat down in my cosy living room where all the furniture had been arranged in a tight circle. As we waited for Yano, a Yonsei, who had called to say she would be late, everyone began to write their responses to two introductory questions I had posed concerning their feelings of participation in this study.

I introduced the first topic by saying that the sense of family support had emerged as a theme from the individual interviews. "What does family support mean to you?" I asked. At first it was quiet, but Mona opened the conversation by addressing Chiyo. Looking at her, Mona said, "Your family seems to really support each other." Caught by surprise, Chiyo responded "Ours? We fight a lot. Everyone's such individualists." Yano laughingly shared that her parents fight too but they're always there for their children. She felt that because they were that way for her, she needs to be there for her children. "It's all passed down, isn't it?" said Mona. But Chiyo added, "That hasn't got anything to do with being Japanese or not . . ." with a questioning tone in her voice. "No" seemed to be the consensus, just family values the group concluded.

So what was the difference between Japanese (or Japanese American- the terms were used interchangeably) family values and those of non-Japanese? Bonnie shared her views on commitment to family and friends, implying that orientals have a stronger sense of commitment. Everyone listened intently to her stories. Shigeko wondered aloud if that was an individual or a group trait. "You can find Caucasian families that would have the same values," she continued, and M. Kana nodded in agreement. Families that valued family tend to bond together regardless of race or cultural background, they suggested. And those parents would recreate the same atmosphere among their "circle of friends," therefore creating a universal valuing of family.

Mona entered the conversation telling us about visiting with friends and talking about husbands. (That got an immediate rise of interest.) Her husband was brought up in a "completely Japanese way" never doing any housework. When her mother-in-law died, she thought that she could "train him again" (lots of laughter). Her German friend said, "we're just like that too." So the conclusion was that every nationality brought these ideas to this country and that it was more of a gender issue. "Italians too," Mona added. M. Kana told of receiving a letter from a Japanese foreign student who said that her husband has been a better husband since he's been in America! Some women thought that these role expectations were generational too. Shigeko and Chiyo talked about their sons taking paternal leave for their newborns creating a sense of hope for the future.

Imoto noted that the women who had intermarried would have a blending of cultures. Noting that her siblings who married Japanese Americans and those who intermarried have raised their children quite differently. She hadn't considered the "Caucasian influence" and found it hard to explain. She saw her brother as being strict and relying more on family than her sister, who married a European American. Her sister, Mindy, wasn't certain that being Japanese made the difference in viewpoints. Comparing the behavior of children in Hawaii to how she had been reared, respect for parents was emphasized in their home. As Imoto and Mindy were speaking about the strictness of their upbringing, there was a lot of nodding from other participants.

I shared how my son's teacher told me to my surprise, that my son was very respectful. Mona added with certainly that children "know how to behave in public." Then Bonnie compared these behavior expectations to her teaching style. She was brought up to expect children to see adults as more authority figures than pals and expects her students to treat her in the same manner. She wondered whether her desire for order and discipline was culturally based. Chiyo agreed sharing the "I was the sargeant mom."

In an attempt to solicit feedback from the women present, Imoto shared a difference she perceived between Japanese American and European American parents; the expectations that children should not bother adults. She spoke of a situations involving her nephew and a neighborhood man. "I questioned her (Imoto's mother) about that . . . well, not to her face (laughter) . . . what would be wrong with Jimmy going over there?" European American children interact freely with adults even demanding attention, Imoto noted recalling the behavior of her boyfriend's niece. Bonnie agreed that she doesn't allow her children to bother neighbors or go into their yards unless they have been invited. She compared her control of her children to a "bungee cord" approach. Yano agreed, explaining that her approach to her children's freedom to socialize is that "you have to wait until you're invited". Since other neighborhood children "just come over" her daughters couldn't understand Yano's rule. "But yet there's something in me that says," admitted Yano, "you don't impose on other people." Others readily agreed. "Those are regular values, or just being thoughtful," concluded Chiyo.

Mindy then shared that she went to Hawaii because she wanted to see if she "fit in" (feeling somewhat alienated in the midwest) but found that there were Japanese cultural expectations not practiced by her family. For example, taking presents when you visit someone (*omiyage*), or giving *koden* (gifts of money at funerals) were obligatory. M. Kana and Shigeko helped explain the traditions. Later, Mona admitted that she still feels guilty if she doesn't take something when visiting friends. Chiyo teased her, "You're still the Issei lady." I pointed out that Mona brought the dessert for the group session. "You're so busy," Mona replied, "I wanted to help." As the women informally gathered for lunch, I noticed that M. Kana joined Imoto and Mindy, along with Ellen, a Japanese American graduate student from Utah, who was assisting me. They commented about the family photos (brought by participants) which were displayed in the dining area and then took their food in the living room. M. Kana was eager to learn about the backgrounds of these women and indicated to me before she left how pleased that she was to be able to meet these young women. I felt that there was a sense of curiosity, connection, and camaraderie across generations by the end of the session.

Vignette B

Five women sat in Anna's sunny suburban living room this August morning. Akiko, Obasan and Anna were Sansei while Erika (Akiko's daughter) and Fusako were Yonsei. Fusako grew up in a Chicago and presently taught at the elementary school where Obasan's son attended. Obasan and Akiko are cousins although their families had not remained in close contact and all three Sansei had grownup in the same city. Their grandparents and parents knew each other but while growing up, they attended different schools since they lived in separate parts of the city. The group began to share photos they had brought. Anna's picture of her grandmother, dressed in a kimono taken at the time of her arrival from Japan, prompted recollections of the gatherings of Japanese American families in Madison that occurred periodically.

At these community gatherings, the Issei played hana, a Japanese card game, and enjoyed conversation in Japanese while the Nisei, as young parents, socialized. The Sansei youngsters played games and entertaining themselves. At least this was the way Akiko and I remembered it. But Anna and Obasan interpreted these occasions very differently. "I was told exactly how to behave, so I was afraid to do anything but sit still," recalled Obasan. Her parents, especially her father made it very clear that children were to be respectful and well behaved, doing nothing to bring shame to the family. Anna also felt restricted since she perceived her role as a *gopher* for her grandmother, to be a model child politely assisting the elders. Neither felt that they had the right to go off and play independently. The environment, they felt was tense. It was ". . . never say the truth. Always be polite," said Obasan.

This was one example of the kind of behavioral expectations that the women began to interpret as obligation. Fusako, also shared her feelings of being responsible for her parents and grandparents. Perhaps, she noted, this was because she was the oldest child (as is Anna and Akiko). Her sister didn't feel as obligated to care for her family. "I'm the only one that lives near my parents," said Akiko, as she told of her mother's weekly visits when Erika was young. "She invested a lot of time in you kids," she said, looking at her daughter. Erika admitted that today as an adult, she has a close relationship with her grandparents and sees them on a regular basis.

Many of the expectations were communicated indirectly, without confrontation, sort of "under the surface" according to Anna and Obasan. Anna recalled that she felt she could be assertive outside the home but within the family there was a facade, or "the old way" as she put it. Mothers didn't speak with their daughters about personal or intimate matters. "I didn't confide in my mother," said Akiko, "In fact the only thing she told me about sex was, 'Don't sit on boy's laps.'" This brought laughter and some relief to a somewhat intense conversation. The three Sansei women seemed to concur that often there were secrets within the family between individuals or that some would put "favorable spins" on information in order to maintain family harmony.

But it was also pointed out that the Yonsei generation was much more out spoken and expressive about feelings, and that was considered a move in the right direction. Akiko shared that she took responsibility for rearing her children to be strong and independent. Obasan agreed that her children were very independent individuals. Anna thought that this family role playing had actually prevented the natural development of interpersonal relationships within the family by dictating prescribed roles. "You're supposed to love your sister, honor your father," she said. But, she contended, once families moved apart geographically, there were no interpersonal relationships to hold families together, only roles and obligations. Akiko pointed out that building family relationships takes effort, both to reach out and to remove "baggage" that may have developed over the years. Nods indicated that this was true. The conversation then moved on to comparing visits to Japan, where Obasan developed a comfort level never before experienced in the U.S. and Akiko found that the Japanese were more interested in her European American husband than her as an "American."

I later wondered if the conversation would have been so open and forthcoming if some of the Nisei women had been present. It was unfortunate that Obasan's daughter Leia, did not attend because with her outspoken personality she might have become a catalyst for a stronger blending of the Yonsei voice. But in their quiet way, Erika and Fusako readily participated and I also notice attempts made by all three Sansei women to bring them into the conversation. Even during lunch the conversation was continuous and compelling so I rarely had to introduce topics or focus on or clarify issues. And I might add, it was Mona's daughter Akiko who brought the fresh fruit salad.

Family Cohesion Across the Generations

When internment destroyed the Japanese family structure and postwar dispersion forced Japanese American families to relocate and to conform more readily to mainstream expectations, a new concept of family cohesion and responsibility was constructed. This process may have been accelerated for some midwestern Japanese Americans due to isolation from active ethnic communities. Support and mentoring came primarily from the nuclear and extended Japanese American family during a period of adjustment and inevitable cultural conflict with mainstream models of family relationships. As illustrated in the vignettes, confusion about and overlap of the "Japanese way" and American values was evident. The development of family cohesion and the expectant harmony that accompanies positive inter-personal relationships within a family was a pervasive concern for most Nisei women. But harmony was not always easily attained.

Maintaining family cohesion would take the deconstruction of obligatory family structures based on gender and lineage (patrilineal from the eldest son) which are not necessarily reinforced in western culture, and replacing them with a sense of family responsibility shared by siblings. Sylvia Yanagisako (1985) describes how kinship networks in Japanese American families evolved from a stem family system to a conjugal family system facilitated by Nisei sisters. Data in this study indicated that a reconstructed Japanese American family structure would focus on the following: 1. the development of a caring, unconditional support system for all family members, nuclear and extended (particularly grandparents) 2. the instilling of a sense of responsibility to the family as a whole (though not necessarily to prevent shame) based on respect for it's members, and 3. the building of interpersonal relationships within the family that are based on individual relations rather than traditional roles. It appears that this process of transformation has begun to occur for these Japanese American women.

Family Support Systems

There seemed to be a pervasive feeling across the generations that even if siblings were not geographically or even emotionally close (although many in this study were), there was an unwritten expectation of support for each other. And support for the care of elderly parents was undisputed. The sense of belonging that came with family membership was interpreted as a commitment and in some cases as an obligation (especially to parents) to be there when needed for family members. Some participants expressed a longing and even guilt when discussing children or siblings who have alienated themselves from their families (There were very few). And sometimes when one generation is not close, a desire for the next generation to maintain a closeness or a bond was expressed.

Several Nisei participants interpreted the support given by Japanese American families to its members as being positive family values that were universal and not necessarily Japanese. Various comparisons were made to other ethnic groups (Germans and Italians) that illustrated the sense of assimilation felt by some of these midwestern Nisei women. They recognized likenesses with more emphasis than ethnic differences and focused on mainstream European American values. This can be interpreted as a desire not to see themselves as different from others (us and them dichotomy), while an alternative orientation would be for the women to see the Japanese influence on their values and norms as inclusive in their "American" identity.

Two examples come to mind in which the significance of family and the expectation of unconditional support is reinforced across generations. Sansei Akiko told a delightful story about her words to her future son-in-law. She told him that he was not only marrying her daughter, but he was marrying her whole family. "He calls us the hunky-dory family," she says with a laugh, "He's got all the family things that are real important . . . It is just assumed that we're going to spend it (holidays) together." Akiko recalled how her mother, Mona worried about building a relationship with her grandchildren so that she visited every weekend when they were young. "That lasted about a month," Akiko quips.

To reinforce the extended family, Sansei Amelia shared the motivational words called "Love yous" that she and her European American husband tell their sons every night at bedtime. The following "positive affirmations" have been altered with pseudonyms:

> Your mama loves you and your daddy does too, and grandma Aya loves you, grandpa Peter loves you, grandma Rita loves you, grandpa Jerry loves you . . . (cousins from both sides of the family are named) . . . You love yourself most of all. You have a strong mind and a kind and gentle heart. You're a healthy young man. You're very smart, very wise. You're a creative thinker. You have lots and lots of good ideas. You're very successful because you try and try and try. You have a great sense of humor and you're lots of fun to be with. You're a beautiful person, inside and out and every day you're getting better and better and better. Today was a good challenging day and tomorrow will be even

better. Now it's time to rest, relax and sleep. Think pleasant thoughts of today and have positive dreams of tomorrow.

Such reinforcing verbal messages were not necessarily evident in the upbringing of many Sansei, yet they illustrate the desire to reinforce a positive sense of family care and commitment for future generations. Often, much was left unsaid due to the reserved family interactions that were the norm. Speaking openly about one's feelings was difficult at best for many Nisei and certainly it was not modeled by most Issei. Thus, what would be considered positive reinforcement of a child's self-esteem was rarely demonstrated by Issei, Nisei and some Sansei parents. In my household, for example, children were not asked about their feelings regarding a certain subject, a rule or expectation, instead, it was assumed that children would comply. Open expression of personal feelings was discouraged and considered self-serving, while concern for the harmony of the household was highly valued. In essence, you showed support for the family by being a member, yielding to what was best for everyone rather than for an individual.

Family Responsibility

The pervasive role expectation passed down from Issei mothers to their daughters was still primarily focused on marriage and child rearing. The Nisei women expected to fulfill family obligation, by caring for elderly Issei but, as supported by data from individual interviews, the traditions of multi-generational households was coming to a close. Many of the Sansei and Yonsei did not live with their grandparents, although they may have been psychologically close.

In multi-generational households, along with the demands of child rearing, Nisei women like Chiyo and Chizu were juggling the needs of Issei parents to maintain their Meiji Era culture with that of a husband who was negotiating work and schooling in mainstream European American society. Sometimes they did this in addition to maintaining a job outside the home or in the family business. As the Issei grew older and the Sansei became young adults, Nisei women began to recognize the tension between their expected responsibility to care for elders and the need to allow their children to be independent and free of the obligation they felt to their parents. But at the same time, they wanted their Sansei children to have a positive relationship with grandparents and themselves built on caring more than on a sense of filial piety. This set of conflicting messages was reflected in the vignettes by what Anna called "prescribed" roles and what Akiko regarded as baggage. Building family cohesion would take effort and cultural knowledge.

The Sansei and Yonsei participants appeared to focus on some of the cultural differences they had noticed and experienced attributing them to their Japanese American ethnicity. It was noted by some that Japanese Americans have a greater commitment to family compared to their European American peers. This sense of family obligation appeared to have differing effects on several of the Sansei participants; resentment for some and family pride for others. Both Sansei and Yonsei felt that Japanese American parents were stricter, acting more as authority figures than the parents of their European American peers. They also mentioned that expectations for being respectful and not bothering others were often stressed. Responsibility for elderly parents and grandparents was considered a family expectation and necessity but not regarded with the same feelings of obligation across the generations. Nisei felt compelled to care for elderly by tradition, while Sansei and Yonsei expressed a greater desire to do so because they genuinely cared about their parents and grandparents.

One example of how the expectation to care for the elderly was perpetuated came from Bonnie's description of her Issei grandmother's care. In her words:

> I watched my grandmother go through a real lengthy illness where they finally made a decision not to hospitalize her or put her into a nursing home because of the language barrier. The older she got the more she reverted back to Japanese. And so we opted to have a visiting nurse come in and a rotation of aunts and cousins (began). My mom would go down and spell one aunt who had the brunt of the responsibilities and another aunt who lived in Evanston would come down and help her out when she could. And then one of my cousins and her husband lived in the house for awhile, but that really wasn't going so well . . . They opted to move on someplace else. And then my mom would go down once a month to spell my aunt and I would go down on weekends to spell my mom. There were a lot of people (involved).

Some of the Nisei women, having experienced this type of responsibility, have told their Sansei children that they would choose not to live with them but prefer going to a nursing home. "You can put me in a nursing home, that's OK," Lani's healthy Nisei mother told her. Another Sansei Amelia, moved closer to her retired parents thinking that perhaps someday they might live with her and her family but found parents that were reluctant to consider the possibility. Even the oldest Nisei in the study, who is eighty and still living alone, told her daughter that she's still not ready to move in. The important factor here is that, since most Nisei speak English as their first language, the linguistic and cultural barriers don't exist for them as it did for the Issei.

Family Relationships

The conflict of divergent child-rearing approaches of Issei mothers with that of their Nisei daughters created turmoil within the households. But Sansei mothers, by in large were free to rear their children without daily input or contradictions from their mothers or mother-in-laws. And Yonsei participants appear to maintain some of the same beliefs about responsibility to family and child rearing although only two in the study were parents.

Since her own family did not stress "familiness," Nisei Chiyo shared her hope that her own children would at least grow up bonding. Like other Nisei women, she worked to perpetuate positive interactions among her adult children and their families. Others who grew up in close-knit families, also worked to pass that model of family connection and mutual support on to their children. This desire to build and maintain family cohesion would eventually reach extended families as siblings grew older, married, had their own children and perhaps even moved to different geographic locations. This concept of family is less rigid and role prescribed as the Meiji Era Japanese family kinship patterns described by Yanagisako (1985) which placed Japanese women in the homes of their husbands being held to obligatory standards of service and respect for elders and the *ie*, or the household.

Adopting western cultural standards, Nisei women in multi-generational households chose to place significance on the nuclear family and the husband-wife relationship rather than on traditional hierarchial patterns of honor and control. This caused some strife and cultural conflict within households, especially where Nisei women lived with their mother-in-laws, who expected to become the matriarch of the family. The transformation of roles and relationships allowed little outlet for the Issei, who had limited contact with other Japanese American elders in the midwest, unless they lived within the small ethnic neighborhoods like the one in Chicago. Japanese communities were not readily available to help Japanese Americans maintain traditional family patterns and to reinforce Asian cultural values, although ethnic communities have persisted throughout the generations (see Fugita and O'Brien, 1991). The Nisei desire to have their Sansei children integrated into mainstream society, rather than promoting ethnic identity, appeared to be a priority.

In some cases, the parent-child closeness skipped a generation, and strong grandparent-grandchild relationships have developed. Several Sansei and Yonsei women discussed their grandparents with a deep sense of awe or intimacy. Yonsei Leia spoke of her "genius" grandfather who was prominent in the field of medical research, which inspired Leia to go into medicine. "He was such an immensely busy and highly achieving human being that I was just in awe of him," she said. Recalling tender moments when he would rock her as a toddler and sing Japanese songs, Leia felt that she had a special bond with her grandfather. She didn't realize how important he was until her grandfather passed away when she was in high school and three thousand people attended his wake.

There are several possible reasons for the development of strong grandparent-grandchild relationships that may have been a function of linguistic difference, ability and opportunity to work outside the home, desire to develop inter-generational communication and respect, and preference for family childcare. Some Sansei recalled acting as translators for their grandmothers during public outings, while others lamented at their inability to speak Japanese and communicate with grandparents. Nisei parents generally had to work and needed childcare but most preferred to use relative rather than babysitters. Or, as described by women in all of the generations, they would usually select outings where they could take their children or where families congregated and children were welcome.

The Transformation of Amae

Most of the Nisei and some of the Sansei in this study were familiar with this word or had experienced the concept of *amae*. Nisei Chizu and Sansei Connie made reference to their contact with Japanese nationals when explaining the meaning of *amae*. As a wife of a university professor, Chizu spent many years entertaining graduate students from Japan. "Their children were spoiled rotten," said Chizu, "They let them do any old thing. It's just shocking . . . up and down the house, on the bed, no discipline. But when they go to school, poof . . . they change just like that. The teacher really takes over. That's the big difference in it." Connie worked for years as a receptionist for her husband's optometry business and would see Japanese nationals with their children in their waiting room. "The kids were very spoiled," she explained, "and they would *amaeru* and ran all over . . . very disrespectful."

One example of the transformation of *amae* was described by Nisei Chiyo, who recalled that although the word *amae* was not mentioned, the concept was practiced in her family. It was most evident to her in the mother-son and grandmother-granddaughter relationships that Chiyo observed in her home. Her mother-in-law treated her husband like a prince, responding to his needs and constantly defending him. She would fawn over her granddaughter who had serious allergies. While Chiyo was attempting to teach her daughter Anna self-control and independence, and assuming that her husband would become self-sufficient, her mother-in-law was trying to establish an inter-dependency between herself and her son and granddaughter. Needless to say, there was tremendous friction and culture clash. The two women had different child-rearing goals and were working under different sets of rules for establishing family life under the same roof.

When Anna first became a parent she recreated the *amae*-like relationship she had with her grandmother until she realized it's perils. She explains:

> I started out an over-mothering, over-protective mother. I carried around a diaper bag that weighed twice as much as the baby. I was prepared for any contingency and potential danger (real or imagined). I controlled every aspect of their lives. Then, during toddlerhood, my two very different children forced me to stand back, and to back off for different reasons.
>
> My son hated to be "bossed around." One day, I found myself wondering, "Why am I fighting with a two year old about socks? What conceivable harm could it do if he wore two different socks? Who cares which socks he wears?" The answer, of course, is that he cares alot, but no one else, including me, could care less.
>
> My daughter, on the other hand, enjoyed being coddled and appreciated all of the services her mother provided. But after finding myself tying her shoes for her long after she could do it herself, I said, "Wait a minute here, at this rate I'll have to go to college with her to tie her shoe." She saw no reason to do things herself, she had no reason to do things herself. So I had to let one kid have more control over his life and make the other one take control of hers. And, I think, it has been good for all of us.

Nisei Mona interpreted *amae* as a responsiveness of a mother to her children's needs. She believes that while growing up, she and her siblings didn't ameru too much because there were too many kids. Mona also explained that whenever the children asked for help her Issei mother was right there. Mona laughingly compared herself to her mother saying, "I always say, 'wait until I finish this,' but she never said that." Mona is amazed that the problems of seven children were always more important to her mother than anything she might have been doing at the time. Keeping her own mother's dedication to children in mind, Mona has also devoted much of her energies to her children and grandchildren.

Sansei Imoto and Grapdelight also mentioned their mother's responsiveness and doting behavior but did not attach this behavior to the concept of *amae*. Imoto described it in this way:

> My mother will also ask me about ten million times if I want something to eat when I'm home. I'm not sure how to describe this behavior, but I notice that my sisters and I do the same thing; ask people ten million times if we can do anything for them. I know that this is behavior that my family typically engages in because when my boyfriend is over he's rather amazed at all the offers I get for things and is surprised that I don't want to accept. I guess it is also understood that in my family that you should say no ten million times.

Grapdelight noted that it's a common perception that grandparents want to live near their grandchildren, but she believes that her mother really wanted to be near her, more so than her children. In describing her mother's behavior she said:

> My mother, still to this day, I mean I don't move because she'll say, "what's the matter?" If I just go like this (a gesture) . . . "what's the matter, is there something you want?" She's very watchful, too watchful, every nuance of my voice, of my movements, of everything . . . the way I choose my words . . . It always has been.

In dealing with her own children, Grapdelight has responded with as much commitment. Her oldest son was very demanding and required constant adjustment and attention on her part. "He had his own agenda about life from the time he was born," she shared, "He completely ran my life for the first four or five years, I mean completely because he was so intense in his needs to have something exactly a certain way." Grapdelight chose to work only 30% time knowing it might negatively affect her as a professional, but finding it necessary for the welfare and development of her children. "I wrote all those words like motherhood and family responsibility when asking to switch to part-time employment," she shared.

The *amae*-like parenting behavior, as well as a strict and authoritative parenting style, was evident across the generations, as expressed by the voices in the child-rearing vignette. Some Nisei and Sansei mothers had dependency relationships with their children while others attempted to break away from the indulgence and psychological control of their children (see Doi, 1974; Mass, 1986) considering that approach as spoiling children, and moved to a more authoritative and stricter method of child rearing. In some cases there were mixed messages for the children when mothers continued to *amae* and fathers became strict authority figures. There were, as a result, mixed messages about dependency and conformity to family expectations while extending oneself to become self-sufficient and independent.

In an attempt to decipher these seemingly contradictory perspectives Sansei Connie offered this explanation: "It was our parents, not so much the fact that they were Japanese, but they were from that Meiji Era. That Meiji Era was very strong in the discipline, I think, or so it seems that way." It is possible that the discipline of the Meiji Era referred primarily to societal constraints (stoicism and endurance) once children went to school and not to child rearing in the home, but was remembered and interpreted by participants as expectations for all children regardless of age by Issei and Nisei parents. Age of the child may also be a consideration in terms of the degree in which *amae* is acceptable, possibly more appropriate for younger children than older siblings.

Japanese societal norms put strict constraints on the behavior of children in public (including school) and Japanese Americans, particularly Issei mothers, may have been unaware of the difference in societal context. Compliant public behavior included *haji* (shame), *ha-zu-ka*-shi (embarrassment or reticence) and *hi-ge* (self-denigration) which are part of the *enryo syndrome* expressed by Issei and some Nisei (Kitano, 1976, p. 125). But these norms were understood by the Issei, experienced by many Nisei but generally unfamiliar to the Sansei and Yonsei. A few Sansei recall parents warning them to not bring shame to the family but for most this message was implied, if even expressed in family relations. Nisei parents understood the impact of racial visibility in an overtly discriminatory society and attempted to prepare their children to avoid confrontation by inculcating compliant behavior in their Sansei children.

Several of the Nisei and Sansei participants recalled being told directly to avoid doing anything that might bring shame to the family, but in many cases, as Lani described, not bringing shame was always implied. "Family pride was very important since you were a visible minority, you could be singled out," Sansei Bonnie explained. The lessons taught by her parents, who encountered blatant racism, to blend in were clearly instilled. "One must survive in society therefore, *When in Rome, do as the Romans do*," she was told. Family pride is a virtue Bonnie is passing on to her Yonsei daughters. And since each family might be one of only a handful of Japanese American families in the community, behavior of any of the children reflected upon the other families as well as their own.

The reality of being a visible minority and the need to not bring attention to oneself and one's family was brought up by several other Sansei and Yonsei, while others do not recall having this discussed in their families. Imoto's family broke the ice by integrating their neighborhood. She recalled her father warning his sons that, "if you're with others who misbehave, you'll get caught. They'll remember your face." People in the community where Sansei Mitzi lived referred to her physician father as a "Jap" without sensitivity to it's derogatory inference. Mitzi's younger brother wasn't truly aware of his ethnicity and had trouble understanding the cruelty of his peers. Then one summer a Japanese American cousin visited from Los Angeles and couldn't believe there were no other Japanese in town. The visitor felt that everyone was staring at him when they swam at the local pool, a perception that changed the understanding and consequent reality for Mitzi and her brother.

Growing up in the suburbs of Chicago, Yonsei Jane's family had little association with the ethnic community. When they occasionally did, Jane felt that the Sansei and Yonsei were cliquish, causing her to not want to associate with them. "They were Japanese in a sense that they associated with other Japanese Americans but they were not Japanese in the sense that they knew culture . . . They were just like any other high school kids," she explained. Jane interpreted ethnicity as an understanding of Japanese cultural traditions rather than on values and world view acquired from family and reflected in behavior. "My parents weren't very Japanesey," said Jane, "we were told *Don't stick out* or *Don't rock the boat*." She recalled how her father warned her brother during the 1960's not to participate in the demonstrations because he would be visible and remembered. Having that Asian face could make you vulnerable in some contexts, desirable in other contexts, as Sansei and Yonsei discovered during the period of civil rights and affirmative action.

Sansei Bonnie and Yonsei Fusako both taught school in primarily upper-middle class White neighborhoods and felt very visible as minority educators. Bonnie recalled being referred to as the "token minority" in her school by a rather insensitive administrator, who was eager to diversify his school district. He had no idea that his comment could be considered negative or be insulting and had no compulsion about stating this in Bonnie's presence. Both women were cautioned by their families not to become conspicuous as they were in the work force as professionals. Fusako remembers her father's suggestion not to buy a Japanese car because that would reinforce her ethnicity and perhaps cause others to see her as being foreign. She laughingly shared the story pointing out how many other White teachers had Honda's in the school parking lot.

The transformation of *amae* appears to have occurred as a result of two factors: the weak understanding of Japanese child rearing norms by Nisei and Sansei and the impetus to integrate third and fourth generation Japanese Americans into mainstream society because of the status as visible minorities particularly during the post World War II years. Kitano (1961) also points to the accessibility of media and professional advise on child rearing, unavailable to Issei due to linguistic differences, that Nisei were able to utilize. And several Nisei participants did indicate that Dr. Spock was a household name during their parenting years. Thus, *amae* in the traditional Japanese sense caused more confusion in terms of child-rearing approaches than it contributed to developing a strong mother-child relationship for midwestern Sansei and Yonsei. But if *amae* were to be interpreted as an unconditional commitment to the nurturing development of children, then that priority of children in midwestern Japanese American families has been evident throughout the generations in this study.

Wedding portrait, 1970 (grandmother in background)

4. How Japanese Are We?

The Civil Rights Movement provided the impetus for some women to investigate their roots. What does it mean to be Asian American or Japanese American? How do race and ethnicity intersect? Why have we been called the Model Minority? Will Japanese Americans continue to assimilate until there is no Japanese American culture? Like many young Americans during the 1960's and 1970's, the Sansei were searching for their personal identities and in doing so, they began to investigate their ethnic heritage. They began to question the stereotypes placed upon them.

De Vos & Romanucci-Ross (1975) note that ethnic identity includes both subjective emblematic expressions of culture as well as a sense of belonging and group continuity. They explain: "Ethnicity is determined by what a person feels about himself, not by how he is observed to behave" (p. 17). But how one feels about oneself, one's self-concept, is in part determined by how that person is treated and accepted by others. Did midwestern Japanese American women "feel" Japanese? Did they feel American? Does "American" only mean European American? Did they feel a sense of affiliation with other Japanese Americans? Did they recognize the relevance of their race in relation to their ethnic minority status in American society, considering the socio-political contexts of their race and ethnicity? How much did they know about the historical oppression of their ancestors during World War II? By listening to their individual and collective voices we will gain some insight into the women's sense of ethnic identity.

There are two theoretical approaches to ethnicity which are considered quite divergent: the *primordialist*, which focuses on "communities of culture" maintaining that ethnic cohesion is based on sentiment, beliefs and worldview, and the *instrumentalist*, which emphasizes "communities of interest" based on the functional aspects of ethnicity (Espiritu, 1992, pp. 4-5). Primordialists focus on cultural content and the learning of traditions and beliefs of an ethnic group while Instrumentalists might be more concerned about how ethnic groups could network in order to maintain political benefits. Both approaches, according to Espiritu (1992), assume that "ethnic groups are largely voluntary collectives defined by national origin, whose members share a distinctive, integrated culture" (p. 5). Those who choose to maintain an ethnic identity gain both psycholological and material support from their ethnic affiliations. But when economic ties disappear and sentiment for one's native culture no longer exists, ethnicity, it is assumed, will also vanish and acculturation will occur. Espiritu also argues that ethnicity is often imposed on groups. Both the primordialist and instrumentalist perspectives were represented in this study.

The midwestern women in this three-generation study have constructed their personal identities across different historical periods, in different geographical settings and with different familial and community influences. They have built their self-assessments on how they feel about themselves as well as their interpretation of how they are perceived by others. "How one identifies oneself is so private and individual," wrote Sansei Imoto, "I realize that identity will be in part a reflection of the group experience but I feel how it is played out is based on personal interpretation and implementation of learning and upbringing." She sees ethnic identity as the "intermingling of values and behaviors in the basic realms of personal, family and community." Individual interpretations of one's family and community cultures may create differing views on ethnicity or "Japaneseness" leading to divergence in identity development even among family members.

Feelings of Japaneseness were described by most study participants as having an understanding of and experience with Meiji Era Japanese culture, as interpreted by family members. One Sansei woman, Obasan, and her Yonsei daughter Leia indicated that they clearly differentiated between Japanese culture and Japanese American culture. At the beginning of the study, Obasan wrote, "I believe we have a distinct cultural history and set of customs apart from the Japanese." At the end of the study when I asked the participants to identify their rating for Japaneseness again, she explained:

> I've changed my ranking since my trip to Japan. I feel as if I've attained a balance between my "Japaneseness" and my American self. In some ways, I understand and like my *Japaneseness* and have less understanding for my American self. I still feel very proud of my Japanese-American heritage but now I have something in addition to this ethnic-American historical identity. When I was in Japan I was let in as an insider. My actions were consistently rewarded without suspicion. I am well aware that I am not Japanese and never will or want to be but what I found was a family feeling that I've never experienced in the U.S.

It is that ethnic-American historical identity that I related to at the Smithsonian exhibition which will evolve as post-war generations of immigrants and their children create a new era of Japanese Americanness. As Yonsei Leia explains, "I think there's a big difference between Japanese ethnicity and Japanese American ethnicity. They are two paths which diverged at the turn of the century." So how would this Japanese American-ness be defined? In order to understand the women's own definitions, I asked them to share the Japanese part of their identity as Japanese Americans. Japaneseness was characterized by race and culture; sometimes interchangeably.

Cultural or Functional Compatibility

The theory of cultural determinism, posited by Caudill and De Vos (1973) and further refined in the work of Kitano (1969), attributes educational success to cultural values that promote upward mobility. "Basically, this theory posits that the current status of Asian Americans is a logical outcome of their unique cultural characteristics" (Suzuki, 1977, p. 164). Asian family values such as hard work, family cohesion, patience and thrift were considered compatible with middle class American values. De Vos & Wagatsuma (1973) list the following traits as being culturally compatible with American mainstream values: politeness, respect for authority and parental wishes, sense of duty to community, diligence, cleanliness and neatness, and the setting and achieving of long range goals (p. 238).

In their study of cultural compatibility within the public school setting, Tabachnick and Bloch (1995) suggest that the term culture is problematic and refers to a dynamic process rather than a static concept. They explain:

> Culture is, therefore, always in need of discovery rather than being describable for all members of a group in advance of knowing any specific individual members and the particular sociocultural contexts in which they enact their cultural identities and behavior. This perspective does not deny shared group outlooks, worldviews, rules for behavior, values or recognition by insiders and outsiders of membership and affiliation with the group. But it does avoid decontextualizing membership in a culture or the meaning of culture for individuals within and across particular groups. (p. 205)

The meaning attached to Japanese American culture for Nisei and Sansei in California may be significantly different from the interpretation of Wisconsin Nisei and Sansei. What may be perceived as mainstream American culture by midwestern Japanese Americans may be considered more Japanese than European American by Japanese Americans reared in San Francisco's Little Tokyo. Indeed, to define a particular culture, one needs to identify the speaker within a given context. And for these reasons, as well as the difficulty defining Japanese culture of the Meiji Era, from Issei immigrants, some Japanese American scholars find functional compatibility to be a more plausible explanation for Asian American success.

Kitano (1969) credits the success of Asian Americans to the functional compatibility and interaction between the two value systems and predicts that future generations would become increasingly assimilated both structurally and culturally (In Suzuki, 1977). His position of functional compatibility maintains that Japanese cultural values are not the same as mainstream American cultural values but that the Japanese have one value of adapting or accommodating to situations (an adaptation syndrome). Kitano believes that the Sansei of the 1970's also prescribed to this orientation. In describing family cohesion, Kitano (1971) writes: "For all of us who live in Asian families, that cohesion as told to us by the White man is really a myth--the White man really thinks that the [Japanese American] families think together, do things together, and everyone obeys, etc." (In Tachiki et al., 1971, p. 85). Kitano (1976) elaborates on this issue explaining that the myth of deference, conformity and compromise has allowed Japanese Americans to be accepted without hostility of the larger society.

Suzuki (1977) endorses the view that the socialization process into mainstream society, rather than cultural compatibility accounted for educational success. He claims that upward mobility had been limited by the channeling of Asian Americans into lower-echelon jobs as a result of racism and discriminatory policies. Suzuki's (1977) revisionist theory explains that, due to racism, Asian American children were socialized to be passive and obedient in school, traits that were rewarded by European American teachers, and that the lack of employment opportunities for their parents caused Asian Americans to invest in education as the only feasible way for them to attain upward mobility. But the opportunity for Asian Americans to reach parity in the job market remained a problem. Even statistics touting high family incomes for Asian Americans failed to consider the number of family members (including siblings and extended family members) contributing to that income. Thus, the myth of Asian Americans as the "model minority," both educationally and economically, was perpetuated.

In later works refining his revisionist theory, Suzuki (1980) defines the term deculturalization as a combination of the processes of acculturation and discrimination. He contends that Asian American students suffer from low esteem, are overly conforming, and tend to have their academic and social development narrowly circumscribed as a result of the Anglo-centric curriculum, which distorts the Asian American experience (p. 93). Creativity and verbal expression are often stifled due to teacher reinforcement of stereotypical behaviors like docility and conformity. In the workplace, subtle forms of discrimination continued to relegate Asian Americans to lower-echelon powerless positions. Some Nisei and Sansei have, in order to ameliorate the effects of deculturalization, renewed their interest in ethnic identity and the emergence of the Asian American movement.

Sue and Okazaki's (1990) perspective of relative functionalism also places the valuing of education by Asian Americans firmly into a societal rather than cultural context. They believe that ". . . for factors that influence achievement levels, single explanations cannot adequately account for the observed performance patterns. Thus, research on heredity, culture, child-rearing practices, educational experiences, and personality, among other topics, has yielded interesting but inconclusive results" (p. 913). Upward mobility in areas of leadership, entertainment, sports and politics, where education does not necessarily lead to positions or careers, was limited to Asian Americans. As a result, Asian Americans turned to education. "That is, education is increasingly functional as a means of mobility" (p. 917). This perspective seems to have merit given the socio-political context in which the Nisei were living.

Ethnicity as a Cultural Construct

Lisa Lowe (1991), writing about Asian Americans, describes her conception of the passing of culture from generation to generation; "Culture may be a much 'messier' process than unmediated vertical transmission from one generation to another, including practices that are partly inherited, partly modified, as well as partly invented" (p. 27). Espiritu (1992) points out that new forms of ethnic cultures are always being created based on "cultural traditions that are symbolic or mythical, or that no longer exist" (p. 8). Therefore, as culture becomes transformed, the original source and content of the tradition or belief may become blurred or lost by continuous re-interpretation, or even misinterpretation.

Some of the Sansei in this study who interpreted ethnic identity as relating to the transmission of Japanese cultural traits were unsure of what was Japanese compared to the midwestern, protestant ethic. For example, when discussing the indirect, stoic Japanese communication style, Sansei Kim pondered:

> I think I was always trying to figure it out. What part of me was Japanese; what part of me was an American? Did it matter? Then there's a whole other dimension too... It is the midwestern ethic, the protestant ethic... I think, that plays a strong part. I have a friend I've known since I was two years old, who I grew up with and we're still friends. So I see her family often, this Wisconsin stock... They're Catholic so it's the Catholic, midwestern ethic... I don't know how it differs from the Japanese American side... but it's this midwestern stoicism that also plays a part.

Two Yonsei, Fusako and Yano, make the distinction between race and ethnic identity. "Since I am 100% Japanese, I feel strongly Japanese, yet I am removed from the culture because I am 4th generation," said Fusako. "However, I am very interested in preserving what I do know and learning more. For example, I hope to visit Japan and learn Japanese someday." Yano put it into perspective: "I think about myself as just a person first. But since the birth of my children, my ethnic identity is becoming increasingly important to me." She felt connected to the values of her grandmother who was a Shinto priestess. It seems as though Yano interpreted individuality as being separate from race and ethnicity and that ethnic identity was related to a cultural heritage with traditions and a value system.

Many of the Nisei women made clear differentiations between their European American western culture and the Japanese eastern culture of their Issei parents. Nisei Masako explained how she didn't like to be identified as having the same culture as Japanese from Japan. She writes:

> From childhood on when people talk about Japan and Japanese I feel self conscious sometimes since they may lump me with Japan when they shouldn't. And acquaintances ask if I came from Japan so I explain my parents immigrated here; I was born here and I am an American citizen.

This dichotomy of cultural difference led some families and individuals to move toward one culture while avoiding or rejecting the other. For differing reasons and personal choice, some participants found themselves moving closer to their cultural roots of Japan while others found themselves more attuned with western philosophy and cultural patterns. These divergent views are illustrated by two Sansei women, Anna and Mitzi.

Anna noted that while growing up her family put a "low priority on things Japanese," stating, "my mother and grandmother, many times, voiced relief that they were free of the many Japanese obligations. They were into assimilation and didn't look back... There was little nostalgia for the old country in our family." She offered this analytical assessment of her low ethnic identity rating:

> My low Japanese ethnicity scale rating is due to: 1. Default, that is, many other components of my personal identity have far overshadowed the Japanese identity component. 2. A fundamental culture clash over individual rights and responsibilities, what degree of control one has (should have) over ones own destiny, what choices one is entitled to make over ones own life. 3. It has never been a matter of rejection, I have never wanted to "not be Japanese." It always seemed to be irrelevant.

Sansei Mitzi, at the other end of the ethnicity scale, became increasingly immersed in Japanese culture. She has taken three courses in Japanese language, five years of ikebana, obtained a brown belt in judo plus a first degree rank in Jodo (stick fighting) and is a member of the Japan America Society of Wisconsin. Several trips to Japan, associations with Japanese athletic clubs, Buddhist churches and speaking as a minority professor on topics of Asian Americans has kept Mitzi involved in a heritage that eluded her while growing up in Iowa.

Japanese culture in terms of "high culture" was a source of fond memories for some Nisei. M. Kana indicated that she hadn't felt that Japanese but because her mother was well cultured she found herself emulating her behavior. For example, M. Kana explained, that when you put a bunch of flowers in a vase, you never just "pound them in," but rather, you place them with care. These were the finer parts of Japanese aesthetics, *ikebana* (flower arranging), that she absorbed and appreciated. Nisei Chizu's mother also taught her *ikebana* and *origami* (paper folding) which she passed on to her daughters and granddaughters. Access to Japanese culture differed for her two Sansei daughters, Mariko who lives in Tennessee and Mika who settled in California. Mika noted that after having grown up in the midwest, "It was an odd experience being around so many Asians at first." She continued, "As I grow older I feel less conflicted about my cultural heritage in an American society." Mika hopes to instill Japanese culture into her young daughter. At the same time, Mika considers herself politically very American and progressive.

One of the most interesting and perhaps strongest connection to the Japanese ethnic community was the active participation of Sansei Lani and Kikuye in the Chicago based Nisei Ambassadors Drum and Bugle Corps. The corps, according to Lani (who provided me with a wonderful videotape of the corps reunion), reinforced the Japanese value of working hard for the collective good, rather than for individual gain. Kikuye, who also now lives in California, has become active in the Japanese American community and became president of the local JACL (Japanese American Citizen's League).

Although most of the Sansei and Yonsei women appear to be highly Americanized on the surface, underneath they share some common values and unanswered questions about their heritage. Often these are manifested as feelings about their ethnicity but are not easily recognized or defined. Both Jane and Lesye mentioned the work of David Mura (1991) as a reflection of their ethnicity. Although Jane found some of the experiences portrayed in his book *Turning Japanese* unfamiliar (They both grew up in Skokie but attended different schools) she attributed this disparity to his more "artsy" background. Lesye attended one of Mura's performances with her Korean and Chinese friends and discovered that they did not relate to his stage personas as she did. But a movie called *The Wash* created the "most acute experience of realizing my Japanese American-ness" according to Lesye. She wrote: "I saw how the family dynamics in the movie were so familiar to me. It occurred to me then that I had never before seen a movie that I identified with in that way before."

Nisei Chiyo pointed out that while Sansei were growing up, Nisei were still trying to negotiate both cultures, wanting the best from American society for their children, yet coping with cultural norms (like *enryo*-holding back, and *giri*-obligation) that they themselves didn't fully understand or necessarily agree with. They had no parenting models for communicating this cultural conflict to their children. Since Japanese behavioral norms in which they had been reared included low verbalization (family conversations were rare) and the reluctance to discuss intimate issues, many of the Nisei mothers were not able to articulate these cultural differences to their children.

Ethnicity as a Racial Construct

The view of race and ethnicity as one joint category can be interpreted from a purely genetic perspective classifying Japanese and Japanese Americans within an Asian or mongoloid race (a dated anthropological term) and placing emphasis on inheritance through bloodlines. Several Sansei mothers in the study eluded to this classification noting that their children had "mongolian spots" on their bodies when they were born indicating Asian racial features. Those adopting this genetic position might be concerned with the high rate of racial outmarriage especially by Japanese American women, causing the Japanese gene pool to become diluted over the generations. In fact, Japanese American historian Ronald Takaki suggested that perhaps with the progressively larger numbers of outmarriages, Japanese Americans might become blended in, no longer able to maintain a racial/ethnic identity.

Panethnicity, which is characterized by solidarity among ethnic subgroups occurs for socio-political reasons because these groups of differing national origins are often considered one people by non-Asians (Espiritu, 1992, p.6). Ethnic identification is a choice for European American Americans but not for people of color in the United States. This categorical racial identity prevents Asian Americans, regardless of heritage or citizenship, to fully assimilate into a non-ethnically characterized American society. Kitano and Daniels (1988) also address the issue of the visibility of minorities. They write, ". . . no matter how acculturated or talented a Sansei may be, the physical features identify him or her as an ethnic. For Japanese and other Asian Americans, acting positions remain primarily as stereotypes" (p. 74). Sylvia Yanagisako (1985) places this definition within the context of racial identity. "What makes a person racially Japanese is substance rather than conduct," she wrote, "Hence, even the Sansei . . . whom the Nisei view as very Americanized and as exhibiting almost no Japanese social conduct and interactional styles, are considered fundamentally, and in essence, Japanese" (p. 173).

This perspective originates in ancient Japan with the belief in racial homogeneity, or in the concept of Japanese blood (*chie*) and the genetic transmission of culture and language (Minnari & Befu, 1991, p. 35). Since race and ethnicity were combined categories, even Japanese Americans were expected to know the Japanese language and culture. Nisei and Sansei living in Japan were often turned down for teaching positions of English, in preference for European Americans. Reischaur (1977) a longtime scholar of Japanese history labeled this genetic theory a racist theory of the unity of race, language and culture (p. 37).

Most of the women in this study identified themselves with other Japanese, Asians and Asian Americans, as racial minorities but not culturally as a member of any of the groups. Their knowledge of Japanese culture (either Meiji Era culture from family traditions or contemporary Japanese culture via study or travel) was relatively weak which lead to a lack of clarity in conceptualizing Japanese American ethnic culture. As a result, some participants found justification for not seeing themselves as very ethnic and for adopting a color-blind perspective. The following descriptions from participants will show the divergent views on ethnic identity.

When Yonsei Leia accompanied her mother to Japan, she discovered that as a biracial Japanese American she was still considered a *gaijin*, or foreigner. This was both a surprise and disappointment for her. Yonsei Alana articulated the same feeling of alienation in her words: "When in Japan and being half Japanese, it just doesn't cut it. My last name may not be written using my family's *kanji* (written characters) because I'm not 100%." These two responses place Japaneseness in the racial category based on genetics rather than on culture or nationality.

Several participants discussed the color-blind perspective in relation to their Japaneseness. Sansei Grapdelight felt that race "should not matter" and recalled rejecting Japanese food and culture while growing up. Sansei Akiko shared that when she told her European American friend that she was planning to attend a group interview with exclusively Japanese American women, her friend couldn't understand why because she considered Akiko White. "I think even my friends now don't view me as oriental," she explained, "they don't look at me as being different than them because I've been around so long, I guess. . . I don't speak with an accent so they forget that I am oriental and I guess that's fine." Several other participants shared that they had siblings who embraced the color-blind philosophy considering themselves to be White, or not different from their European American friends.

Others like Sansei Lesye explained how she separated her race as an Asian American from her ethnic identity as a Japanese American:

> Asian American is central to my identity. Japaneseness--I just haven't been in places with much community so it's not a strong identification. But I know I have bunches more in common with other Sansei than with other Asian Americans. I look at events going on around me with a racial identity lens--that's constant. This is because Asian American activism is a central part of my life now.

Sansei Mimi used the term Asian American interchangeably with Japanese American when she described her work at an Asian American Clinic in California. For Mimi, cultural traits, like reserve, respectfulness (especially of elders) and commitment to the group or collective could be attributed to all Asians. Both she and her sister Amelia indicated that their visibility as a racial minority was more salient to their identity than their ethnic identity which "is most often *not* part of my day-to-day awareness." After having grown up without an active ethnic community (a few Japanese American families got together occasionally), Mimi found a comfort level in a west coast Asian American community which she described by the terms brotherhood, sisterhood, "one big family," and "being treated in a family way."

Was this feeling of acceptance a function of racial identity or cultural compatibility or both? In further describing her relationship with this clinical counseling group, Mimi remarked:

> Others had a skeptical view of me because I was from the midwest... Was I really Asian? In their own way they tested me to see if I would laugh at the same things... Would show the correct respect to the pastor?... Would I sort of like play the correct role of a woman?... Was I really an Asian woman, which I knew how to do and also it came naturally... and because everyone was behaving that way, it was easy to behave that way also.

Once she was accepted, Mimi found that she was included as one of *them* and that acceptance was a permanent status. "There was nothing I could do to get out of it," she admitted. This kind of collective interdependency was a new experience for Mimi, something unfamiliar and in contrast to the individualism and independence of her family and midwestern community. So it would appear that race was the first indicator, a marker by which she was invited to participate, but cultural understanding and appropriate behavior was the deciding factor as to whether she would be accepted (fit in) or not.

Biracial Yonsei Erika spoke of how she came to identify with her Asian or Japanese side (The terms were used interchangeably), as a response to racist comments and behavior of others. She felt alienated from her European American peers and sought ways to cope with this feeling. In discussing her feelings of being an outsider as a teenager, Erika said:

> I often think about my Japanese side. It wasn't until college that I stopped feeling different from everyone else. Most often the indications that I got (before college) were in the form of racial slurs. Occasionally there would be a boyfriend who was interested in the *non-White* foods we ate. Otherwise it was not acknowledged. I guess because I was young when the racial slurs started, I couldn't get past that until college.

Now as an artist, Erika has used her questions and insights about being biracial in her creative work. Her prints incorporate Japanese symbols and styles with an assertive message about racism in American society. Like many of the women in this study, she has found her own way of coping with her developing and often conflicting identity as a Japanese American woman. The following quote, called *Ninjabitch*, provided the context for her recent showing of black and white prints:

> Being human, I feel the need to identify and express myself as an individual. Through my art work I can satisfy this need. As I mature, I am beginning to perceive a focus amid the chaos. The overriding desire to push further the concept of defining and refining three pieces of my identity: I am Japanese. I am Japanese American. I am a Japanese American woman. For me these are very complex ideas, I have found it very difficult to separate these things from the White world in which I was raised. Not that I feel the need to get away from Whiteness (as if it were possible) but to simply identify that which is different. I choose images that exhibit ideas about: racism, White/mainstream misconceptions about Asian culture, what Japaneseness means to me, what it means to be Yonsei (4th generation), for example, 2nd generation European Americans are considered American where as (I think) because of their unique appearance (looks) Japanese Americans are still Japanese.

There has been an evolution of coping from the alienation Erika's grandmother experienced during internment to the assimilationist upbringing of her mother's generation to the willingness of Yonsei to creatively express the shared racism. It appears from the comments of Leia and Erika, that race and ethnicity are extremely salient to their self-identities. As biracial Japanese Americans, they are seeking to reconnect with a rich yet unarticulated ethnic heritage.

Assimilation, Acculturation and Identity

O'Brien and Fugita (1991) believe that when discontinuity between home culture and that of the school and society occurs, parents can teach their children to accommodate by one of three methods: 1) ignoring the immigrant culture and attempting to fit into the host society (cultural assimilation), 2) accepting an alternative without losing their own traditions (acculturation), or 3) constructing new cultural norms altering the cultural content of both societies (transformation). But, based upon Gordon's (1964) definition of structural assimilation, O'Brien and Fugita (1991) caution that equality in the workplace, neighborhood and interracial marriages would be required for total assimilation to occur (p. 83). It is also possible to utilize all three methods at differing times, in differing contexts, so that a group or individual might adopt several strategies to meet changing sociopolitical conditions. This may, in fact, explain what happened in the case of midwestern Japanese American women across three generations.

Montero (1980), in his study of ethnic affiliation over three generations (Issei, Nisei and Sansei), examined the relationship of the impact of economic advancement on Japanese Americans and the cohesiveness and solidarity of their ethnic community. "Does departure from the community (geographically, psychologically, or both) smooth the road to success?" Montero pondered, "In short, what is the relationship between socioeconomic advancement and assimilation into the larger American society?" (p. 80). Montero's (1980) study focused on four indicators of assimilation: visiting patterns with relatives, ethnicity of favorite organization, ethnicity of two closest friends, and rate of intermarriage. Comparative results between the Nisei and Sansei indicated that there was a definite trend away from ethnic affiliation. Higher occupational and educational status played a significant part in the mobility away from the ethnic community. Sometimes a limited number of professional positions were available to Japanese Americans in locations near ethnic communities. Therefore securing jobs at their educational level meant moving to other cities away from kinship ties. As a result, the extended family became less involved in the family that moved away from the community.

Montero's four indicators of assimilation cannot be adequately applied to midwestern Japanese Americans since access to relatives for regular visitations, access to Japanese American organizations, and access to other Japanese or Asian Americans were all limited by geographical isolation and could not be considered personal preferences or lifestyle choices. Inter-marriage, which was high for third and fourth generations, was perhaps the only reliable indicator of assimilation.

Assimilation, according to Kiefer (1974), requires two distinct processes; the disappearance of outward behavior traits that distinguish an ethnic group, and the disappearance of exclusive and discriminatory behavior by members of the host culture (p. 86). Thus acceptance by others as well as willingness to relinquish one's native culture is necessary for assimilation to take place. Kiefer (1974) prefers to use the term acculturation, meaning "the learning by members of one cultural group, of skills and values native to another group" (p. 86). She reminds us that acculturation is highly situational so that "minority group members seldom lose their native culture or become absorbed by the majority culture" (p. 87). This interpretation would be consistent with Lebra's nonlinear model of acculturation.

Kiefer's (1974) ethnography, which examined patterned meanings attached to behaviors across three generations of Japanese Americans, considered both cultural contexts and human interaction processes (p. 231). It was part of a three culture study on Mexican Americans, Japanese Americans, and European Americans, which was based upon a cross-cultural study by Margaret Clark (1968) on intergenerational relations. In Kiefer's (1974) discussion of Nisei and Sansei views of history, she remarks that the Nisei had to switch back and forth "with the same agility that they switched languages" between Japanese and European American viewpoints (p. 69). But the Sansei, especially those who became politically active, struggled with their ethnicity. In Kiefer's (1974) words:

> The activist Sansei are afflicted with the malaise of a stigmatized ethnic identity, vague but real guilt over their own prosperity and comfort, and dissatisfaction with their dependence on parents and community. The civil rights movement has helped them to diagnose the disease - racism - and to devise a cure - ethnic self-consciousness and self-determination . . . the ethnic identity movement is an adaptive strategy based on a creative interpretation of history and the common personal needs of many Sansei. (p. 78)

Lebra (1974) cites three factors that differentiate nonlinear acculturation models from linear ones. In a nonlinear model, the new culture is added to the old one, while partial replacement of the old culture by the new one would occur in a linear model. In a nonlinear model acculturated people are free to choose from different cultural alternatives according to a given situation, while those using a linear model would accept one cultural standard thereby rejecting the other. And in a nonlinear model, the acculturation process is contingent upon the context and therefore a function of social relationships, roles, audiences or reference groups, while a linear model would entirely embrace an individual.

The switching back and forth between cultures created a confusion that made the development of identity difficult for many Japanese Americans. Nisei Lindberg Sata (1973) mused about his position as a "hyphenated" American (p. 150) and wondered if the survival needs of his Issei parents were so high that they "minced words in those brief communications" or that members of his generation "simply lack comprehension of what was actually being said" (p. 151). His identity was built upon advice given from parents, like *ga-man* (perseverance) and *shi-ka-ta ga nai* (It can't be helped) which "encouraged a fatalistic stance in matters related to expectations for equality and human dignity" (p. 151). Sata considers language and communication central to the understanding of self and notes that what a person says, what he thinks he said, and what the listener perceived may be three different things. The poorly educated Issei communicated with the bilingual Nisei in such an ineffective manner that "what is taken to be a dialogue between generations is often an alternate monologue" (p. 151). With generational and linguistic barriers and limited knowledge about American customs, the Issei found it difficult to transmit their culture in an authentic manner.

Sata (1973) called his lifestyle a form of cultural paranoia. He brings to light the feelings of doubt that people of color experience when they are unsure of the attitudes on race of others in their company. So often, they are the ones always accomodating others in order to gain acceptance and to prevent conflict, only to find out that their efforts may not have gained the intended outcome. Sata's explanation is bittersweet:

> My parents, being mindful of helping the family achieve an acceptable place in society, constantly reminded me of the need to co-exist with others unlike myself. Without conscious awareness, I began to function as a human chameleon, sensitive and adaptive to the response of others and only secondarily aware of those feelings within myself. More often than I care to remember, I have attempted to relate with others honestly and openly, only to discover that, when I least expect it, either my racialness would be denied, which is to deny an important aspect of my identity, or I would be reminded that, because of my racialness, I was less than equal. (p. 154)

Derald and Stanley Sue (1972, 1971) coined the phrase "marginal man" describing a person who has trouble reconciling the differences between two cultures and, as a result, experiences an identity crisis, feeling isolated and alienated from both cultures. There are three ways in which Asian Americans (the Chinese in the Sues' study) and other minorities can deal with the stress of cultural conflict: they can remain allied to their native or ethnic culture, they can reject their Asian ways and attempt to become over-westernized, or they can attempt to integrate aspects of both cultures. The individual can choose to conform to their immigrant parent's values and become (Chinese or Japanese) "traditionalists," they can reject Asian parental values and adopt western values becoming a "marginal man," or they can integrate both value systems becoming "Asian-American" (Sue &

Sue, 1973, p. 113). The Asian-American does not have a model therefore, he is in the process of integrating his past experiences with his present condition (p. 117).

The marginal man would be considered a "twinkie" or a "banana"; translated, yellow on the outside, White on the inside. These derogatory terms, like "oreo" for the African American, were designed to identify and characterize those who have sold out to mainstream ideology and lifestyles. Used primarily within ethnic groups, they depict those who choose not to identify with their racial heritage but will still face discrimination and prejudice because of their racial visibility.

Colleen Johnson (1976) concludes in her cross-generational study of ethnicity that ". . . the principle of the second generation is that of ethnic ambivalence, while the principle of the third generation is that of ethnic commitment" (p. 27). Because there was a negative evaluation by the dominant group, the Nisei (second generation) experienced identity confusion, marginality, status ambiguity, and generational dissonance which created ethnic ambivalence. The Sansei (third generation) experienced greater tolerance and messages of accomodation from their Nisei parents so that there was more congruence between parental expectations and societal expectations. As a result, Johnson (1976) believes that the Sansei could succeed in the dominant society while still preserving kinship and ethnic solidarity (p. 27). She writes:

> The Sansei's ethnicity finds its expression in the operation of bounded, ethnically-dominated social groupings where kinship loyalties have increased rather than decreased in the progression from second to third generation. Furthermore, ethnicity is found in a value orientation where collective values more reminiscent of Japan outweigh the lonely pursuits of ego-centered interests so typical of the American middle class. (p. 28)

Hansen's Law (1952) or the "principle of third generation interest" posits that, "what the immigrant's son wishes to forget, the grandson wishes to remember" (p. 15). Johnson (1976) rephrases this perspective as "what the Nisei rejected explicitly, the Sansei can accept with commitment" (p. 32). She points out that this acceptance of ethnicity by the Sansei is not rooted in Japanese heritage but rather in a viable functioning group which provides self-esteem, not stigma (p. 32).

Johnson's research did not include midwestern Japanese Americans and was conducted almost twenty years ago, yet it shares some conclusions with this study. Ethnic ambivalence could describe the attitudes of many Nisei in this study, and an increase in ethnic awareness and commitment could describe some of the Sansei and Yonsei, but actual affiliation and active participation in ethnic groups differed due to lack of access to large ethnic communities.

The reliquishing of one's ethnic ties for midwestern Nisei became a necessity, a conscious choice to assimilate, rather than a desire to reject one's cultural heritage. There was a need to become an invisible minority. Within the family, a private acknowledgement of Japanese culture was nurtured to some degree, but the external goal was directed at assimilation and westernization. For example, Nisei Mia described how avoidance of overt racism was necessary and achieved by maintaining a low-key profile in public. The impact of internment had a strong effect on the resettlement of Japanese Americans after the war. She explained:

> When I first went to St. Louis from camp, and this was (below) the Mason-Dixon line . . . we had to, we were very careful about how we performed or acted in crowds. . . We were still not (considered) as bad as the blacks. We were considered White. There were quite a number of (Asian) students there at the time, but we never vocalized. . . But we knew, just that instant that we had to be, you know, low profile. We couldn't stand out.

Masako articulated the feelings of many Nisei: "I also felt like I wanted to be American. I knew my face and background were Japanese, but I felt that I really was a true American." Masako lived a bicultural life with her immigrant parents, but to rear her Sansei children, she chose to embrace western cultural norms and to see herself and her family as "all American." The worldview of Nisei parents in this study focused on individualism and independence more than collectivism and interdependence, the cultural orientation of the Japanese.

Many of the Sansei women regarded their race and ethnicity as personal traits, without thought to group identity or the stereotyping and discrimination which often accompanies minority status. They held the optimism of their parents and grandparents, believing that they had settled in a kinder, more accepting midwest, where post-war opportunities were greater for Asian Americans. Without the overt racism and minimal contact with other Japanese Americans, these Sansei did indeed feel "all American," exactly what their parents were seeking. As a result, intermarriage was common, or as one participant said, "Growing up, there weren't any other Japanese to choose from." Seeing themselves as assimilated, many Sansei assumed that differences between themselves and their European American friends were merely individual rather than cultural. But even though they may have been unaware of Japanese cultural traits, midwestern Sansei were still faced with the reality of their Asian racial characteristics. Racial identity became more salient than ethnic identity. They were not spared from prejudice and discrimination.

Masako's Sansei daughter Amelia Bedelia recalls the time when she was passed over for the role of Portia in a high school play while being told that she was the best actress for the part. A blond girl got the part and Amelia was given the role of the soothsayer, with a dark cape over her head. This kind of discrimination was hard to accept because she had always considered herself assimilated and accepted by most of her classmates. Amelia does remember, though, that she always felt a sense of striving to overcome racial barriers. Her parents reinforced the fact that she was American, not Japanese, not foreign. When occasional derogatory remarks like "chink" or even "nigger" arose, Amelia's father advised her to "tell them that you're American with a Japanese face."

The Yonsei also considered themselves to be assimilated, yet they continued to face prejudice as their parents and grandparents had. Yonsei Leia spoke of her awareness of racism and the ways she tried to become accepted by her European American peers:

> I made a lot of friends, however there were people there who instantly had something against me . . . and I didn't really, well, pick up on it and it was so blatant, and it really started me to think what factors were out of my control that people were holding against me. And of course race became one of the big issues. . . I knew that there was some reason that people weren't accepting me as an equal and so I didn't really think it was race, so I tried to figure out other reasons. I tried to be more active, involved (in school activities). I was involved in everything under the sun. I was friendly to the point of nauseam. I was just trying to be as perfect as possible and in some ways it did help me. I gained a lot.

It was only later in college when she began to develop positive racial and ethnic identities that she began to appreciate her biracial, bicultural heritage. The Yonsei in this study were the ones to actively seek knowledge about their Japaneseness in positive, reaffirming ways. The need to be accepted as White was being rejected for a healthy ethnic identity. It appears that the ethnic identity movement associated with the civil rights movement of the sixties lay dormant in the midwest until the Yonsei generation. Only two of the study participants considered themselves politically active regarding issues of race and ethnicity.

Measuring Ethnic Identity

Ethnic Identity scales have been designed by quantitative researchers to measure the ego identity and acculturation of Japanese Americans (Kendis, 1989; Masuda et al., 1970). The statistical significance of these data were derived using nonparametric statistics and total ethnicity scores were compared across the generations.

Basing their work on Caudill's 1952 study of Japanese Americans in Chicago, Masuda, Matsumoto & Meredith (1970) created an ethnic identification instrument to assess Japaneseness across three generations. Data from their self-administered questionaire indicated that there was erosion of positive ethnicity in 30 of the 50 items with considerable behavioral assimilation. There also was "a considerable residue of ethnic identity in the third generation Sansei and considerable acculturation of the Issei" (p. 207). Some of the variables found to influence the magnitude of ethnic identification were social contacts, mobility, education and socioeconomic status.

In 1973, the same authors did a comparative study of the ethnic identity of Japanese Americans in Honolulu and Seattle and found that for all three generations (Issei, Nisei and Sansei), Honolulu respondents exhibited lower ethnic identification than corresponding Seattle generations (Matsumoto, Meredith & Masuda, 1973, p. 72). Some causes for this discrepancy were attributed to greater racial discrimination of mainland Japanese Americans, the political and economic strength of Hawaiian Japanese Americans, the multiracial composition of Hawaii which leads to greater social mobility and assimilation, personality differences (citing Arkoff, 1959 and Fujita, 1956) and differing interpretations of ethnic identity (Meiji Japaneseness for Seattle respondents and neo-Meiji Japaneseness for Honolulu respondents).

Connor's (1977) study compared Issei, Nisei, and Sansei with a European American sample in an attempt to assess the degree of acculturation of the Japanese with "American" psychological and behavioral patterns. Data were gathered using an Incomplete Sentence Test, the Edwards Personal Preference Schedule, An Ethnic Identity Questionnaire and A Survey of Contrasting Values. Connor concluded that the Issei had marginal acculturation due to their lack of fluency in English (p. 160). The bicultural Nisei believed that they were culturally midway between their parents and their children, therefore, they could combine the best of both cultures. But, the Issei and Nisei viewed the Sansei as completely Americanized (exhibiting European American behavior patterns) and the Sansei rated themselves being over 70 percent acculturated (p. 163). Based on the Edwards Personal Preference Schedule (EPPS), Sansei were found to be "more deferent, more abasive, less dominant, more affiliative, less aggressive [and had] a greater need for succorance and order" compared to European Americans even though they held more "American" values and behavior than their Nisei parents (p. 164). Combining his finding with those of Lois Frost (1970) on Japanese American child rearing, Connor (1977) concluded that there was a continuation of dependency needs fostered in Japanese American families.

A comprehensive study of Japanese American ethnic maintenance was done in 1989 by Kaoru Oguri Kendis. Although ethnicity is considered as an ascriptive status, "one is born into it," by some researchers, Kendis takes the perspective that ethnicity is self selected. Restating De Vos' view of the relationship between personal survival and collective continuity, Kendis writes: "De Vos has stated that in its deepest sense ethnicity is a desire for survival of oneself indirectly through the continuation of the subculture that one strongly identifies with" (p. 32).

Kendis (1989) places ethnicity on a continuum from high to low intensity, describing "high" ethnics as those who view themselves more as a member of a group (as Japanese Americans) and "low" ethnics as those who see themselves as individuals whose success or failure depends on personal merit and effort. High ethnics were able to articulate behavioral and value differences between themselves and mainstream European Americans while low ethnics more often mentioned material differences in music or art (referring to Japanese aesthetic forms). High ethnics found greater differences between Japanese American and European Americans in areas of reciprocity, generosity and hospitality (obligatory gift giving, one kind being omiyage) (p. 36). Japanese American Sansei held values of close family bonds and monetary and psychological support of children. These values led to childrens' longer dependency on parents and a stronger commitment to care for aging parents.

In the area of interpersonal relations, high ethnics felt that there were "unwritten rules of behavior" for Japanese Americans that separated them from their European American counterparts. These were described in terms of their "comfort level" being with Japanese Americans or mainstream Americans. Kendis (1989) outlines this nebulous but significant measure of ethnicity.

> Ways of relating to people are largely learned unconsciously during the socialization process, something one grows up with, and a person is less likely to be aware of differences in the ways he and others relate than in more obvious differences such as the use of chopsticks instead of a fork. It is much more difficult to change the way one relates to others than to change the

particular utensil one uses for eating. A person interacts with others in the way he assumes to be natural and human. (p. 42)

Interpersonal differences between high and low ethnics fall into the categories of aggression, directness and individualism. These traits are valued in White society and would be considered acceptable and practiced more readily by low ethnics, according to Kendis' continuum. Low ethnics see themselves as more western in their behavior and interaction style. But high ethnics, being more in tune with Japanese inter-personal relations, would interpret the same behavior as being pushy, hostile and rude. High ethnic Japanese Americans prefer to avoid conflict, are reared to be aware of other people and to take measures not to hurt their feelings by directly confronting problems (the concept of "saving face"). Conformity rather than a trait characterized as "rugged individualism" would be preferred and admired by high ethnics.

High and low ethnics can be distinguished by their view on individuation and their differing ethnic style. "To put it simply, and perhaps simplistically," writes Kendis (1989), "high ethnics say 'I'm different because I'm Japanese American', while low ethnics say 'If I am different it's because I'm me'" (p. 73). Ethnic style, according to Kendis, is learned, though not consciously taught, and is not an innate characteristic. Ethnic style can be best described as an unspoken, taken-for-granted, subtle set of rules of behavior and expectations shared only by members of an ethnic group.

The Japanese American ethnic style is characterized by the following elements: 1) sensitivity to feelings of others, 2) saving face, 3) avoidance of confrontation, 4) etiquette and formality (i.e. *enryo*) and 5) group orientation and conformity (p. 75-83). It is important to note that this style may be based on traditional Japanese cultural values but they are different from the behavior of Japanese nationals. In fact, Kendis' informants provided a definition of *enryo* ("a holding back of the expression of one's desires so as not to cause inconvenience to anyone" p. 79) which matches one given by participants in this study. Michi Weglyn (1976), in describing the enryo syndrome, succinctly describes it as "reticence, restraint and desire to be inoffensive" (p. 274). This appears to be a transformation of the original purpose of enryo (modesty in the presence of one's superior), which was applicable to Japanese in Meiji Era Japan.

Although neither type of ethnic identification instrument was appropriate for this postmodern qualitatively oriented study, the section of Kendis' (1989) instrument on feelings of being Japanese American came the closest to my intent for this portion of my research. In previous studies there was an assumption that participants held a clear differentiation between that which is Japanese (or Japanese American) from that which is European American (or mainstream western). I believe that for many participants in this study, particularly the Sansei and Yonsei, little thought had been given to differentiating Japanese culture from midwestern mainstream culture. As a result, the purpose of the ethnicity measure was to elicit the personal definitions of Japaneseness from the participants and to jointly construct a notion of Japanese American ethnicity. The participants in this study were asked to rate themselves on a scale from 1 (low) to 10 (high) ethnicity, based entirely on their personal feelings and interpretation of Japaneseness (Table 1). This was done at the beginning and at the end of the study so that comparisons could be made. No definition of Japaneseness was provided, therefore participants were given a space to make comments about their interpretation. One's heritage and the culture associated with it can be internalized in many ways. Being Japanese American, or having membership within an American ethnic group, was not presented as an entity separate from the culture of contemporary Japan or the culture of the Meiji Era (the heritage of most Issei immigrants). Japaneseness was entirely open to interpretation.

Table 1 Self-Reported Ethnicity Ratings by Participants at the Beginning of the Study on Midwestern Japanese American Women, 1994.

NISEI		SANSEI		YONSEI	
Chiyo	2	Grapdelight	1	Leia	2
Mariko	4	Obasan	2	Jasmine	2
Mia	5	Anna	2	Shigeko	3
Masako	7	Shigeko	2	Emily Akemi	3
Mona	7	Mimi	3	Yano	4
Chizu	9	Amelia	3	Jane	5
		Akiko	3	Erika	5
		Lesye	4	Fusako	6
		Connie	5	Alana	7
		Kim	5		
		Mariko	5		
		Bonnie	5		
		Imoto	5		
		Lani	7		
		Mitzi	8		
		Mika	8		
		Kikuye	9		

Data from the ethnic identity scale should be considered interesting but inconclusive due to: 1) the varied interpretations of the term

Japaneseness and, 2) the low number of responses at the end of the study. But when combined with the other data presented in this section, it would indicate that overall, the women in this study felt with differing intensities both ethnic pride and marginalization (Sue & Sue, 1972) as Japanese Americans. Although many have positive feelings about their heritage and some appear to exhibit subtle Japanese cultural behaviors, few have chosen to make Japanese culture an active part of their daily lives.

Since a standardized measurement scale was not used, it is critical that these data are interpreted in relationship to the other data gathered in the study. Throughout the study the term Japaneseness has been raised in differing contexts (group interviews, literature, ethnicity) and participants have been invited to elaborate, describing what being Japanese means to them. The use of this scale is just one more concrete measure by which participants share their views. In fact, this information has been used in conversations as a means of stimulating further interpretation and feedback. For example, in an individual interview, one participant indicated that she really wasn't very "Japanesey" and inquired about how other Sansei women had felt. Using the feminist interview technique, I was able to share that there was a large range of responses from 1 to 9 and continued to probe her feelings on why she felt the way that she did. In a sense, she was apprehensive that she might be unique and not suited for participation in a study of this nature. Together we sought to find the variables that created such diverse responses.

In each of the generational groups, there was a wide range of responses (Table 2, Figure 1). For the Nisei, the range was from 2 to 9. Four of six Nisei (67 percent) responded 5 or higher. Comments made by Nisei at the beginning of the study who rated themselves high (7 to 9) included: "I was brought up strictly Japanese" and "My mother was a Japanese school teacher." Chiyo, who rated herself a 2 wrote: "The Japanese image is always with me. They had grown up in a bilingual and bicultural environment, experienced incarceration and segregation with their own ethnic group, then relocated to the midwest as young adults. The Japaneseness is within, and the depth is hard to measure." Another Nisei woman who chose not to select a rating wrote: "I greatly value and appreciate my cultural background and I want to preserve as much as I can that which is good and positive. I've tried to pass some of it on to the next generation and to their offspring."

Several Sansei who rated themselves as 5 expressed pride in their heritage while also feeling disconnected from Japanese culture. Sansei Connie succinctly described it: "I am an American of Japanese descent, and as long as I look Japanese, I feel a pride in my Japanese origin."

And those Sansei who rated themselves in the 7 to 9 categories also expressed strong pride in their heritage but included more knowledge of Japanese culture.

Table 2 Frequency and Percent of Responses to an Ethnic Identity Scale of Midwestern Japanese American Women by Generation, 1994.

Resp.	Nisei		Sansei		Yonsei		All	
	Freq.	Percent	Freq.	Percent	Freq.	Percent	Freq.	Percent
1	0	0.0	1	5.9	0	0.0	1	3.1
2	1	16.7	3	17.6	2	22.2	6	18.8
3	0	0.0	3	17.6	2	22.2	5	15.6
4	1	16.7	1	5.9	1	11.1	3	9.4
5	1	16.7	5	29.4	2	22.2	8	25.0
6	0	0.0	0	0.0	1	11.1	1	3.1
7	2	33.3	1	5.9	1	11.1	4	12.5
8	0	0.0	2	11.8	0	0.0	2	6.3
9	1	16.7	1	5.9	0	0.0	2	6.3
10	0	0.0	0	0.0	0	0.0		0.0
Count	6		17		9		32	

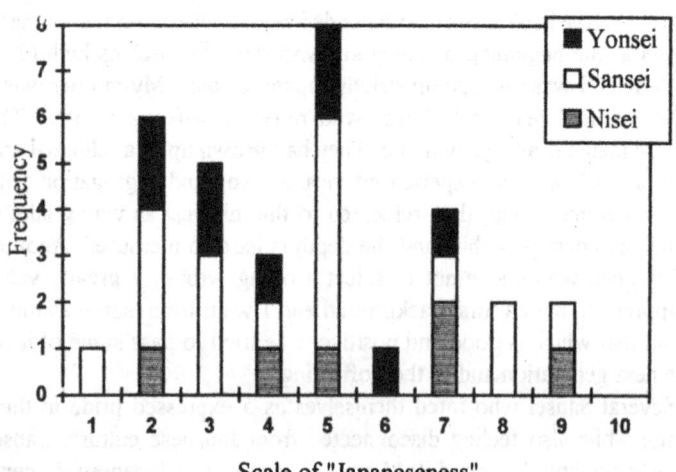

Figure 1. Responses to an Ethnic Identity Scale by Midwestern Japanese American Women by Generations

Four of nine Yonsei (44 percent) responded 5 or higher on the Ethnic Identity Scale. Of the Yonsei who rated themselves 2 or 3, several considered themselves to be "fully Americanized" and said that they had few, if any, Asian friends. They were just beginning to notice their Japaneseness. Yano, who rated herself a 4, mentioned that ethnic identity had become increasingly important since the birth of her children. But some of those who rated themselves in the 5 to 7 range felt more Japanese, had studied Japanese, and a few had visited Japan. One of the biracial women selected the highest rating of seven. Her father has been very active in the Milwaukee Japanese American League and she lives in California. This revival of ethnic awareness and the associated interest expressed by many of the Yonsei contrasts somewhat with the ambivalence shared by some of the Sansei.

Descriptive statistics, by generation, were determined (Table 3). The associations among the means and medians for the three generations were what might be expected. The six Nisei respondents had a median score for Japaneseness of 6.0 (mean = 5.7), the highest of the three generations. The Yonsei had the lowest median score, 4.0, (mean = 4.1) and the Sansei were between with a median score of 5.0 (mean = 4.5). Although the relationship among the means and medians were what might be expected - i.e. highest Japaneseness among the Nisei and lowest among the Yonsei - there was no attempt to test the statistical significance. As explained above, this scale was not rigorously developed and there was no measure of reliability. A formal statistical hypothesis test would not be appropriate in this case.

Table 3. Sample Size, Mean, Median, and Standard Deviation of Ethnicity Ratings by Generation of Japanese American Women, 1994.

	n	mean	median	standard deviation
Nisei	6	5.7	6.0	2.50
Sansei	17	4.5	5.0	2.37
Yonsei	9	4.1	4.0	1.76
	32	4.6	4.6	2.24

The relationships of the variability of responses as measured by standard deviations, was counter-intuitive. The most diverse responses were those of the Nisei women (s = 2.50) and the least varied responses were among the Yonsei women (s = 1.76). Again, there was no attempt to test the observed differences in variance for statistical significance. However, the decreasing medians and, particularly, the decreasing variances among the three generations do point to some interesting questions with a scale which would better lend itself to statistical analysis.

When looking across the generations by family configurations, one begins to see some trends (Table 4). Of the eight families represented, four of the mother-daughter dyads rated themselves the same. Since the Nisei all spoke Japanese and had attended Japanese school, it might be assumed that their ethnic identity would be higher than their daughters' or granddaughters'. This was not the case with Mariko and her daughter Kikuye. It is also interesting that another daughter who did not participate in the study was considered by both not to be particularly interested in anything Japanese. Kikuye, along with her friend Lani participated in the Nisei Drum and Bugle Corps while growing up. She settled in California and actively participates in the local Japanese American Citizens league chapter. Similar descriptions of low ethnic interest was reported about Akiko, Kim, and Jane's sisters. The difference between Mika and Mariko's ratings may be attributed to present geographic location. Mariko noted that she feels somewhat isolated from her Japanese heritage since she lives in the south, while Mika's ethnic awareness has expanded since settling in San Francisco.

Table 4. Ethnicity Ratings by Family Configuration Across Generations of Japanese American Women, 1994.

Nisei		Sansei		Yonsei	
Chiyo	2	Anna	2		
Mrs. K	*	Connie	5	Jane	5
Mona	7	Akiko	3	Erika	5
Mia	5	Kim	5		
Mariko	4	Kikuye	9		
Masako	7	Mimi	3		
Chizu	9	Mariko	5		
		Obasan	2	Leia	2

* Information not provided by participant.

Throughout the research period, I attempted to continually investigate the meanings that participants placed upon being Japanese, or their sense of Japaneseness. When I asked participants to select a numerical rating once again that represented their feelings of Japaneseness at the end of the study, I received few responses. This request was made along with the literature packets sent out to all participants; therefore, several women who wrote comments tied their remarks to the literature. Seven women replied (five Sansei and two Nisei). Compared to the individual ratings reported at the beginning of the study, two ratings remained the same, two went down, and three went up (Table 5).

Table 5. Comparison of Ethnicity Ratings of Midwestern Japanese American Women at the End of the Study, 1994.

Participant	Change of Rating	Direction of Change
Chiyo (Nisei)	2 to 5	increase 2
Masako (Nisei)	7 to 6	decrease 1
Mini (Sansei)	3 to 5	increase 2
Mariko (Sansei)	5 to 3	decrease 2
Obasan (Sansei)	2 to 7	increase 5
Amelia Bedelia (Sansei)	3 to 3	remain same
Connie (Sansei)	5 to 5	remain same

The Sansei woman whose rating increased by five points wrote about attaining a balance between her Japaneseness and her American self. The two women whose ratings went up reported that they were more aware of Japanese culture as the study progressed. Of the two ratings that had gone down, one woman's was due to feelings of being isolated from any Japanese American community, and the other woman, a Nisei, recalled how embarrassed she was that her parents were so different from her classmates' parents. The embarrassment reinforced her strong desire to assimilate. This response may have merely been a reflection of her reminiscences and not particularly a comparison with her feelings at the beginning of the study. In fact, there is no indication that any of the seven women who responded even considered their ratings at the beginning of the study.

Since this procedure of self-reporting was informal and optional (as were other portions of the study) and the actual responses were so few (seven of the 34 participants), I feel that the data reported should be considered interesting but insignificant. There was no correlation (-.07) between pre and post ratings on the ethnic identity scale for the seven participants who provided ratings both times.

Identifying with Japanese American Literature

Responses to the literature portion of the study produced some enlightened reactions from participants regarding their ethnic identity. As indicated in Table 4, there were eighteen participants who responded in writing to the questions accompanying the literature selections written by Japanese American authors and poets. They included: five Nisei, ten Sansei, and three Yonsei women. The written answers ranged from lists and short comments to long analytical descriptions of feelings and beliefs. The comments reinforced existing feelings of the participants and also brought new awareness to some of them.

Several of the participants expressed a strong sense of feeling validated and seeing a self-reflection in the literature. Sansei Lani eloquently described her response at length. Lani is an only child who was reared in Chicago in the same house with her grandmother, aunt, uncle, and cousins (living in separate flats). She participated in the Nisei Drum and Bugle Corps, so she had many Japanese and culturally diverse friends at school and in the band. She described herself as extremely quiet and compliant when she was younger, but in the course of her life and career as a librarian she has developed the art of storytelling and finds joy in being openly expressive. In Lani's words:

> My first reaction was strong and immediate: the wonder and novelty of seeing a part of me, my Japanese-American self, before me in literature, in words on a page, the reflection that I have been missing my whole life. In my comfortable life in a Caucasian culture and society, I'm not even aware that the void exists. Seeing these words I feel sadness at the resulting lack of affirmation and feeling of invisibility that this brings. . . . My second reaction is the recognition of similarity of experience, and the relief one feels to know that one is not alone. Others have felt the same, others have struggled with like issues. . . My third reaction is the accompanying recognition that, in fact, no one has the same experience, and that my own life was its own, unique and different. . . My fourth reaction was one of pleasure in seeing the creative and artistic side of the Japanese American feminine. I have not seen this much at all in my life. It needs to come out much more!

Later, Lani succinctly rejoiced: "Reading the literature gave me a shot of ethnic energy. . . My ethnic identity has a mirror!"

The most senior Nisei participant M. Kana responded with praise and analysis. M. Kana had been active in camp and during the post war years in the midwest as a music teacher/choral director for her church. During the study group sessions, she had been eager to meet some of the younger Sansei and Yonsei women. She wrote: "I am glad we have Nisei and Sansei who have the talent to put into poetry and stories their experiences that give insight to their heritage and legacies that they have inherited for others to read. The depth of knowing about their Japanese ethnic identity depends a lot to what they have experienced in their homes with their parents, at their schools, and in their community where they were brought up."

In one family, the responses were reflective and consistent from one generation to the next (It appeared that they wrote their responses independently of each other). Sansei Mika, a lawyer presently living in California, summarized her general response this way: "Very evocative, familiar pieces. They recall parts of my experience. I used to feel caught between two worlds and cultures. But as I grow older I feel blessed to be part of two rich sensibilities. . . Reading through the literature confirms my feelings that as I grow older I feel less conflicted about my cultural heritage in American society. "

Mika's mother, Chizu noted that the selections had "true meaning to our daily lives and touched the ethnic identity." And her sister, Mariko, a mathematics teacher living in the south, described her response to many of the selections as a "special kindred bond." All three seemed to be in touch with and appreciative of their Japanese heritage while cognizant of their assimilation into mainstream American society.

In a revealing personal response, Sansei Obasan, a professor in Wisconsin, wrote: "Many of the authors' insights reassured me because they have been unshared thoughts of my own. Until recently I have been reluctant to explain my *Japaneseness*." Obasan was able to share her journey in ethnic awareness with her Yonsei daughter, Leia. They even traveled to Japan when Obasan was conducting research there.

Sansei Amelia, a mother of two biracial boys, described a new ethnic cultural lens in her words: "I am more inclined now to see the differences between my Caucasian husband and myself as cultural as opposed to individual." Amelia's comment was enlightening as it exemplifies one of the common themes that emerged from this study. She also noted that she identified with some pieces while others offered her insights into her mother and grandmother. Sansei Connie, a grandmother from the Chicago area, described the dichotomy that others had felt in her words: "My reaction to the literary selections was that a common thread ran through most of the pieces, that of the influence of both of the cultures. . . sometimes clashing, yet often times meeting to produce a new individual." Sansei Mimi, Amelia's sister, also saw the individualism and wrote: "I was interested to see how vastly different the internal experiences of the authors were." In a sense, they were describing the diversity and individuality in this group of midwestern Japanese American women too.

There was one participant who didn't relate to many of the pieces. Grapdelight had been reared as an only child in a Cleveland neighborhood populated by war veterans. I was surprised by this information, so she assured me that her family did not perceive any discrimination. She had been reared, in many ways, to be color-blind. "Not surprisingly, I suppose," wrote Sansei Grapdelight, "I felt distanced from many of the readings. They did not, for the most part, clarify my own experience, nor did they give me insight into my heritage." She appears to be closer to her father than to her mother which could explain why she found the selection called Issei Men from *Proud Upon an Alien Shore* to be particularly moving. "I had not thought much about Issei men," Grapdelight wrote, "having known my own grandfathers only through black and white photos. Nor have I actually met many Issei men. So the images of the men *stealing warmth from pale cups* gave me a sense of these pioneers." In several of the families, including my own, this was precisely the case: Sansei knew their grandmothers but not their grandfathers. I was lucky in a sense, because one of my maternal grandfather's friends, who was a bachelor, became our family *Ojisan* (familiar term for uncle) after both my natural grandfathers died in camp. Thus I was able to grow up with an Issei male figure in my home. When *Ojisan* was in his late nineties and my son was a toddler, they seemed to have made a unique personal bond though neither could speak English very well. They could communicate beautifully in gestures and smiles.

Of the twelve selections, *Beyond Manzanar: Views of an Asian American Woman* was the most popular piece, mentioned by eleven of the eighteen participants (three Nisei, seven Sansei, and one Yonsei) as having particular impact. Sansei Mika indicated that the selection was not very relevant to her while the rest of the women identified with it in a variety of ways. Their responses and interpretations were expressed by the following themes: love and respect for Issei women, dignity, and strength of Houston's mother, an understanding of the struggle for individualism and the building of self-concept, a feeling of wanting to be American, an appreciation for the quiet inner strength characterized by the segment, and a sense of being bicultural. Nisei Mia quoted Houston's words: "Because I am culturally neither pure Japanese nor pure American does not mean I am less a person. It means I have been enriched with the heritage of both" and added, "This sums it all."

Seven of the eighteen women (one Nisei, five Sansei, and one Yonsei) found *Family Dinner* to be particularly meaningful. Relating to the idea that the mother served as a "buffer" between her (the author) and her father for the "words we don't say," Imoto wrote, "I remember feeling as I read that this very accurately described my family. Although I don't believe that these dynamics belong only to the Japanese ethnic group, they may be slightly more common in Japanese families." Imoto revealed a recurring question articulated by several participants throughout the research process: What is Japanese and what is universally true of American families in general, families of all ethnic backgrounds?

Occasionally during the interview process, a participant would preface her statement by saying, "I don't know if this is Japanese or not, but . . ." My response as the researcher was that cultural traits can be members of several categories, and that in a postmodern framework, there are many truths rather than clearly defined dichotomies. Group behavior or personal characteristics can be Japanese, Japanese American and mainstream European American simultaneously without conflict or exclusivity. By understanding the etiology of one's behavior traits, one can begin to build a sense of self-identity. Ethnicity and gender characteristics, likewise, can be, I believe, complementary or mutually reinforcing even if it is unclear which is the source. For example, the Japanese trait of *enryo*, or the holding back and putting the concerns of others first, can be interpreted as a "female" characteristic even though it also has roots in Japanese culture. This cultural trait would certainly be compatible with gender expectations for Issei and some Nisei women. And many Sansei and Yonsei were familiar with the behavior, seeing it in themselves or other family members, but were unfamiliar with the Japanese term *enryo*.

It was also interesting that Sansei Lani and Mariko both described the reverse situation where they attended a family event at the home of their European American spouses. "I was initially apprehensive," wrote Lani, "not knowing how relatives in a small, central Illinois town would take to a person of a different race, but I found everyone in the family, and in the town itself, to be friendly and welcoming." With a sense of humor to break the tension, Mariko gives this account: "I can remember meeting my husband Don's parents for the first time. They are *hakujin* (White) and I was very tan in the summer and my mother teased that I should put on lemon juice to lighten my skin. I was so nervous that I could hardly talk!" The knowledge of one's racial and ethnic difference, along with the apprehension about how one would be received, created a tension with which most of the women in the study could identify.

Masks of Woman, mentioned by four participants, was described by Sansei Anna, Chiyo's daughter, as an "excellent metaphor of the Japanese woman, my mother and my grandmother, and many Japanese American women. But not for me." On the other hand, Sansei Mariko related to it because, as she explained, "I, too, wear many masks that hide the real me." M. Kana, who happens to be a personal friend of the poet, offered the following background information: "Mitsuye Yamada's parents were very cultured people and her poem *Masks of Woman* reveals her exposure to the Japanese culture and her understanding of "*Daruma*," "No Mask," and the "*Onnibaba*." Anna wrote an extensive analysis of how masks can be effective or detrimental depending upon the intent of the wearers and the cultural contexts in which they are worn. This is her cross-cultural appraisal:

> Wearing masks works very well in Japanese culture. All of the players are reading from the same script so there really is no confusion. If everyone knows her lines (role) and follows stage direction (traditional rituals) then it makes for a cohesive play (culture). It's obvious that the whole system is weakened if any one person will not (refuses to) or cannot (is incapable of or unfamiliar with) play her role correctly. American culture, and certainly cultural diversity, depends strongly on not having strict roles and rituals, and on the ability to accommodate a wide range of cultural roles and rituals. A mask is a real liability in intercultural relationships because, in those cases, it is crucial to know another person's true feelings and opinions. A mask just becomes confusing pretense.

Six participants (two Nisei, three Sansei and one Yonsei) responded to *Through Harsh Winters: The Life of a Japanese Immigrant Woman*, one stating that she did not relate to it. I had thought that perhaps the Nisei would relate to this selection since they have had direct, long term relationships with their Issei mothers, but it appeared that the issues raised in this piece touched the other generations. Nisei Chiyo found that it reflected her marriage and her parents' marriage saying: "It was papa who spoke and mom tuned off and chose the subtle road." Sansei Imoto, who was one of the younger siblings in a large family, concurred with the author's point that she had to switch communication styles for her family and her friends and community. Having worked in a school setting, Imoto saw this happening not just with Asian children but with other ethnic groups. "A more successful or resilient child recognizes the switch in settings and can adjust accordingly," she explained. Both

Imoto and Yonsei Yano, a teacher and former family daycare provider, felt that they had been socialized to be quiet, non-assertive and less direct than required in mainstream American society. They spoke about struggling with it individually, and since Yano is a parent, she was particularly concerned that her daughters understand "the importance of being quiet and respectful but to also speak up." Both stressed personal responsibility for learning to switch when necessary.

Of the other literary selections, the following number of participants responded to the individual pieces; *Proud Upon an Alien Shore* 6, *I am Sansei* 6, *Sansei* 5, *Maternal Tsunami* 4, *The Loom*, 4, *Eleven A.M. on my Day Off*, *My Sister Phones Desperate for a Babysitter* 2, *Mirror Mirror* 2 and *A Mother's Touch* 1. Responding to the strong desire to be a mother described in *Maternal Tsunami*, Sansei Mimi wrote: "I felt the same way when pregnant with my first child. I had longed to be a mother for many years, and felt that my true identity was being a wife and mother long before I married or had children." Mimi, it should be noted, has chosen to have a part time career as a practicing psychiatrist in order to rear her children. This commitment to and pride of rearing children was echoed by many study participants.

When Mia reiterated the words of author Houston stating that since she was neither pure Japanese nor pure American and therefore she was not less a person but enriched by both heritages, she illustrated the strong self concept of many of the women in the study. Even though most of the respondents saw themselves as having some affinity with the Japanese American authors, they also maintained a sense of individualism that separated them even from other participants in the study. To many, especially the Sansei and Yonsei, they were American first, with a Japanese heritage. For the Nisei, they lived in a society that defined them racially as Japanese first, so they found it necessary to become as "American" as they could.

Asian American Stereotypes and Identity

The perpetuation of the "Model Minority," the "Exotic Oriental Woman," the "Dragon Lady," "Suzi Wong," and the "Yellow Peril" or "Jap" stereotypes have contributed to the racism and sexism still faced by Japanese American women. The historical contexts for burgeoning racism has led to the development of different kinds of Asian stereotypes. As long as American soldiers have been stationed in Asia (commonly referred to as the "orient"), stereotypes of Asian or "oriental" women as either sensuous and compliant, or cunning and controlling, have emerged (Yamada, 1983). As Asian "war brides" began to emigrate with their American husbands, these stereotypes have continued, through the World Wars, the Korean War, and the Vietnam War (Yoshimura, 1971). After Pearl Harbor, when Japan became the official enemy of the United States, west coast fear of the "Yellow Peril" or enemy "Japs" who were indistinguishable from citizens of Asian heritage, fueled racism and stereotyping (Ogawa, 1971).

Later, during the civil rights movement of the 1960's, Asians began to be perceived as compliant, model citizens compared to more demonstrative African American population. Then, during the 1970's and 80's when the American auto industries were experiencing competition from Japanese auto companies, increased acts of violence against Asians peaked in Detroit with the murder of Vincent Chin, who was thought to be Japanese. Japanese were seen as an economic enemy of America's free market, and the stereotype of the Asian "worker ants" began to emerge. Although some of the stereotypes referred to specific ethnic groups, all Asians and Asian Americans were lumped into these categories.

Each Asian stereotype will be further defined in the following paragraphs. The "Model Minority" Stereotype, as presented in the media, maintains that Asian Americans have attained high educational levels leading to upward mobility and subsequently higher median family incomes compared to Whites and other minority groups. "Asian students are seen as academic superstars who manage to graduate at or near the top of their classes, win a disproportionate share of the awards in national academic competitions, and then are *over-represented* in our elite institutions" (Suzuki, 1989, p.13). This stereotype evolved at a time when minority groups were becoming identified as sociopolitical forces that challenged the White mainstream structure of society. "The image of Asian American success did not appear in a vacuum" writes Osajima (1987, p. 166). He continues:

> The definition of a new racial identity emerged at a moment of tremendous racial upheaval in America. . . On the political level, Asian American success constituted a direct critique of Blacks who sought relief through federally supported social programs. (pp. 166-167)

Much controversy surrounds this issue, resulting in the labeling of it as a myth by Asian American scholars (Ogawa, 1971; Suzuki, 1977 & 1989; Osajima, 1987; Sue & Okazaki, 1990; Lee, 1996). "A number of Asian scholars remained skeptical about the validity of the model minority thesis . . . [their analysis of the 1970 census data] reached the conclusion that the model minority characterization of Asian Americans was inaccurate, misleading and a gross over-generalization" (Suzuki, 1989, p. 14).

This stereotype of all Asian and Pacific Americans leads government officials and educational institutions to believe that Asian Americans don't deserve social services and affirmative action programs. Despite scholarly work on the mental health of Asian Americans (Sue, 1973; Sue & Sue, 1975), there still remains a perception that Asian Americans have become effectively assimilated into mainstream culture as model citizens. Sing (1989) puts the dilemma succinctly:

> Some say that while Asian Pacific Americans are often high achievers, the "model minority" myth perpetuated by the media obscures serious problems in Asian Pacific communities, including poverty, substance abuse, mental illness and domestic violence. The myth makes it more difficult to get help in dealing with these problems from government and the private sector. (p. 12).

Amy Tachiki (1971) points out that the mass media selectively overlooks factors such as middle management ranks, de facto segregation and delayed promotion in jobs. Japanese Americans in the work place have experienced these "glass ceilings" for many years. In most strident, terms Tachiki (1971) explains:

> The danger in upholding this success myth is that it reinforces the underlying value structure that created it . . . the Asian model of assimilation frees the White majority from assuming responsibility for its own oppressiveness, since it implies that non-White minorities have to earn their rights to American society and it shifts the causes for minority problems away from the society and onto the minority communities. (p. 1)

But perhaps the most insidious use of the model minority stereotype results in two effects: it exploits all Asian Americans and it is used as a tool of oppression against other minorities (Albert, 1980, p. 103). This pits racial groups against each other in a destructive manner for all minorities.

The "Exotic Oriental Woman" Stereotype portrays the Asian woman as "graceful, delicate, a cultured woman of the Orient" (Ogawa, 1971, p. 59) or "the submissive, subservient, ready-to-please, easy-to-get-along-with woman" (Yamada, 1983, p. 37). Sing (1989) points to stereotypical media images like the 1914 film "Madame Butterfly" and Miyoshi Umeki's coy geisha role in "Sayonara" made in 1957-58.

All Them Orientals Look Alike by Julie Sittig

The Japanese woman has been defined from the White male perspective as a combination of the inscrutible, evil and powerful "Dragon Lady" of the orient and the "Suzy Wong" sexual stereotype (Sing, 1989). Yoshimura, (1971) in her essay *G.I.'s and Asian Women*, uncovers how Asian women have been dehumanized as the "enemy" by the psychological conditioning of American soldiers designed to make them insensitive to Asians as people.

During World War II the Japanese and Japanese Americans were referred to as the "Yellow Peril" and labeled "Japs," which is considered a derogatory term when placed in this historical context. For example, Daniels and Kitano (1970) note the intensity of anti-oriental feelings reflected in the 1905 San Francisco Chronicle headline "The Yellow Peril - How Japanese Crowd out the White Race" (p. 47). In 1943, with wartime hysteria, headlines from the Los Angeles Times announced; "Jap Boats Flash Messages Ashore" and "Caps on Japanese Tomato Plants Point to Air Base" (Armor & Wright, 1988, p. 20). Even today, some non-Japanese Americans use the word "Jap" without knowledge of its racist connotations.

Study Response to Stereotyping

Although most of the participants were aware of the various stereotypes of Asian Americans and Japanese Americans, they had spent little time thinking about how they might be affected by them. The Exotic Asian woman stereotype brought laughter to some who truly thought it ridiculous that others might cast them as such. Yes, some of the Sansei and Yonsei participants had dated men who were, as one participant termed it, "Japanophiles" and/or men who were particularly attracted to Asian women for their physical, racial features and the assumed role of the subservient female. But the participants did not necessarily consider themselves to be the "Madame Butterfly" type portrayed by Miyoshi Umeki in *Sayonara*. Some indicated that body type may influence this perception. For example, a petite frame might fit the classical stereotype while a medium build with *daikon* shaped legs (like a Japanese radish) might not be considered "cute" (as in petite or diminutive). Sansei Kim, a dancer, recalled that she faced stereotyping from choreographers in New York, who had a quota for how many "Asian types" in a dance company. For the first time, she was confronted by being classified as a member of a group rather than being judged by her individual abilities and achievements.

Most women who spoke of their mothers as mentors, described them as strong in character, intelligent and independent thinkers, an image contrary to the stereotype of Asian women. Nisei women had seen their Issei mothers play multiple roles of housekeeper/cook, field worker or businesswoman, and servant to their fathers. Sansei women saw their mothers maintaining a household while working in the community. Their Nisei mothers began to expect respect, independence, and joint decision-making. Yonsei women saw their mothers as career women who were also dedicated to their families.

The model minority stereotype was not necessarily seen as a negative since most of the women had internalized the expectations of their parents to be well behaved and to achieve by "Doing their Best." These were considered positive traits by most of the participants. They had little awareness of the political controversy this stereotype had generated. As high achieving Asian students they were being compared with lower class Black and Hispanic students. High academic achievement of Asians especially in technical and mathematical fields became accepted as norms without actual analysis of the reasons for this perceived phenomenon. Several participants indicated that their teachers assumed that they would excel in math and science, when, in fact, they had little interest and average aptitude in those subjects. One Yonsei spoke of the reverse dilemma having to justify her going into medicine to other activist Asian American students who were protesting the model minority stereotype. Asian American activism is a relatively new experience for many midwestern Japanese American women, one in which some of the Yonsei are beginning to participate. The Sansei, who perhaps were finished with college when the ethnic studies movement began to take shape nationwide, did not readily embrace political action, perhaps because they hadn't developed a sense of group identity. Sansei Anna shared that, for her, the women's movement was more relevant than the civil rights movement because she interpreted the workplace discrimination she had experienced as being attributed to her gender rather than to her race. Some Nisei, even after being interned by government mandate and having been reared with a respect for authority, find political action an untenable road to follow. There are exceptions, though, like Nisei M. Kana who is active with Amnesty International. But others, like Sansei Bonnie and Yonsei Jane, recall their Nisei parents' warnings not to demonstrate in public because "your oriental face will be remembered." Unfortunately, growing up in the White midwest did not bring assurance of a color-blind society. Sansei and Yonsei had to contend with covert racism and now in the late 1990's, there is a backlash against affirmative action and other programs from which they, as visible minorities have benefitted.

I was quite intrigued by a few comments made by participants who indicated that their siblings or daughters had chosen not to participate in this research study because they didn't consider themselves to be very ethnic. As one Sansei woman said of her sister, "She thinks that she's White." Another Yonsei participant shared that when she became sensitive about racism or discriminatory treatment, her sister and cousins told her to "Get over it." They preferred to remain color-blind. Then, I recalled that my mother said the same thing of me as she thought back to my adolescent years. Did the women in this study participate because they were interested in their own ethnicity and already had some awareness of its impact on their lives? What were the reasons for those who chose not to participate?

I had one indication from the woman who rated herself a one on the ethnic identity scale. She was reluctant to attend a group interview session explaining that it was difficult for her to discuss personal family issues with others. She sent me a copy of a story she had written about being color-blind and finally apologized for not fully participating saying that if she had thought through her feelings more carefully, she would have declined to participate. It was this Sansei participant who gave me the most insight into the culture conflict felt by many of the women. Her description of her mother's child-rearing style indicated a strong *amae* relationship which she consistently resisted as a youngster. Other participants have also shared their frustration dealing with either a mother or a father where there was little or no communication and many repressed feelings. Several participants implied and even stated that they thought their family relationships were dysfunctional. Yet they were able to rise above it, reflect intelligently about it, and find a path for dealing with this culture conflict. In some cases, they were eager to hear what other Japanese American women had to say, perhaps hoping to hear a familiar voice.

In view of Michael Thornton's (1992) belief that there would be "inner drama," when objectively assigned and subjectively appropriated identities come into conflict, it appeared that any internal conflict, or "inner drama" participants may have felt was difficult for them to understand. Perhaps since many had not experienced direct racism in the midwest, and had rarely discussed their ethnicity and or racism with family members, some chose to ignore or failed to recognize their assigned identity as Japanese Americans. They adopted a comfortable color-blind perspective instead. When midwestern Sansei and Yonsei grew up feeling a sense of belonging within a White community, and they felt uncomfortable and out-of-place while visiting west coast ethnic communities, they assumed that they were being accepted because of personal, individual attributes. This self-selected identity ignored issues of institutional racism and discrimination. But when they discover that society is not necessarily color-blind or that there may be "glass ceilings" in the workplace because of their race and ethnicity, their sense of security and belief in a democratic society may be challenged. These women may begin to realize how their race and ethnicity are integral parts of their personal development.

When Sansei and Yonsei investigate their ethnic histories, study the socio-political contexts in which their Nisei parents and Issei grandparents have lived, and ponder how they have or are going to help their children develop a sense of identity, their own beliefs and values may become altered. It is a process of growth, knowledge and change. Racial prejudice and discrimination have been a part of their heritage and family histories that cannot be changed and should not, I believe, be overlooked. How one interprets these historical events, and the meanings attached to their significance will lay the foundation for future generations. It is a dilemma of victimization and family storytelling which can enrich or disturb the younger generations of listeners. Even though it is public record that slavery existed and that American Indians were forcibly removed to reservations, so it is with the story of internment, they can be communicated as impersonal political events or as stories of people's lives.

The trend from silence about ethnic history may be changing to one of active investigation of how the negative attitudes of racism affect the identities of people of color. The articulation and construction of what it means to be Japanese American needs to be inclusive of all Japanese Americans across the nation. Since there were few midwestern Yonsei in the study, further research on their feelings of Japaneseness is warranted. Consideration might also be given to whether the participants are biracial or full Japanese American. How much one knows about cultural traditions of the country of one's ancestors may not be as salient of an issue as how one is stereotyped by society or how limits to achievement and opportunity are shaped by society. Within all the generational groups in this study, there were some who rejected and some who accepted their ethnicity, but their interpretations of Japaneseness have been transformed. They have been transformed to incorporate Japanese, midwestern, middle class, mainstream values and beliefs as well as experiences with racism and discrimination. These experiences have emerged as a diverse, not a single, portrait of midwestern Japanese American women.

Class, Gender and Ethnicity

The Nisei who settled in the midwest after the war came with few material assets to start a new life. One of the requirements for leaving camp before the end of the war was that internees had assurance of a job (or enrollment in school) on the outside, in essentially White communities. Later, as Nisei left to join relatives and friends across the country, employment was not always waiting. Chiyo recalls walking city blocks upon arriving in Chicago, seeking employment at whatever business looked promising. As M. Kana pointed out, family assets were frozen and often west coast businesses were sold so that, economically, Japanese American families were essentially starting over in the midwest. Some families went to camp from a lifestyle of tenant farmers, so what little property they may have had was most likely sold or given away. Each person was allowed one suitcase of belongings upon entering camp. Even those evacuees, mostly Nisei, who were employed in camp earned less than GI pay according to Weglyn (1976):

> Despite early Army statements which had placed the evacuee wage scale in the $70-$80-a-month bracket, internment policy planners (who included Eisenhower, DeWitt, and McCloy) had bucked under vigorous public protest which insisted that no internee be paid more than the prevailing $21-a-month GI pay, bringing to pass a situation tantamount to creating a class of serfs in a free society since evacuees

> were accorded none of the fringe benefits enjoyed by servicemen . . . throughout the internment period, the evacuee wage scale remained unaltered, providing less than sixty cents a day, or $12 to $16 a month, to the vast majority of the employed. . . Although GI wages climbed to $50 a month, the $19-a-month professional pay (given doctors, surgeons, dentists, administrative aides, architects, and others of "exceptional skills") remained constant throughout the war years. (pp. 115-116)

Thus, upon leaving internment camps, Issei and Nisei would have been considered low income by most standards of the time. It took *gambare* and *gaman*, working hard and persistently, enduring the challenges of a postwar society resistant to integrating Japanese Americans, just to live.

Although possessions were meager upon leaving camp, Japanese Americans brought with them a cultural capital based upon a Meiji legacy of honor and hard work (Bourdieu, 1986). In their new midwestern communities, regardless of educational level, most adults worked at whatever was available while extended family or split shift arrangements were made for childcare. Families sometimes lived together since housing was not always available to Japanese Americans due to discriminatory practices.

From these meager beginnings, most families rose to middle or upper class status due to their persistent focus on education and professionalism. Mei Nakano (1990) writes of Nisei women in the work force dedicating time and effort first to their children's academic success and community involvement, then to earning tuition money for their children's college education. This was not an uncommon scenario for midwestern Japanese American women, many of whom held degrees themselves. There is a legacy of Japanese linear kinship patterns, (male oriented) that has changed over the generations to a stem pattern of shared responsibility and inheritance for both sons and daughters (Yanagisako, 1985). Thus, for Issei parents, the significance of the number one son as benefactor and protector was held in high regard. But as the Nisei became bicultural, this obligatory responsibility changed so that, as Yanagisako (1985) discovered, it was the Nisei sisters who maintained family ties and assured a sense of family cohesion. Eldest sons were still considered special, as evidenced by some of the participant's accounts, but there was also an associated sense of liberation for Nisei and Sansei women.

Opportunities for women to get an education or enter a career were available, though sometimes not particularly encouraged, but they felt less pressure to achieve than their brothers may have experienced. They were always encouraged to "Do their Best" and become well educated but the emphasis was not directly on jobs and upward mobility. There was no intention on the part of Nisei parents to have women carry on the family name or reputation. Women could achieve as individuals for personal reward and self-satisfaction, so many became self-motivated and successful. Gender roles and expectations intersected in new, less restrictive ways, mostly to the benefit of Sansei and Yonsei women.

Motherhood was still held in high regard, but not in lieu of an education or a career. Many of the Sansei participants either married later after having completed their education (including graduate) or after becoming established in their careers. Most indicated that their families felt that having children was very important. For example, Kim described how interest at Japanese gatherings seems to focus on children, compared to another communal setting she experienced where children were regarded as no less or no more important than adults of all ages. Conversations were between individuals on a variety of topics rather than group discussions about (or sharing) about children and their activities. I also found that when I contacted many of my participants, (and even when I occasionally spoke to their husbands), they eagerly shared information about their children, assuming that I would be most interested in them, almost in a family way. Unless I asked specifically about a topic, like internment or work history, the stories about children constantly and naturally emerged. This may have been a function of the study topic, child rearing, but the interview methodology used encouraged open-ended conversation.

5. The Work Ethic: *Do Your Best!*

The model minority stereotype of Asian Americans characterizes Japanese Americans as high achieving "model" citizens largely due to perceived compliance, politeness, and "work-a-holic" behavior. Since stereotypes are generalizations made about a group based upon observed behavior, one begins to wonder if there is a kernal of truth in any of these assumptions. Do Japanese cultural norms of role perfectionism, *gambare* and *gaman* create expectations for Japanese Americans to be thorough and meticulous in their approaches to work? In this chapter I will examine some of these Japanese cultural concepts.

Gambare, to Persevere

Gambare has been associated with educational achievement from the feudal Meiji period when the *sensei* (teacher) was highly respected and the original model of "scholarly goodness," Ninomiya Sontoku, worked hard and diligently against adversity to become a well educated philosopher (White, 1987, p. 51). This work ethic originated from the teaching of Confucius and Buddha and the value of work was taught as part of the *Meiji* school curriculum (Kitano, 1976, p. 131). The attitude that work is a desirable goal in itself may still be part of the socialization of third and fourth generation Japanese Americans.

A variety of scholars have attempted to define the Japanese words *gambare* and *gaman* sometimes using them interchangeably. "Literally," writes John Singleton (1991), "*gambaru* is a verb that means *to persist, hang on, or do one's best*. In its imperative form (*gambare*) it is used to encourage cooperative activities" (p. 121). O'Brien and Fugita (1991) describe it as the "bearing up" of an individual to adversity (p. 78). Merry White (1987), who has written extensively on the Japanese educational system, defines *gambaru* as meaning "to persist," as it is invoked by Japanese mothers, teachers, and peers (p. 30). Hendry (1986) attaches the terms endurance, patience, tolerance, and tenacity when describing *gaman* in relationship to Japanese child rearing.

While conducting the pilot study (Adler, 1992), I asked three graduate students from Japan to describe the concept of *gambare* and found that they also equated it with a kind of perseverance in the context of working hard and "doing your best" at any endeavor. "When children make the effort, parents say '*gambate*.' They are asserting that the children are making the effort," one Japanese student explained. Another added, "Children say, 'I'm *gambaru*' or '*gambate masu*'. . . I'm trying as much as possible." Making the effort is more important than the actual achievement and will be accepted by the parents even without a clear outcome. In other words, *gambate* has no fixed goal . . . you just go on farther and farther. *Gambaru* is an aspect of self-discipline. White (1987) describes the cultural perspective; ". . . [The] Japanese see fully engaged discipline as refining and enhancing the self" (p. 30).

Family and Cultural Influences on Learning

In addition to using *amae* as a technique for creating acceptance and security, Japanese and Japanese American mothers may also create home environments that reinforce learning as an ongoing process and set a foundation for the acquisition of knowledge that will enable their children to perform well on school related tasks. What is the nature of the family environment that stimulates Japanese and Japanese American children to both value education and succeed academically? Are there effective instructional methods or "home curriculums" culturally embedded in the family lives of Japanese Americans? Although these questions are not directly part of this study, they pose a line of inquiry that may contribute to the understanding of beliefs Japanese American women have about child rearing and education.

Price and Hatano (1991) have constructed a taxomomy of roles that families play to enhance the cognitive development of children. Children move from a novice to an expert status in their acquisition of domain-specific knowledge depending upon the influence and facilitation of the family. Price refers to this as "family-mediated curriculum selection" (p. 7). The roles that family environments provide include: forum and audience, apprenticeship, instruction, bottleneck-mitigator, and bottleneck remover. Price and Hatano (1991) explain: "Cultural-familial values and purposes have a selective influence on the forms of expertise that children seek, practice, and take in pride. They affect the choices children make of domains in which to become expert" (p. 10).

What happens when expertise in one realm is so divergent from another that they rarely intersect or that over time school expectations dramatically change? For example, Asian American children become experts at keeping their emotions concealed and controlled. But in American society (represented by the mainstream classroom), students are encouraged to express their feelings and opinions. Participation in group discussions becomes a domain in which Asian American children lack facility. Furthermore, their parents may be inculcating behavior patterns that prove counterproductive in changing times and differing contexts. Passive, compliant behavior may have benefitted the Nisei in 1930 or the Sansei in 1950, but will the same behavior and cultural orientation prevent the Yonsei from effectively engaging in cooperative group activities in the 1990's?

During the post World War II years, Issei and Nisei strongly reinforced the importance of schooling because it was believed that education was one of the few means for overcoming, or at least circumventing, societal and workplace discrimination (Suzuki, 1977). "Since very few other options existed," writes Suzuki, "they very likely saw schooling as one of the only avenues left for their children's upward mobility. This almost desperate faith in schooling was undoubtedly reinforced by the traditional veneration accorded to education in Asian societies" (p. 173). This process, along with the rewarding of compliant behavior in school and the underdevelopment of the Nisei's verbal-linguistic skills, led to the selection of lower echelon white collar occupations, especially in the technical-scientific areas. This analysis, Suzuki believes, seriously challenges the widely-accepted notion that Asian Americans have achieved middle class status and have been almost completely assimilated into the American mainstream (p. 174).

The seriousness in which the Japanese and Japanese Americans regard education is illustrated by the long term commitment parents make to their children's achievement, development and schooling (Le Vine & White, 1986). Referring to both groups, Trueba, Cheng & Ima (1993) point out that "the parents' most important obligation is to start early in life preparing children for higher education . . . Education is a common topic of family discussion and a serious preoccupation" (pp. 31-32). Slaughter-Defoe, D. K., Nakagawa, K., Takanishi, R., & Johnson, D. J. (1990) endorse approaches that emphasize cultural/ecological perspectives suggesting that the socio-economic status and the subsistence strategies utilized by families are related to the achievement socialization of children from ethnic minority families. The immigrant Issei taught their bicultural Nisei children to value education and to respect the *sensei*, or teacher, legacies of the *Meiji* culture. Simon (1987) explains that ". . . To Japanese women, motherhood is a profession, demanding and prestigious, with education of the child the number-one responsibility." A report from the U.S. Department of Education, describing this uniquely Japanese maternal role, claims, "much of a mother's sense of personal accomplishment is tied to the educational achievements of her children..." (Simon. 1987, p. 46).

Effort over Ability Orientation

The distinction between effort and ability has been examined by a variety of scholars whose research compares Japanese educational perspectives with "American" or primarily European American orientations to education. Focus is maintained both on the schools and on parenting practices related to producing effective learners. Their work has lead to conclusions about the differences in achievement between "American" and Japanese students but has hardly addressed the achievement of Japanese American students or the inculcating of Japanese cultural beliefs by Japanese American parents. In fact, it is unclear whether Japanese American students were part of any "American" research samples. But their work is valuable in that it helps us understand the differences in worldviews.

Hess, Azuma, Kashiwagi, Dickson, Nagano, Holloway, Miyake, Price, Hatano & McDevitt (1986) found in their longitudinal study of Japanese and American maternal influence on learning, that there are different goals and techniques for socializing children for intellectual growth and development. In their words:

> Japanese mothers interacted with their children in ways that promote internalization of adult norms and standards, whereas American mothers were more oriented toward application of external authority and direction. American mothers relied more on verbal explanations and on the use of techniques encouraging verbalization by children. Japanese mothers seemed to emphasize more following the correct procedure as a route to understanding; the concept of "from form to mind" seems to fit their behavior in teaching tasks. (p. 163)

If a Japanese 4 year old child in their study made a mistake while doing the sorting task provided by the researchers, the mother would give the correct information and perhaps some additional information about the task. In a similar situation, the American mother would interact with the child requesting verbal responses about the task. Japanese mothers then focused on the procedural aspects of the task while American mothers stressed conceptual grasp of the sorting principles (Hess et al., 1986, p. 154). In assessing the beliefs about the causes of success and failure, Hess et al. found that Japanese mothers put more confidence in internal factors, expecting their children to assume responsibility for achievement and performance in school, while American mothers felt that external guidance and support was more important (p. 161). Poor performance was also attributed to lack of effort by Japanese mothers and their children. They were less likely to blame the training at school as a cause of low achievement. American mothers and children tended to see poor performance in mathematics as caused by all three variables: effort, ability and school instruction.

Holloway (1988) notes that there were distinctions between Japanese and American notions of effort. "Not only is performance viewed as hinging on effort rather than ability in Japan, but the notion of effort includes a positive orientation toward the intrinsic benefits of such persistence" (p. 331). Holloway's thesis maintains that Japanese schools and homes foster a state of task involvement, as opposed to ego involvement. "In task involvement, ability is judged with reference to one's previous level of performance, and hence is seen as dependent on effort" (p. 334).

Both Japanese teachers and mothers use unobtrusive control strategies that do not threaten the adult-child bond by overt demands for compliance (Holloway, p. 338). There is a strong reliance on procedural knowledge in the approaches used to build persistence. Repetitive practicing of procedural skills fosters that task involvement vital to sustained learning. In contrast, according to "self-worth theory," American adults view effort and ability as inversely related, concluding that effort is a compensation for lack of ability (Holloway, p. 328).

Stevenson's (1992) work on cross-cultural achievement in mathematics, indicates that a greater emphasis is placed on innate ability by American parents than Japanese parents. American mothers of elementary school aged children, placed less emphasis on academic achievement, indicating that doing well in school was merely one of many different kinds of accomplishments they expected of their children. Asian mothers repeatedly reported that their child's primary task was to do well in school and that their own job was to "do everything possible to ensure that success. They regarded education as critical for their children's future" (p. 72).

In the subsequent report of this longitudinal study, Stevenson, Chen and Lee (1993) report similar results: "Eleventh graders in Japan and Taiwan remained strong adherents to the belief that hard work was of primary importance, and their American peers retained their strong belief in the importance of ability as a modifier of the effects of effort" (p. 57). Their data indicates that 72% of the Japanese students versus 27% of the American students felt that studying hard was the most important factor. Of the Japanese teachers, 93% selected studying hard as a significant factor compared to 26% of the American teachers. In contrast, 41% of the

American teachers chose innate ability compared to 7% of the Japanese teachers (p. 57).

Cross-Cultural Perspectives on Education

Currently in both cross-cultural research and in the public media, comparisons of academic achievement have been made between Japanese and Americans students. This is a misleading comparison because the educational systems differ in their goals. Furthermore, the societal and familial influence on education differs in each country. This section will focus on some of the differences and will examine the impact of family and social norms on Japanese and American educational goals and practices.

It should be noted that in some studies, the "American" samples have included Asian American or specifically Japanese Americans. For example, in the Tobin, Wu & Davidson study (1989), the "American" preschool was located in Hawaii and included some Japanese American teachers and students. This may be true of Stevenson's samples, although no breakdown of the Minneapolis sample was provided. Also, studies in this and the next section range from preschool to college. Slaughter-Defoe et al. (1990) point out the paucity of research, especially at the early childhood level, on Asian Americans and achievement socialization since 1970. The authors were only able to identify six of twenty-five studies that included elementary and middle-school aged Asian American children, while the majority concentrated on high-school aged or adults (p. 366). Between 1970 and 1980, only ten studies were focused on Japanese American families (p. 367). Five studies did not differentiate between Asian groups and only one (Onoda, 1976) included lower-achieving Asian Americans.

Further research on the range of academic achievement among Asian Americans challenging the model minority myth was conducted by Stacey Lee (1996). Lee maintains that not all Asian American students are high achieving, compliant and academic *nerds*. There is diversity in student motivation, achievement and sense of ethnic and Pan-Asian identification. In describing the problems associated with this myth, Lee (1996) writes:

> The model minority stereotype is dangerous because it tells Asian Americans and other minorities how to behave. The stereotype is dangerous because it is used against other minority groups to silence claims of inequity. It is dangerous because it silences the experiences of Asian Americans who can/do not achieve model minority success. And finally, the stereotype is dangerous because some Asian Americans may use the stereotype to judge their self-worth; and when this happens,

we/they may, as one student reminds us, "just lose your identity ... lose being yourself." (p. 125)

Simons (1987) calls attention to the role of the *kyōiku mama* in preparing Japanese children for the competitive school systems in Japan. To illustrate the strong commitment Japanese mothers make to the education of their children, Simon (1987) tells of a Japanese businessman's apology to the host of a dinner party for his wife's absence. "I'm sorry she couldn't come tonight" he explained, "My son has an exam tomorrow" (p.48). Responsibility for the Japanese mother to care for her child before his exam supercedes support of her husband in professional contacts. In America, the reverse would be more common where childcare responsibilities might be left to a babysitter (which is rarely used in Japan). Japanese mothers also feel ashamed if their children do not do well in school, taking it as a personal critique of the effectiveness of their mothering skills. Shame and saving face play a significant role in motivating success in school. "The child is taught early that he must do well or people will laugh at him - and laugh at his mother as well," writes Simon (1987, p. 48).

In her article on Japanese families as "mirrors of society," Anne Imamura (1991) describes the family as an important "nucleus of stability and nurturance in Japanese society" (p. 47). Motherhood is recognized both informally and institutionally through required maternity leaves and re-employment incentives. The mother becomes a supporter, a selector of appropriate schools and tutors (including juku, or cram schools), and a partner with the schools. But the emotional and psychological support a Japanese mother provides for her children and their educational pursuits is most crucial. "While the child is studying," writes Imamura (1991), "mother is close by rather than off doing things that interest her. Indeed, living up to the model of mother as all-sacrificing constitutes a primary motivation for success in contemporary Japanese society" (p. 45).

Sato & McLaughlin (1992) point out that there are culturally embedded differences that affect the teaching process. The Japanese see the goal of education to be more inclusive, encompassing a range of competencies including social, aesthetic, and interpersonal skills. "Skill in human relations is considered essential to the educated person," write Sato & McLaughlin (1987, p. 360). Much of the class student and teacher time is spent on activities designed to develop peer socialization, peer supervision and peer teaching and learning skills (p. 361). Japanese teachers work to build social cohesion and social responsibility. "The fact that Japanese students advance to each grade with age-level peers regardless of achievement reflects the priority Japanese society places on group identity and cohesion" (Sato & McLaughlin, 1992, p. 361).

This holistic approach to education dominates the Japanese educational system. "The Japanese view academic knowledge as just one part of the more comprehensive goal of developing *ningen* (human beings)," explain Sato & Mclaughlin (1992). This phenomenological approach is fundamentally different from the western conception of education. They describe it this way:

> *Ningen*, a concept that transcends basic skills and academic achievement, assumes a holistic conception of students' growth and learning . . . Japanese educators . . . believe that the broad educational goals set for children cannot be accomplished "if there is a separation and/or a differentiation of heart and body, and if knowledge is provided only through language." (p. 361)

Since the Japanese view people as their greatest resource, teachers are given much respect and esteem. Japanese teachers are responsible for aesthetic, physical, mental, moral, and social development at all levels from preschool to graduation. School activities cover areas including student guidance, personal habits, motivation, interpersonal relations, and on- and off-campus behavior (Sato & Mclaughlin, 1992, p. 361).

Addressing the needs of the whole child, or making him *ningen-rashii* (or human-like) means, according to Merry White (1987), helping the Japanese child maintain harmony in human relations. To make a cross-cultural comparison, she adds:

> To perform well in school and other settings is important, but that is mostly regarded as a visible demonstration of a capacity to be a good (social) person. Americans, by contrast, tend to give much higher priority to individual skills and attributes, "independence" key among them, and see one's interpersonal skills as more superficial, "social graces," a *means* rather than an *end.* (p. 23)

By contrast, engaging in *amaeru*, or pursuing the indulgence of the teacher, might be interpreted by western standards as a form of immature behavior or selfish individualism (p. 23). Interpreting the Japanese concept of *amae*, outside of its cultural context contributed to the prevailing interpretation of *amae* as spoiling, or allowing misbehavior, by westerners including some Nisei and Sansei.

In Japanese child rearing and educational training, both goals for personal growth and the means for attaining success are clearly identified. Personal attributes of a good child are; *otonashii* (mild, gentle), *sunao* (compliant, obedient, cooperative), *akarui* (bright-eyed), *genki* (active,

The Work Ethic: Do Your Best!

spirited, energetic), *hakihaki* (brisk, prompt, clear), and *oriko* (obedient, smart). Means by which a child's development is advanced include *gambaru* (to persist), *gaman suru* (to endure hardship), *hansei suru* (to reflect on one's weakness), *amaeru/amayakasu* (to depend/to indulge), *wakaraseru* (to get the child to understand), and *rikai saseru* (to get the child to understand logically) (White, 1987, p. 27). The mother would use strategies that are more nurturant while the teacher would use didactic methods. Together, they work on goals of self-fulfillment and social integration.

Lewis (1988) agrees that education in Japan during the primary years is focused on the whole child. In one of the classrooms Lewis observed, 67 goals and objectives were displayed. Of them, only eight referred to academic work. The others related to social development (18), personality development (14) and the development of habits (17) (p. 166). The teachers concentrated their efforts on developing persistence of tasks, setting up routines to avoid stress, and having children share authority for classroom management. Procedural training was designed to help children feel settled and to maintain an efficient classroom.

One key feature of the Japanese early childhood classroom was the extent to which children shared authority for classroom management. Children conducted class openings and closings as well as monitored classroom behavior of their peers (pp. 162-163). They even evaluated groups of classmates on their performance. Lewis (1988) writes:

> Some teachers described the groups as key structures in keeping children on-task, in ensuring that children who lacked skill in a given area (be it gymnastics or reading) would have ready access to a more skilled child, and in promoting the class's ability to initiate new tasks with a minimum of classroom disruption" (p. 163).

The emotional bond between teacher and students was also evident in the Japanese classroom. Reflection and self-critique were frequently part of the curriculum too (p. 168).

At the preschool level, much instruction surrounds helping the children develop social skills and fostering identity as a member of a group. Tobin, Wu & Davidson (1989) describe the role of the school and how it differs from that of the family:

> Japanese children learn dyadic relations at home and group relations at school . . . The role of schools is to transform dependent, selfish toddlers into group-minded youngsters . . . To be Japanese is not to suppress or sacrifice the self to the demands of the group but rather to find a balance between

individualism and groupism, between *giri* (obligation) and *ninjo* (human feeling) (p. 71).

Too often western observers misinterpret Japanese groupism and see it as the opposite of individualism. American preschool teachers would eagerly endorse the development of the individual child as a primary goal of early education, and relegate the development of cooperative skills as secondary and dependent upon individual readiness. To the Japanese teacher, the sign of a well developed individual is the positive manner in which she embraces groupism.

While western child development specialists and teacher educators value the ability of preschool teachers to relate to children in a nurturant manner, the Japanese make a clear-cut distinction between the teacher role and the mother role. Tobin, Wu & Davidson (1989) write, "Teachers are not parents, and to the degree a Japanese teacher allows herself to slip into a maternal relationship with a child in her care she has failed in her role as a teacher" (p. 62). Japanese teachers in their study were observed doing paperwork while children were encouraged to solve their own interpersonal problems.

Teacher intervention in peer relations occurred infrequently in Japanese preschools. The structure of the classroom, with a ratio of one teacher to thirty-some students is designed to force children to develop ways of relating to each other without adult assistance. Some class activities are also designed to expect cooperation and communication. For example, a teacher may invite children to paint at a table where there are more children than available paint brushes. This pattern of structural organization requiring peer cooperation continues throughout elementary school.

Lois Peak (1991) points out that Japanese parents and teachers consider themselves to be specialists with distinct and dissimilar roles and, therefore, rarely share concerns about the children with each other. The formality of social relations between teachers and parents in Japanese society also contributes to this perspective. A mother would never consider criticizing a teacher or sharing any problems about her child. American preschool teachers, on the other hand, actively seek information about children in their classes and feel free to offer advise or make recommendations to parents.

Japanese American Academic Achievement

Research confirms that, as an ethnic group, Japanese Americans are highly educated (Sue & Okazaki, 1990; Suzuki, 1977; Sue & Kitano, 1973). Suzuki (1977) notes the high level of Nisei and Sansei college graduates compared to European Americans. Nakano (1990) points out that in 1973, 88% of the Sansei population had completed some college training (p. 220). The 1980 census indicates that for Japanese Americans between the ages of 25 and 64, 37% earned high school diplomas, 15.6% earned college degrees and 2.6% received doctorates or equivalent years of education. At the high school level, it was below that of Whites (39.9%) but considerably higher than other Asian groups. At the doctoral level, it was slightly better than Whites (2.6% to 2.1%) and well below other Asian groups with Chinese being the highest at 7.1% (Barringer, Gardner, & Levin, 1993, p. 172).

This educational success has it's roots in the philosophies brought by Japanese American immigrants. The Issei held beliefs and customs of the Meji Era in Japan, where both the parent and the *sensei* (the teacher) were highly respected and honored. "A model of scholarly goodness for Japanese children, from the Meiji period to the present," wrote Merry White (1987), "has been Ninomiya Sontoku, a Tokugawa-period philosopher whose statue still stands in many schoolyards" (p. 51). Harold Stevenson (1992) further defines the Japanese perspective explaining that:

> This attitude stems from Confucian beliefs about the role of effort and ability in achievement. The malleability of human behavior has been long emphasized in Chinese writings, and a similar theme is found in Japanese philosophy. Individual differences in potential are deemphasized, and great importance is placed on the role of effort and diligence in modifying the course of human development. (p. 73)

Some research (Sue & Kitano, 1973; Mordkowitz & Ginsburg, 1987) indicates that Asian American families have a profound effect on the academic achievement of their children and that education is regarded as requisite for economic and social success. Hard work and effort along with guidance and monitoring of behavior have lead to achievement in American schools that surpasses other minority groups. Mordkowitz & Ginsburg's (1987) study on high achieving college students tie academic success for Asian American students with high expectations of academic success, parental monitoring of students' time, respect for teacher authority and education, investment in educational opportunities, avoidance of peer conflict, and a strong belief that effort would be rewarded.

Both self-discipline and a role perfectionism became norms learned by Asian American students through parental influence. Befu (1986) describes role perfectionism as a Japanese cultural concept that implies a "commitment to do well against all odds" (p. 25). Despite the lowly level of menial tasks, one is still expected to put forth his utmost effort. "The cultural ideal of endurance enables a person to overcome the feeling that a role is unworthy," writes Befu (1986, p. 25). Mothers engage in role perfectionism through personal example, or modeling, as they teach their children to work hard at every task. Whereas the education of children is a Japanese mother's first priority, American mothers, according to Befu (1996), have competing roles and priorities. Japanese American mothers, in studies like the ones mentioned previously, also appear to have a strong commitment to the education of their children.

Schneider & Lee (1990) examine the academic success of East Asian students in American schools (Chinese, Japanese and Korean 6th and 7th graders in Illinois) using a model that combines the macro socio-cultural factors of native culture and socio-economic status in host country with the micro interpersonal interactions of the teacher, parents and students (p. 363). They write:

> We hypothesized that children develop academic self-expectations based on their parents', teachers', and peer groups' educational expectations for themselves and their past experiences. Aware of others' expectations, it appears that children set certain self-expectations or standards for their own achievement and translate these standards into performance through their effort and persistence in coping with particular learning situations or tasks. (p. 362)

> We also hypothesized that East Asian parents were more likely to stress certain norms such as industriousness, diligence, and respect, which reinforce particular behaviors highly valued by teachers. (p. 364)

Findings indicate that East Asian parents tend to structure the home learning environment for their children by strictly controlling the out-of-school time, directing it at academically related skills (Schneider & Lee, 1990, p. 374). For some study participants, parents established and monitored specific periods of time for study. These study habits were reinforced by teachers who then tracked the students into top-level classes starting with high reading and math groups in the primary grades. Teachers rewarded behaviors like being quiet, industrious, disciplined, and orderly, viewing East Asian students as highly cooperative. Peers also identified East Asian children as "good" students therefore reinforcing a positive image.

Powers, Choroszy & Douglas (1987) investigated the relationship between attribution theory and achievement motivation in Japanese American and Anglo students at the university level. "Attribution theory," they write, "suggests that attribution of success to one's effort tend to increase achievement motivation since effort is perceived as internal and under volitional control . . . Since ability is often perceived as internal and not under volitional control, it would not be expected to be related to achievement directly" (p. 17). Their findings indicate that Japanese American students attributed success in mathematics to external causes more than Anglo students, and they attributed failure more to lack of ability and poor educational environment than their Anglo-American peers. The data also indicates that Japanese-American students were less achievement motivated, had less self-esteem and more anxiety than their Anglo peers.

Using an instrument called SOAR (Survey of Achievement Responsibility) which consists of a group-administered questionaire, Mizokawa and Rychman (1990) investigated the causal attribution for success and failure of over 2,500 Asian American students. Their findings indicate that Asian American students identified as low-income (by subsidized lunch status) seem to believe that hard work leads to achievement. Koreans hold the highest effort attribution scores and Southeast Asians (except Vietnamese) have the lowest scores. Interestingly, all groups except the Japanese attribute more effort to success outcomes than to failure outcomes. The Japanese have an even distribution of effort to success and failure (p. 440-442).

The rationale for this explanation of upward mobility was that discriminary laws and practices denied Issei access to unions and to White businesses. As a result, they were forced to become independent farmers or to open their own businesses. "Since very few other options existed," writes Suzuki (1977), "they very likely saw schooling as one of the only avenues left for their children's upward mobility. This almost desperate faith in schooling was undoubtedly reinforced by the traditional veneration accorded to education in Asian societies" (p. 173). This process along with the rewarding of compliant behavior in school and the underdevelopment of the Nisei's verbal-linguistic skills, lead to the selection of lower-echelon white-collar occupations, especially in the technical-scientific areas. This analysis, Suzuki believes, ". . . seriously challenges the widely-accepted notion that Asian Americans have achieved middle-class status and have been almost completely assimilated into the American mainstream" (p. 174).

If researchers narrowly define the criterion for "success" solely in terms of income level, then statistics could be used to dispute Suzuki's viewpoint. Based on the 1980 census, statistics indicate that both median household and family incomes were considerably higher for all Asian Americans (except Vietnamese) than Whites. The Japanese with the smallest family size, held the highest per capita family income at $9,068 compared to other Asian groups and that of Whites with $8,667 (Barringer, Gardner, & Levin, 1993, p. 151). In terms of parity with Whites, Japanese were found to be the only Asian groups that had reached and maintained equity with White incomes.

But further research on the nature of the family's influence upon career choices of Japanese American children would help explain whether cultural valuing of education, ability to "function" in society, or both were primary catalysts for academic achievement. Issei parents might have socialized their children to seek an education regardless of (or without knowledge of) the opportunities available in society. During the postwar years, many college educated Nisei returned to family businesses on the west coast while others migrated to other parts of the U.S. in order to pursue career goals. Family responsibility and general livelihood might have taken precedence over career advancement and upward mobility.

Yamamoto (1968) elaborates on this perspective noting that even in the face of job discrimination, the Nisei became high school and college graduates "... just for the sake of being educated" (p. 135). He explains:

> Even though men with college degrees could only obtain work as gardeners and as fruit stand vendors, they still went to college. Great emphasis was placed on education and knowledge which were considered virtues. One could be respected for what one had learned and knew regardless of one's occupation or material rewards. (p. 135)

Education for Japanese Americans might or might not have proven "functional" in the job market of the 1960's, but it certainly was a "personal possession" that society or government could not usurp from any person, of any race or gender!

Educationally Oriented Participant Group

The thirty-four current study participants are diverse in many ways, but they are uniformly well educated. All hold high school diplomas, one has an associate degree, and twenty-eight (82%) have undergraduate degrees (two of the six that do not are recent high school graduates and are both in college). Sixteen (47%) hold graduate degrees which include two medical doctors, two Ph.D's, one lawyer and one engineer (Table 6). Since participants were recruited through informal networking and the core of women from the pilot study were well educated, it is possible that this study is biased in favor of more educated women.

It was suggested by several of the participants, that many of the families who remained in the midwest rather than returning to their ethnic communities on the west coast after the war, were particularly independent and self-sufficient with family members who reinforced assimilation. Since employment and education were the two main contingencies which allowed

Table 6. Participant Education and Occupations.

Participant	Education	Field of Study	Current Occupation
Nisei			
Chiyo	High School	.	retired
Mariko	High School	.	retired
Mia	Bachelors	Music	retired
Mona	Associate	-	retired
Masako	Masters	Library Science	retired
Chizu	Masters	-	retired
M. Kana	Masters	Music	retired
Mrs. K	.	.	retired
Sansei			
Grapdelight	M.D.	Pediatrics	physician
Obasan	Ph.D.	Audiology	professor
Anna	Bachelors	Mathematics	systems analyst
Shigeko	Masters	Social Work	retired
Mimi	M.D.	Psychiatry	psychiatrist
Amelia Bedelia	High School	.	telephone supervisor
Akiko	Masters	Education	teacher
Lesye	Masters	History	college administrator
Kim	Bachelors	Dance	modern dancer
Connie	High School	.	retired
Imoto	Bachelors	Social Work	social worker
Mariko	Masters	Mathematics	teacher
Bonnie	Bachelors	Education	teacher
Lani	Masters	Library Science	librarian
Mitzi	Ph.D.	Nursing	professor
Mika	J.D.	Law	lawyer
Kikuye	Masters	Education	college administrator
Yonsei			
Leia	Bachelors	Zoology	student
Jasmine	High School	.	student
Shigeko	Bachelors	Psychology	counselor
Emily Akemi	High School	.	student
Yano	Masters	Education	teacher
Jane	Masters	Mathematics	demographer
Erika	Bachelors	Art	student
Fusako	Bachelors	Education	teacher
Alana	Masters	Engineering	civil engineer

internees to leave camp, many who did relocate in the midwest came for opportunities in higher education. In 1941, one hundred-nineteen Nisei were in colleges in the midwest. By 1943, there were six hundred thirty-four andduring the years 1945-46 it rose to one thousand, three hundred thirty-two (O'Brien, 1978). In the first group of four hundred relocated students, there were twice as many men as women mainly because "ability to support one's self while attending college was an important requirement" (p. 74). In addition, preference was given to sons first in most families, but after February 1943, "many Nisei men left college to enter the armed services" (p. 74).

Midwestern families sometimes chose to integrate into mainstream society and, in some cases, even disassociated themselves from smaller Japanese American communities like the one in Chicago. Two Yonsei women and two Sansei women from different families told how their parents purposely moved to suburban White neighborhoods in order to be "accepted as individuals" rather than as members of an ethnic population. Some families also moved into White suburbs where Japanese Americans could buy homes (discrimination in real estate was common) and where schools had high reputations for academically challenging programs. This information was shared matter-of-factly and seemed not to contradict their feelings of pride in their ethnic heritage.

The connection of child rearing responsibility with educational achievement was evident, although not as intense, with many of the current study participants. Japanese American mothers did not necessarily measure their own self worth by the academic achievement of their children, but most did invest time and energy into making certain that their children were readily achieving at school. The focus seemed to be more on setting expectation levels, monitoring behavior and grades, and facilitating learning in general rather than direct teaching, tutoring, or intervention at school. Sansei Connie pointed out that there may have been some contradictions with the messages she and her husband sent out to their children because they wanted them to "try their best," achieve, but also be happy. "We were lucky," she said, "by trying their best they were able to do fairly well."

Voices from Group Conversations

"*Do your best* is what we always heard," said Nisei Mona, "Do your best even if you're a streetsweeper or you work at McDonalds!"

"Were we conditioned that way?" asked Nisei Chiyo.

"I think we were," echoed a few women.

The Work Ethic: Do Your Best!

"I don't think we were pressured," added Yonsei Leia, "but we were expected to *Do our Best*. For me, this intense effort wasn't external. I was self-driven. I know I learned that from my mother."

Laughingly, Chiyo said, "I guess we were obligated to not be a bum!" Others agreed. They couldn't imagine themselves as Japanese American bums.

"You can see it through the generations," Nisei Mia suggested.

"Yeah," Leia added, " My uncles worked hard too. And they wanted to live up to their father's standards . . . my brilliant grandfather."

"I think girls are a little bit freer . . . in choosing their own fields," said Nisei Chiyo, "Girls don't feel pressure to accomplish in academics."

"I didn't even think about college," said Nisei Mariko, "because my parents stressed education more for boys than for girls."

Nisei Mona, who was valedictorian of her high school class and who wanted to go to college was quick to reply. "Let me tell you," she asserted, "During that time [wartime] you can go to college, you can put in four years of college, you can come right back on the farm or family business because there were no jobs for orientals. We couldn't get into the job market."

"I had to finish high school in camp by correspondence," continued Mariko. Recalling her husband's sisters, she said, "they went to junior college. I think they thought that office work was for girls, unless they were wealthy; then they went to college."

"My parents were tenant farmers, so they didn't expect me to go on, even though I was inducted into the California Scholarship Federation," Chiyo shared.

"I always wanted to go off to school after I got out of high school," said Mona, "And I had scholarships, you know. But all these Issei people had the idea that girls go off to college to look for a man. Well, where else are you going to look for somebody who's going to get ahead? But instead, my mother sent us to cooking school and sewing school and all that kind of crap." She laughed.

"My father was a progressive man," said Nisei M. Kana, "the year after evacuation when the bank froze our family assets taking away our money for education, my father said, 'I'll give you the privilege of going . . . You are free to get an education.'" He wanted to free his sons from having to go into the family business so they could pursue careers of their interest.

"Was that privilege just for the boys?" Sansei Shigeko asked.

"No," M. Kana replied, "we all worked while we went to school. And the school of education wouldn't accept us. The school of nursing wouldn't accept us at the University! The only thing girls could go into was fine arts or business."

"That's amazing," said Yonsei Leia, "And now two generations later, I'm attending medical school."

"And I'm just starting college," added Yonsei Emily Akemi.

"If you really want to go way back in time," said Mia, "My mother was progressive too, a real free thinker. She used her dowery in Japan to continue her education at a Tokyo missionary school to become a teacher. Then she came to America and worked as a secretary for a Japanese newspaper publisher eventually becoming a teacher in a Japanese language school. She was my mentor."

"My parents expected me to get good grades and go to college," said Sansei Shigeko. "I guess I'm a lifelong learner because I even went on to get a second masters degree. All of my children are college educated." Shigeko also noted that her parents gave her money for earning good grades. Sansei Bonnie and Yonsei Fusako's parents also expected good grades and gave monetary rewards for them. Other Nisei parents declined to give tangible rewards.

"It was not expected that you play the dumb female in the house," shared Bonnie, "That was totally unacceptable. You were in school to get good grades. If you came home with a B there had better be a real good reason on why you're not pulling straight A's. Privileges were taken away if you continued to get B's."

Yonsei Fusako joined in noting that good grades were expectations for her too. "I remember getting grounded even if I tried my hardest," said Fusako, "It was a lot of pressure because I wasn't trying to get A's for myself, I was trying to get A's for my parents. They would help with homework only after I tried 100% and still didn't understand."

Many of the other Nisei and Sansei women expected to pass on the legacy of a college education to their children. After having friends in camp who were "serious about learning" Chiyo's post camp experiences solidified her belief that her own children should have a college education.

"I had to leave camp to go to Chicago to find a job," said Nisei Chiyo, "I mean, if you weren't educated you had to settle for a lesser job so just by economics you realize you want more for your own kids."

"We made it fairly clear," said Nisei Mia, "that we expected our daughters to go to college. That was one legacy we could give them, whatever they did . . . if they had the education they could go on from there and improve themselves, and then get a job and then have the life that they want."

The Construction of the Work Ethic

The interpretation of gambare as a work ethic by Japanese Americans encompassed both the putting forth of consistent effort to "Do One's Best" as well as building internal self-discipline regardless of outcome. But in a reward oriented western society, hard work is expected to lead to results, which can be rewarded or lead to upward mobility. Thus, when Issei and Nisei encouraged their children to "work hard" for the sake of building self-discipline, sometimes it was interpreted as "work hard" to get ahead. This would be consistent with the protestant ethic that maintains that those who succeed in a democratic free market are those who "put their nose to the grindstone," apply themselves diligently, and surpass their competitor in performance. In a sense, Japanese American children were being given two different reasons for developing a strong work ethic, one from their families and one from society at large. The following examples illustrate how these discrepant interpretations might become confusing when parents and children are working under different assumptions.

Sansei Kikuye spoke about learning the Japanese American work ethic from her father with the following story about working in her father's factory. She is trying to instill a respect for "working hard" in her children, but may do so for different reasons.

> When I was growing up the children in my family used to go to my father's factory on the weekends to help . . . During these workdays at the factory, the four of us children were our own work crew. We took pride in completing tasks quickly and finding faster more efficient ways to do things. We packed racks in boxes, counted tips and put them in bags, and assembled racks for shipping. I remember one time when we packed everything as quickly as possible and finished early. As soon as we completed packing all the racks, we started to play around the factory. I'll never forget my father coming back and asking what we were doing. We were very proud and said we had finished packing all the racks. Instead of saying that's great, he said, *Whenever you finish a job early, you should go ask what else needs to be done.* At the time we thought he was crazy! After all, we had worked hard so we could play. But those words of wisdom have held me in good stead throughout my career and I hope to pass them on to my children.

Anna was another participant who held a negative reaction to her parent's expectations to work hard because it brought little acknowledgement of achievement. In fact, according to her recollection, hard work did not help her learn good study habits at all. She equated the process with the "carrot and horse approach" or the "rat on the treadmill." As a result, she "subconsciously sabotaged" her own achievement producing a mediocre academic career. She described it in this way:

Well, it was the carrot and the horse approach. That is, you're never good enough. So you can read, well, so why can't you read Shakespeare? You can add, well, why can't you multiply? You were never good enough, but I wasn't smart enough to realize that, so I was still this horse following this carrot in front of me on a little treadmill. And it wasn't really until I was in college, that I realized that hey, you know, this is really stupid. This is really a stupid motivation to do things. Now, there are many in a similar situation . . . There are a lot who would have said, *Heck, what's the sense? I'll never measure up so* . . . But I didn't.

As evidenced by the last two responses to the work ethic, one begins to see a divergence in interpretation of this cultural orientation. Does one work hard to build character and personal traits of perseverance, or does one put forth effort because it is the socially reinforced way to succeed? Were both the goals that Japanese American parents were trying to inculcate?

In the midwest where an ethnic community did not reinforce Japanese norms, individuals responded to their family expectations in differing ways. In the households of some participants, verbal praise and tangible rewards were relatively rare. Under these conditions, resistance to and rejection of high expectations to work hard were not unusual and might have been predictable. For example, some Sansei remarked how their peers earned money for A's while they were "just expected to earn them," but few remember explicit words of praise or encouragement from their parents.

The work ethic in relationship to academic achievement and learning in general was facilitated by Japanese American parents in differing ways. Three examples of how it was encouraged and communicated came from Sansei Mimi, Nisei Mariko and Yonsei Jane. "My mother always had us do our homework before we could play," said Mimi, "And Dad would sit with us and be doing his 'homework' while we were doing our homework. Later he told me that that was part of his reason for bringing things home; to help us, to encourage us to do our work." Mariko described her husband's method for encouraging her children to be constant learners:

Once in a while when he was around, we used to go to the park, and we'd take the four kids, and we would go just for evening . . . a walk just to discuss things. And then he says, when we get back, everyone's got to write . . . what they thought about. What they thought about was the subject. And Mark, the youngest one, he said, *I don't know. What am I going to write?* He remembers that. Yah, he remembers that today. He said,

The Work Ethic: Do Your Best!

> Yah, I was worried because I didn't know what to write. That's how strict he (her husband) was . . . a very strict parent.

Mariko also recalled how her husband would ask the children about current events at dinner. Yonsei Jane recalled that her father did quite a bit of "lecturing" to his children about their behavior and work habits. She laughingly described this father-child interaction:

> If he saw you after dinner watching T.V. (even after doing your homework) he'd say, *What are you doing? You're watching T.V. You should be studying.* Then you'd say, *Well, I finished my homework.* And he'd say, *Well, you never can get too far ahead in homework, can you? Read the next chapter.* Then he'd always tell us how he studied really hard.

These three examples illustrate the ways in which the value of gambare and education was communicated from parent to child. The participants did not recall if their parents ever gave reasons for inculcating this behavior (like "you'll get a good job someday," or "it will make you strong in character," or even, "good work habits will pay off in efficiency"). There appeared to be high expectations with the assumption that children would comply. This may reflect a style of parental control and discipline that places high value on the psychological relationship between parents and children, in particular, the amae relationship. Children's behavior is therefore motivated by the desire not to bring embarrassment or shame to parents or family. It is also interesting that in these cases, it was the Nisei fathers who were explicit about how children should "Do Their Best" and build work habits, while mothers responded more implicitly. More about gendered differences will be discussed in later sections.

Expectation, Effort and Achievement

In this study, several of the Sansei participants mentioned that there were "low-key" rather nonchalant responses to report cards and other measures of success in school. Although some parents rewarded grades with money (as illustrated in the group conversations) many merely assumed that if effort was be put forth, academic success would follow. Sansei Anna described this perspective in the following way:

> Academic achievement was in a sense for it's own sake. . . One should learn for the sake of learning and that's the only reward. Even report cards, they looked at them and kind of gave them

lip service but that was not ever a big deal. But if there was an A minus, you see, then it was, *Well, it looks like we can improve here*. It was almost a guilt thing.

Several participants including Sansei Grapdelight and Lani and Yonsei Leia, noted that they were self-motivated and internally self disciplined. They knew their parental expectations and met them without external reinforcement. Grapdelight noted that there wasn't a great deal of pressure on her to be successful in school because she was generally goal oriented and loved to learn. "It was intrinsically rewarding to learn," she explained, "They (her parents) considered my work to be going to school. As long as I wanted to do that they would support it. They paid for all of my education." Lani echoed the same experience of parental support, low key discipline, and reinforcement of a strong work ethic: "I was a good girl. I was a good quiet girl and I got good grades and I was exceedingly responsible from an early age so they never had to tell me to do my homework or get after me to study." Yonsei Leia and her brothers knew what was expected of them and described it as follows:

> We're all good students. It was just something that came like, *Well, of course you do your homework, well of course you study, well of course you go into an exam prepared as you were supposed to.* And of course my grandfather was this big researcher. He was so smart, this genius in our family. The least I could do was just to try to live up to that legacy. Do your best.

Associated with this sense of self-fulfillment and intrinsic reward is Befu's (1986) concept of role perfectionism. It implies that doing well against all odds despite the lowly level of menial tasks is still expected and that gaman (endurance) enables a person to overcome the feeling that the role is unworthy. This concept was reiterated in the literature by Japanese American women. This quote, taken from Jeanne Wakatsuki Houston's *Beyond Manzanar: Views of Asian-American Womanhood*, describes the author's conversation with her Issei mother about hardwork that might lead to death. Houston writes:

> When I told her my fears she only laughed and said, *I like to wash clothes. It gives me time to think of other things in my head.* She tapped her forehead. *Besides, I'm not a washerwoman. This is just a chore. I'm your mother.* I did not then understand the weight of her explanation. Being mother was not only enough for her, it was a prized identity. It meant she had a family, and in her world---her peers and community almost

exclusively of Japanese descent—the family was supreme. Thus, the chores and duties which she inherited as Japanese wife and mother were not her identity as such; they were just a means to accomplish the end, which was to keep her family intact, happy and well. She never confused her tasks with who she was.

As Nisei Mona expressed in the group conversation, "*Do Your Best* regardless of the task or role, streetsweeper, clerk, because that thoroughness reflects upon you and your family." Sansei Kim remembers hearing the same message from her parents. Attributing this trait to her father's modeling of tremendous patience and meticulous ways, Kim said, "When I do something I do it well, I do it carefully . . . with a great deal of attention." There are a variety of reasons that Kim and other Japanese American women might develop these traits. Perhaps personality or temperament and parental modeling reinforced the development of task persistence. But Japanese cultural influences in conjunction with sanctions from mainstream society might have also contributed to the development of this role perfectionism and *gambare*.

The behavior of Japanese American children in public (including school) was considered a reflection of the family as a visible minority in a White community. This response may have originated from the cultural norms of *Haji* (shame), *Ha zu ka shi* (embarrassment or reticence) and *Hige* (self-denigration) which are part of the Enryo Syndrome expressed by Issei and some Nisei (Kitano, 1976, p. 125). Japanese Americans were self-conscious in public due to differences in both the linguistic and interactional style. Therefore, compliant behavior in school was regarded as desirable and proved rewarding (Suzuki, 1977).

As Yonsei Fusako mentioned in the group conversation, she was earning good grades for her parents rather than for herself. Pleasing parents and teachers was also very important to Yonsei Yano. She analyzed her academic achievements in the following way: "Because I was well behaved and always tried my best, the teachers liked me. I consider myself an average student but persistent. I did not test well in math in elementary school but received good grades because I tried hard and was well behaved." Sansei Lesye, like Yano, was a compliant, well behaved student in elementary school but changed from being timid and shy to becoming outspoken and political and into "counterculture kind of stuff," after the ninth grade. She attributed this shift to her new found political awareness: "I was against the war in Vietnam and wore a black armband in protest for almost a year. I started hanging out with the 'heads'. And in the last years of high school, I became more of an 'intellectual' type."

Others, like Sansei Amelia and Yonsei Erika, resisted the expectation for compliant behavior. Since Amelia had an older sister who excelled in school, she chose to concentrate on the social realm, "the personality part" to forge her own identity. She started with high aspirations heading for a bachelors, a masters, and then a Ph.D. But after one semester in college, Amelia quit saying, "I'm eighteen. I need to grow up." By the time she returned to college, she found that she had little in common with her peers. When asked if she would ever return to complete her degree, there was still a sense of rebellion. "It's always been something that's been . . . ," she answered, "I really should have that degree, but on the other hand, I really don't want it. I want to be somebody who's made it without having it. So, which again is like going against the grain. That's been my way of life to just kind of buck the system."

Yonsei Erika was smart and had relatively high test scores but found school so unchallenging that she became bored and rebellious. It wasn't parental pressure (they just said "Do Your Best") or school curriculum but rather the negative peer interactions that made school an alienating place for Erika. She experienced racial slurs and harassment from classmates but did not share them with her parents, retreating to her room at home and socially from her peers instead. This reticence to converse about intimate issues and personal feelings was commonplace among other Japanese American families. It might be part of the Enryo Syndrome, where one does not bother or inconvenience others with their problems, that Erika learned from her mother and grandparents. It might also be a teenager's desire for isolation or hurt and alienation after the rejection implied in racist remarks. After having completed her college education, Erika now recognizes her parent's philosophy: "If you do your best, good marks will follow. If you short change yourself now (in high school), you'll regret it later. It will always be on your record, and your record will always be with you or catch up with you later."

In analyzing the varied responses of the participants, it is unrealistic to try to attach one dominant rationale to their responses. A multitude of factors contributed to individual responses to the work ethic gambare. They include: acquired role perfectionism, parental expectations and control, emphasis on effort over ability, response and behavioral expectations of peers and teachers, and psychological bonds with parents and family. Why were these Sansei and Yonsei women told by their parents to "Do Their Best?" Did their European American peers in school have the same mandate from their parents? According to Sansei Connie, the choice of rearing daughter Jane and her siblings in Skokie, Illinois, resulted in contact with predominantly Jewish families who shared the same attitudes about academic achievement as her family. Although socialization was an important part of school life, learning was the prime reason for attending school.

In contrast, Stevenson's (1992) research indicated that, compared to Asian American maternal views on schooling, European American mothers placed less emphasis on academic achievement. Since most of the Sansei and Yonsei in this study attended schools with predominantly European American student bodies, their peers may not have had the same orientation to school work as they did. Were they, then, perceived as the "nerds" or the highly academic students more than the athletic or socialite type of students? As Yonsei Yano and Fusako indicated, they may have been considered "model minority students" by school faculty and administrators. But as Yonsei Leia and Sansei Amelia also pointed out, they made attempts to avoid that label by becoming active in extra-curricular activities like drama and sports. Personally, and to the dismay of my parents, I felt the need to "play down" the academic side of my high school life choosing to value cheerleading over science fair (although I participated in both).

Some of this tension between parental expectation for achievement and the need to be accepted socially in high school might be considered a common, middle class American teenaged dilemma, separate from cultural orientation. In short, as one participant put it, "That's not particularly Japanese, is it?" In some ways I tend to agree, especially since Maya Angelou (1993) so elegantly pointed out that we (human beings) are more alike than different. There are, I believe, some universal issues (like discipline, care and responsibility) that influence all family units. But each family within an ethnic group sanctions some behaviors and not others depending upon the values being taught, the cultural traditions being maintained, and the contexts in which they can be internalized. If a behavior, based upon a foreign culture becomes problematic in a new setting, then that behavior would most likely become transformed over a period of generations. For example, the self-deprecating behavior of Meiji culture (apologizing for poor quality, when that may, in fact, not be the case) and the *enryo*, which some Issei and Nisei exhibited, proved to interfere with communication with westerners. Intensions and perspectives were misunderstood. As a result, Nisei parents, who adopted the low-key, indirect communication style, allowed their Sansei children to become more direct and even assertive in their communication with peers.

Class, Gender and Educational Opportunity

Although all of the Nisei women in this study indicated that they wanted their children of both genders to attend college, they had varying opportunities to continue their own education depending upon the class and beliefs of their Issei parents. The prevailing Issei view was the stem or linear perspective (Yanagisako, 1985) which favors the first born male. Therefore, in Japanese American families, educational opportunities often went first to the oldest son. For example, Nisei Chizu recalled having to wait for a new dress because money was being spent on her brother's education to become a dentist.

Social class of the family in Japan, as well as socio-economic status in American society, influenced whether Nisei women were given the opportunity to attend college, as Mariko and M. Kana mentioned in the previous group conversation. After the war, most interned Japanese Americans lost any wealth they may have accumulated prior to the war, so that most college students had to earn their own way by working. But there were different Issei female role models in the homes prior to camp, which illustrated the social demarcation of class. Several of the Nisei women from wealthy families spoke of their "cultured" mothers who arranged flowers, could serve ceremonial tea, were well versed in the Japanese arts, and for some like Mia and Chizu's mothers, even attended college. But other Nisei women from poorer families recalled how their mothers worked in the fields or family businesses and had little time to spend with them. As Chiyo recalled, even though her parents were farmers, they sent Chiyo to Japanese culture school with the intent of having the family eventually return to Japan.

Sansei role models for this group of participants included many college educated Nisei mothers, but there were career choices that fell on gendered lines. For example, Sansei Mitzi wrote, "They told me at the age of seven years old that I would be a nurse and my brother was to be a doctor, and both of us would go to the University of Iowa and get our education. That is exactly what happened." She recalled that her father began saving for their college education "on the very day we were born" because he wanted his children to put all of their concentration and effort into their studies without having to work as he did. "They considered my work to be going to school," said Sansei Grapdelight, "As long as I wanted to do that, they would support it. They paid for all of my education."

There were also mixed messages of gender expectations regarding education. Since her father was an educator, it was assumed that Sansei Anna would become a teacher, a relatively gendered occupation. (In fact, she even joined the Future Teachers of America in high school.) But Anna also found out that her parents were concerned about her being "too smart" or in danger of "achieving too much academically." She described her dilemma in the following way: "I was a female nerd in high school. My parents worried about my social adjustment (or lack thereof) and my prospects for marriage and family." Other Sansei told similar stories of not being encouraged, but they all have succeeded in earning college degrees.

A different view on academic achievement for women was shared by Sansei sisters Mariko and Mika. Their father was also a college professor who encouraged his daughters to achieve academically, rewarding them with money for good grades. As Mariko said, "My parents had very high expectations. I always met them and they were proud of my achievements." Mika added, "I was brought up to believe that I was smart. This expectation was self-fulfilling. As an adult, I realize that my parents still think that I am smarter than I really am." They both have carried on this legacy of high educational expectations for their children, regardless of gender. In order to insure the *best* education for her child, Mika has enrolled her young daughter in "a top-notch academic, nurturing all girls school."

There also appeared to be less closeness reported between some fathers and daughters which may have had roots in the cultural distance prescribed by traditional Japanese family roles. The combination of authority figure (real or perceived) and lack of physical and verbal expressiveness of some Japanese American fathers may have created a psychological distance that was culturally based. In contrast, a biracial Yonsei woman described how physically close she was with her affectionate European American father, while she highly admired and respected her more reserved Japanese American mother. The nature of individual relationships between daughters and each parent most likely shaped both cultural and gender roles.

For the Sansei and Yonsei generations, the hard work, perseverance, and high educational expectations of Nisei parents and grandparents has placed most of the families into a middle or upper class status. It seems as if the "pay-off" for academic success in terms of upward mobility came for the third and fourth generations when a college education translated to jobs in their fields of study. The careers of these women span a wide range from technical and scientific positions like computer analysts and medical doctors to the social sciences with teachers and social workers. The fine arts, with one participant as a dancer, was not well represented in this study, although one librarian had recently emerged as a storyteller.

Second doctorate in the family, 1995

6. The Transformation of Culture

In the 1980's, President Ronald Reagan spoke of the "melting pot," focusing on a dominant White society in which racial and ethnic differences would be eliminated and a "color-blind" perspective would prevail. Today, in the 1990's, President Bill Clinton speaks of a multicultural American society, a "tossed salad," "tapestry," or "mosaic" of pluralism where diversity is valued and racial differences acknowledged. Though these metaphors are preferrable to the melting pot, they are static models and do not permit changes within and among the individual elements. I would like to focus on the 21st century and propose a new metaphor; a constantly recording videotape or "Ameri-view," to describe the transformation of American culture. It would be a dynamic model, documenting historical accounts of many racial and ethnic groups, interpretations of diverse family cultural traditions, and personal stories of "lived" experiences in American society. In the postmodern sense, the video would portray multiple perspectives, or multiple "truths" about the nature of American society.

Marcus and Fischer (1986) contend that as generations pass and racial groups intermarry, the culture of the immigrants will evolve and be reconstructed in diverse ways. In short, it will be transformed. The transformation of culture can be considered a dynamic process in which individuals and communities of people construct new entities rather than merely combine existing cultural traditions. Sonia Nieto (1992) explains the creating of new cultures by young people of color as follows:

> Their native cultures do not simply disappear, as schools and society might expect or want them to. Rather, aspects of the native culture are retained, modified, reinserted into different environments, and "reissued," so to speak, so they are valid and workable for a new society. These young people do not totally express the original values of their cultures, nor have they been completely assimilated into a new culture . . . transformed values and behaviors resurface in sometimes surprising ways. . . What is "American" is neither simply an

alien culture imposed on dominated groups nor an immigrant culture transposed to new soil. Neither is it an amalgam of old and new. What is "American" is the complex of interactions of old, new, and created cultures. These interactions are not benign or smooth. Often characterized by unavoidable tension and great conflict, the creation of new cultures takes place in the battlefields of the family, the community, and the schools. (pp. 231-233)

This study of Japanese American women describes their feelings of affiliation with the culture of their heritage, or the "native" culture of Japanese immigrants, and attempts to determine how those feelings might relate to their views on child rearing and education. Sense of belonging to an ethnic group was regarded as personally meaningful, to some participants, or a mere categorical membership to others. Personal comments made by participants about their ethnicity uncovered a curiosity about, an embracing of, and a rejection of "Japaneseness." The varying degrees of ethnic affiliation along with interpretations of Japanese culture have, according to data from this study, contributed to the transformation of culture by generations of Japanese American women. The way in which midwesterners have "reissued" Japanese culture, using Nieto's (1992) term, reflects their isolation from ethnic communities.

In her poem *Mirror, Mirror*, Mitsuye Yamada (1986) explains to her son that "American" can mean looking oriental or Asian on the outside, but feeling "All American," or having a national sense of belonging, on the inside. She infers that "All American" includes the interpretation of Japanese cultural beliefs as they are relevant and applicable to individuals of Japanese ancestry. As Japanese beliefs are transformed across the generations and are shared in contemporary society by Japanese Americans, the vision of American-ness becomes more multicultural. Japanese Americans, like any other ethnic group, contribute to the weaving of a more diverse social environment, which makes heterogeneity enriching rather than divisive. In this study participants grappled with the meaning of "Japaneseness." I believe that the more profound question really is, "What does *American-ness* mean?"

The persistence of ethnic culture has been debated among scholars. Specifically for the Japanese American population, Montero (1980), Levine and Rhodes (1981), and Kitano and Daniels (1988) appear to favor the view that assimilation would naturally prevail and that a sense of Japaneseness would fade through the generations. Levine and Rhodes (1981) explain that the Sansei, "may have little reason to retain any

Japanese American identity at all" (p. 146), though they may still appear to be foreign to others. In fact, their endnote indicated that where there are few Japanese Americans, Nisei and Sansei may have difficulty convincing residents that they are ignorant of the Japanese language and owe loyalty to the United States (p. 154). On the other hand, Fugita and O'Brien (1991) maintain that there is a persistence of ethnic community and that emergent ethnicity will change across generations as reasons for maintaining ethnic identification and community change. This change may be a shift from economic and linguistic support to shared experiences and familiarity with interactional styles.

Based on her study of kinship patterns, Sylvia Yanagisako (1985) concluded that Japanese culture had been transformed by Japanese Americans from a Japanese stem-family system to a conjugal family system. In a stem-family system, inheritance and family responsibilities are passed down in a linear fashion to the eldest son, while in a conjugal system the siblings share equal rights and responsibilities for the welfare of the family and elderly parents. Yanagisako discovered that Nisei sisters maintained family responsibilities through closeness and enduring cooperation making kinship patterns women-centered rather than patriarchial. While this was thought to reflect the perpetuation of Japanese culture, it was, in fact, an example of how loose interpretations and assumptions about "native" culture create new beliefs and values upon which contemporary norms are based. As a result, Japanese American families were considered close-knit, cohesive, and respectful of elders, when the responsibility of keeping the family together and caring for parents was originally expected only of the eldest son and his wife. The Nisei interpretation of the Japanese concepts of *enryo* and *amae* may follow similar patterns of transformation. Although the interpretations may not be entirely consistent with the Japanese definition of the term or the historical use of the term in Meiji culture, the manner in which the beliefs are transformed and passed on to future generations is of significant interest.

The Japanese concepts of *amae*, *gambare*, *gaman* and role perfectionism, re-interpreted into the context of Japanese American child rearing, are key components in the transformation of culture that I believe has occurred. Mothers in the study defined their parental roles to include: teaching morality (character), encouraging the understanding of social contexts, inculcating work habits, and instilling a desire to become an intelligent, educated person. The practice of all of this lead to academic success as an outcome, but high grades and scholarships, although important, were generally not considered to be the primary goal. The emphasis of their child rearing was on the process of learning, more than on the product or outcome. "Do your Best" as a recurring theme reflected a call to put forth effort, to build task persistence, and to apply oneself with a motivation for thoroughness and thus excellence. It had less to do with "Being Best," with competition or with the performance of others and more to do with building one's own habits and learning style. Effort also was tied with intelligent behavior in which one persists at meaningful tasks that will solve problems and produce results and are designed to be efficient. Thus hard work would lead, in small cumulative increments, to the process of becoming a competent human being. There was also an implicit assumption that all persons are capable of becoming a competent human being.

The transformation of *amae* combined the psychological closeness of a mother to her children, exemplified in the mother's attentiveness to attitudes, feelings, and needs of her children, with the desire to make them independent rather than dependent. In essence, these women were attempting to teach responsibility and self-sufficiency in learning while being very attentive to the learning environment and experiences of their children. In guiding their children, the mothers helped them understand consequences and evaluate results so that future learning could be attained. Independence was not regarded as simply being free to experience, the sink or swim mentality. Instead, these mothers carefully, inconspicuously, and often non-verbally attended to their children's habit formation. Their approach was often indirect without lots of rules and active problem solving discussions. Mothers felt that they were attentive of and responsive to both the environments in which their children were growing up and to their children's individual ability to cope and adapt.

From the female child's perspective, as several Sansei women mentioned, boundaries and expectations were clear, but it was hard to figure out which method was acceptable or preferable for attaining them. Haphazard attempts or "just good enough" approaches were not acceptable, yet specific instructions for achieving a task were not necessarily articulated. Instead, parents often observed their children, then suggested ways in which a task could be made more efficient, rather than teaching them directly how to do a particular task. This approach was perceived by some participants as somewhat stressful because one was never certain whether one's efforts would bring success, and in addition, one rarely received concrete feedback.

As a function of this confusion in their own upbringing, some Sansei and Yonsei parents have attempted to be more direct, more clear and even more rule oriented with their Yonsei and Gosei (5th generation) children. The less verbal and less demonstrative Japanese communication style made some Sansei and Yonsei more aware of the need to provide encouragement and praise for their own children. New ways of building parent-child relationships have emerged in which communication is more open, yet expectations still remain high. But the sense of commitment to family cohesiveness and the belief that child rearing is a primary responsibility remained intact in these Japanese American families.

Study findings indicate that the relationship between ethnic identity and perspectives on child rearing and education were connected through cultural assumptions that were not necessarily perceived by some participants as Japanese in origin. Therefore, participants could have a low or weak sense of ethnic identity yet believe in educational goals and demonstrate child-rearing approaches that reflect or parallel Japanese cultural assumptions. When a strict dichotomy is not created, (i.e. This is Japanese, this is not Japanese), then an emergent Japanese American-ness based upon selective cultural choices, personal knowledge of family child-rearing practices, and possible misinterpretations of immigrant culture, is likely to emerge.

As the 21st century draws near, American society needs to be acknowledged as the multicultural society it always has been. How that sense of American-ness is reconstructed with ethnic minority contributions is of significance. Nisei, Sansei and Yonsei women need to see themselves and their family members not as just "Americans with an oriental face," but as racially Asian with transformed cultural interpretations of their Japanese heritage combined with western cultural norms of the dominant European American society. I believe that these midwestern Japanese American women were influenced by their Japanese cultural heritage regardless of the degree of ethnic identification and affiliation they may have felt or expressed. They most clearly saw themselves as culturally different from contemporary Japanese but did not disregard a sharing of values originating in Meiji Era culture. They also knew that there was a richness in their cultural worldview that was not shared by their European American friends.

Comparison of Generational Groups

The investigation of how these thirty-five midwestern Japanese American women transformed the culture of their immigrant ancestors was examined within various socio-political and historical contexts. Table 7 categorizes data about each generational group and compares them in terms of: interpretation of ethnicity, cultural integration, experience with racism, linguistic differences, understanding of and experience with internment and redress, response to the civil rights movement, and educational attainment and it's relationship to the women's movement. The table is designed to illustrate a possible progression across the generations so that all categorical descriptions may not apply to all participants of that group. For example, an individual Sansei might fall in the Yonsei category in terms of political involvement, or an older bilingual Sansei might be better described by the Nisei category. This conceptualization would most likely not be applicable for west coast Japanese Americans, where ethnic studies and heightened racial awareness was evident for the Sansei and provided the catalyst for the redress movement. But for the participants in this study, these categories are generally relevant.

Each participant expressed her own interpretation of what Japanese culture meant and rated herself according to her personal feelings of Japaneseness. The meaning of Japaneseness was allowed to evolve, to be jointly constructed by the participants as they shared their views with others. Many of the participants aligned themselves with the primordialist orientation to ethnicity by associating cultural traditions, beliefs, worldviews, and artifacts with being Japanese. In explaining their "Japaneseness" they spoke of cooking and eating Japanese food, speaking Japanese, learning dances or paper folding, wearing kimonos, and seeing things from a collective versus individual orientation. They also spoke of an interaction style which included low verbalization and indirect communication, similar to other research on Japanese American interactional style (see Kitano, 1976: Suzuki, 1980). Other participants, like Sansei Lesye and Yonsei Leia and Erika, adopted an instrumentalist orientation to ethnicity prioritizing Asian American racial identity above Japanese American cultural identity.

The connection to Japanese cultural associations for many of the participants was more sentimental than functional. Since the Japanese American community was so small and somewhat inaccessible to those who did not live in cities like Chicago, most felt little need to depend upon their ethnic group for linguistic, economic, or socio-emotional support. One functional purpose for the coming together of Japanese American families in cities like Madison, Wisconsin during the postwar years was to allow the Japanese speaking Issei to have companionship. But generally, the family, rather than the community, became the primary source of support; therefore, ethnicity was regarded as more of an individual rather than a group identity. Most of the women in this study saw family cohesiveness as having more significance to their lives than group cohesiveness; and therefore, felt little affiliation with Japanese Americans as a collective.

Table 7. Comparisons of Midwestern Generational Groups.

	Nisei	Sansei	Yonsei
Ethnicity	Japanese American, bicultural	American of Japanese ancestry	American of Japanese or multi-ethnic ancestry
Cultural Integration	acculturation, assimilation	assimilation, transformation	transformation
Family & Children	obligation	high priority	priority
Language	bilingual, Japanese and English	mono-lingual, English	mono-lingual, English
Education	high school, college	college, graduate school	college, graduate school
Employment	post-war jobs	career	professional career
Women's Movement	nascent feminism	emergent and active feminism	feminism, activism
Internment & Redress	all incarcerated	few went to camp as children	knowledge by self study
Civil Rights	demonstrate good citizenship, low profile	ethnic awareness, quiet involvement	knowledge of contemporary Japan, political involvement
Racism & Stereotypes	overt racism (West Coast), foreign, "oriental"	covert racism (Midwest), "model minority"	racial awareness, multiracial, "model minority"

Knowledge of Japanese culture decreased over the years because family and community did not reinforce it and, for some, it was more beneficial to alienate themselves from their ethnic culture. As some Sansei and Yonsei report, their parents purposely moved into suburban areas away from the inner city ethnic community. Although housing opportunities and better schools were some of the reasons given for this migration, the desire for assimilation was clear. It did appear, though, that some Sansei and Yonsei renewed an interest in their ethnicity and discovered that they had developed a need for affiliation with a Japanese

American community. This was perhaps best illustrated by the resettlement of some Sansei to the west coast, California in particular.

Linguistic Transformation

When ethnic groups do not maintain linguistic ties to their countries of origin and native language is lost, cultural understanding is also often lost (Ovando & Collier, 1985). Upon relocation to the midwest, the need to assimilate into mainstream culture as quickly as possible provided the motivation to learn English as a survival mechanism that reshaped the Japanese American family. Sansei Anna remembered acting as a translator for her grandmother as they traveled on a bus together. Her grandmother spoke "broken" English at home but relied on her children and grandchildren in public. Sansei Akiko recalled how her Issei grandfather, who was a produce farmer, meticulously copied words from the English dictionary every night so he could learn the language in which he would have to do business. For Issei and some Nisei, the prewar vision of returning to Japan after having made a fortune in America was essentially gone and the cultural and linguistic preparation of children through community Japanese schools became memories of west coast life.

A growing cultural divergence between the predominantly Japanese speaking Issei and their bilingual Nisei children, who were being educated at school by English speaking teachers, was beginning to develop. The bicultural, bilingual Nisei worked in jobs where English was spoken and soon found that the Japanese language they had learned as a child from attending Japanese schools was not reinforced at home by their parents. Although there was limited access to Japanese schools set up by Buddhist churches in cities like Chicago, most Sansei never became fluent in the language of their grandparents. A loss of native cultural understanding proved to be the ultimate result, yet the opportunity for cultural transformation flourished.

One personal example of the difficulty in making cross-cultural translations emerged when I was teaching a dulcimer workshop at Appalachian State University. All of the instructors were asked to present one song that illustrated a particular technique or type of music. Since the workshop repertoire included a multitude of country tunes, I chose a Japanese song played in a minor key, *Sakura*. The common translation was "cherry blossoms," so I sent a copy of this song, found in an American folk songbook, to my father, and asked if the Japanese translation was accurate. I received a long letter critiquing the words, and essentially explaining that there was no direct translation for each word, since the whole concept of *Sakura* dealt with a sense of community sharing of the rebirth of Spring. Cherry blossoms were only a small part of this cultural tradition but had become the English words attached to the event. Thus, when American teachers taught this song, they promoted the narrow definition of "beautiful cherry trees in bloom," rather than the broader view of aesthetic appreciation of nature shared by a community of people. In the same manner, Japanese Americans across the generations have transformed cultural concepts based upon historically and linguistically narrow translations.

The Nisei and some Sansei in this study, who had definitions for words like *amae, gambare, gaman, giri,* and *enryo,* knew approximate meanings but generally did not use them in their conversations with family. In addition, since interactional styles of Japanese Americans (based on Issei interpretation of Meiji Era Japanese culture), tended to be quite non-verbal, explanations of Japanese terms and their associated behavior were rarely shared. Similar to findings in Mass' (1986) study, some Nisei participants associated the word *amae* with spoiling and indulgence, thus parents are seen as giving in to the demands of their children. This approach would lead to a child-centered parenting style creating a dependency in children, which might be appropriate and acceptable in Japanese society but conflicts with western views of independence and self-sufficiency. As visible minorities in the midwest during the post-war years, Japanese Americans were cognizant of how they were perceived in public. Spoiled or dependent children who might misbehave in public could not be tolerated. And Nisei parents needed to teach their children to be independent and self-sufficient since there was no assurance that community networks would guide and protect their children. As a result, *amae* was not seen as a means of developing security and acceptance, but rather as a hinderance to integration into American society. The socio-cultural context of Japanese society was different; therefore, the interpretation of the Japanese concept was transformed from inter-dependency to spoiling, and discouraged rather than encouraged.

Enryo is another Japanese cultural concept that is difficult to define using English words. Some of my Nisei participants implied that I would know what they meant when they said, "You know I *enryo* a lot." The behavior associated with *enryo* is holding back, it is reticence, being non-assertive, inoffensive, and considering the needs and feelings of others before yourself. This is part of a collective mentality in which it is impolite to stand out, calling attention to oneself, and in which the whole group, rather than the individual, is of primary concern. The socio-cultural context is one of group consensus. But in a society where individual rights and assertiveness are highly valued, this type of behavior is considered non-productive, if not wimpy.

Nisei and Sansei participants based their interpretation of the concept of *enryo* on the reticent behavior they recognized in their parents, and they determined that the continuation of that behavior interfered with their ability to integrate into mainstream society. Thus, the clearly reciprocal interaction style of the Issei and some Nisei, to politely *enryo*, was found to be problematic in a society where direct, assertive behavior was expected. In fact, because it proved to be difficult to apply in a western context, it actually contributed to stereotyping. *Enryo* Japanese Americans were seen as hesitant, indecisive, inscrutable, and therefore either cunning or weak.

Giri, or reciprocal obligation which defines Japanese social interactions at many different levels, was translated in varying ways by Nisei and Sansei. Without understanding the cultural contexts for *giri*, Japanese Americans associated specific traditions like *koden*, (gift giving of money at funerals) and *omiyage*, (gift giving when you visit someone) as a form of obligation. In the same manner, respecting and caring for elders, which was traditionally expected of the first son, became an obligation. In western tradition, elderly parents are either cared for jointly by siblings or placed into nursing homes, and respect is earned by all ages rather than arbitrarily granted to parents or grandparents.

After moving to the midwest, away from traditional family and community obligations, some Nisei chose to eliminate *giri* from their daily lives. Sansei and Yonsei in this study still express concern and respect for their parents (just because they are parents) but tend also to resist the feeling that they might be obligated to them. They would rather see their parents as independent individuals who have their own lives and need their own space. In fact, some Sansei, who have moved closer to parents as they rear their own children and as their parents age, have been told by their Nisei parents that they would prefer going to a nursing home than live with them. This came as a surprise to several Sansei women. It was also a way for Nisei parents to free their children from any further *giri*, something that they could not escape, especially when Issei mothers-in-law lived in their first son's home. This family configuration occurred in three of the study families and lead to considerable culture conflict.

The Internment Legacy

The governmental plan to use the internment camps as a site for promoting Americanization helps to explain the desire on the part of some Nisei to readily assimilate after the war. Camps were segregated and controlled communities with impetus from the governmental administrations to shape model American citizens. One camp director, quoted by Thomas James (1987) explaining the rationale for selective dispersion of Nisei after the war, said: "To train these people not just to make a living or pass the time until the war ends, but to make them ready to hurl as projectiles of democracy into the maelstrom of postwar readjustment--this is the sober demand of common sense, as well as the high demand of justice" (p. 112). Even the written curriculum for schools in camps emphasized the Americanization of Japanese American children. American educators who supported sending Nisei to college were eager to connect education with assimilation and democratic values. As James (1987) described it:

> Educators and concerned citizens working to help the Nisei from outside the camps were also protecting the norms of open competition and individual freedom that gave higher education its legitimacy as a democratic institution in American society. The list of advocates included nationally known educational leaders like Robert Gordon Sproul of the University of California and Ray Lyman Wilbur of Stanford University. Besides advocating the interests of the Nisei, educators were defending their own position in the moral order of U.S. society as keepers of enduring values, sorters of intellect, managers of assimilation. In support of the student relocation from camp to college, educators argued that it was essential to avoid the waste of human resources brought about by the evacuation. The Nisei were citizens who would play a role in American society after the war. Sending them to college would cost no more than maintaining them as wards of the government in the camps. Those who went to college, the argument continued, would symbolize to their families and friends in camps that education was still the best route to a successful future. Finally, the process of assimilation would be enhanced among young Americans in midwestern and eastern communities, where the relocated students would be received more generously than on the West Coast. (James, 1987, p. 115)

The objectification of a whole ethnic group as "projectiles of democracy" reflects the political agenda of the time. Nisei were selected to become racial pioneers and ambassadors of good will (James, 1987, p. 128) and encouraged to become examples for others in camp of the possibility of upward mobility on the outside. Geographic dispersion for the purpose of assimilation was a WRA (War Relocation Authority) mandate that began with the camp school curriculum focusing on family relocation. "The administration," wrote James, "also hoped to use the relocation of college Nisei as a wedge for bringing families into the communities where the students had settled" (p. 131). Thus, assimilation for Nisei began well before they left camp and caused conflict between Issei who were "calling for an awareness of collective needs as the college-bound Nisei pursued individual opportunities" (p. 129). Racial oppression lead to patterns of dispersal and liberal sponsorship and obligated the Nisei "to maintain high levels of achievement and conformity to justify the second generation's status as citizens in American society" (p. 121).

Not all midwestern Nisei concur with this theory of planned governmental dispersion and assimilation. Paul Kusuda, a Nisei active in the Wisconsin JACL and the WOAA (Wisconsin Organization of Asian Americans) notes that, (based upon personal experience), the WRA office in Chicago gave very little actual assistance to Nisei relocating in the midwest. The War Relocation Authority was designed to pave the way for Nisei resettlement, by establishing sponsorships among private and religious groups, and to assist them in securing employment and housing in their new communities. "They (the WRA) certainly could have offered more than a one way ticket and twenty-five dollars to entice young people to leave camp," remarked Kusuda. Dispersion occurred naturally at that time because those who left camp were not allowed to return to the west coast, and once resettled, according to Kusuda, assimilation took on a natural process. The National Japanese American Student Relocation Council, a voluntary agency set up in 1942, also "played an aggressive role in persuading institutions of higher education to participate. It set up standards and procedures for college application, then screened candidates and coordinated communication. It raised funds to help the Nisei pay for college, since the government would provide no support" (James, 1987, p. 116).

The internment experience generally separates the midwestern reared Sansei from their Nisei parents, who moved east after internment. This direct experience with a segregated all-Japanese community of Nisei (and some Sansei) contrasts greatly with the predominantly White environment in which many Sansei and Yonsei in this study were reared. Since stories about camp life were rarely shared with Sansei and Yonsei children, three of the Yonsei women initiated studies of internment as school projects, seeking information from their parents and grandparents. In order to prepare her daughter, one Sansei mother cautioned her that internment was a controversial topic that might generate racist attitudes. Most Sansei had not learned about the internment of Japanese Americans from their American history classes.

As visible minorities during the postwar years, midwestern Nisei maintained a low profile in their daily lives, not readily congregating with other Japanese Americans. The prewar, pre-camp bicultural environment of the Issei and Nisei, in which ethnic pride and the continuation of cultural traditions flourished, had been dismantled by the breakdown of the family in camp and the imperative of Americanization. But, along with the caution of being a visible minority of Japanese heritage, there was also a sense of optimism that there would be less racism in midwestern and eastern communities and that opportunities for integration into American society would be greater away from the west coast.

Patriotism meant placing American national identity above ethnic identity and assimilating into a color-blind society. Even though some Nisei privately heard, "Be proud that you're Japanese," from their parents, the real message may have been, "Don't forget that you are Japanese." Thus Nisei parents encouraged their Sansei children to embrace American values and behavior, even when they conflicted with their own family perspectives. In some families, especially when Issei grandparents were present, the messages were mixed and confusing, actions did not always correspond with words, and disagreement in child-rearing approaches created conflict.

Growing up Sansei, I was comfortable in the predominately European American culture of my Nisei parents, my neighborhood, and my school. I never really considered the Japanese traits and language of my grandparents as foreign or ethnic nor had I ever thought about their past history as immigrants in this country. It was not until I was teaching a college class on multicultural education that I asked my parents to share their first hand knowledge of internment with my students. As I look back, I was pretty detached and insensitive to the emotional impact on my parents and grandparents until they reluctantly consented to visit my class. They would do it to help me professionally and they shared two very different personal accounts. It is difficult for any Japanese American, who had not been interned, to fathom the displacement of 110,000 people because of race and ethnic heritage, knowing that we too could have been victims. We can only imagine the indignation and sense of insecurity our relatives must have felt, and try to understand their individual journeys of ethnic identity. We can only imagine the negative impact forced displacement had on the health and well-being of the family as a whole. And rarely, in Japanese American families including my own, has there been a connection articulated between internment and family dysfunction or personal weaknesses. Families moved onward and away from that ignominious past of racial victimization where oppressors frame the experience as protective evacuation and internees know the reality of forced incarceration.

In order to survive psychologically, (see Kitano, 1969; and S. Sue, 1973, for research on Nisei mental health) and rear mentally healthy children, Japanese American parents had to mesh family cultural values of their heritage with mainstream European American social and political contexts. They had to inculcate what would work effectively in mainstream society without compromising basic values and beliefs of their family. This pragmatic modus operandi is difficult to manage when cultural contexts and societal mores differ tremendously. For example, social interactions among Japanese are obligatory and dictated by a hierarchy of social positions, (i.e. respect for age, rank, and authority) which contrasts with western equality and earned respect. During internment, automatic respect for elders waned as young Nisei men, rather than Issei fathers, began to assume family leadership, both economically and politically. Compliance with military authorities was required, though respect was not necessarily felt. After internment, respect for social institutions and their representatives (i.e. school teachers, elected officials, and police officers) evolved as Japanese Americans responded to their vulnerable positions as visible minorities. In today's society, when Japanese American parents teach their children to be respectful of elders or of teachers, they provide reasons for this expected conduct that are congruent with mainstream norms. Peers, media, and societal norms of individual decision-making challenge the traditional Asian respect for age and authority causing mixed messages.

Japanese American children have been taught to develop an individualism and self-respect within the context of responsibility to their family and community. They have been taught that treating elders with respect reflects their kindness, their desire to learn from those who are wiser and more experienced, and their positive relationship with grandparents. Parents provide opportunities for their children to develop personal relationships with elder friends and relatives so that communication and respect for age becomes fruitful and desirable rather than obligatory. As one Sansei, who regretted not having the opportunity and language to communicate with her grandmother, put it, "How can I be respectful to my grandmother when I hardly know her?" knowing her grandmother could have given her the desire and reasons for treating her with respect. And even if the relationship was strained due to cultural and linguistic differences, knowledge of Japanese American group struggles with discrimination and racism would build a foundation for personal empathy, cultural understanding and positive regard for perseverance. So when Japanese American parents are complimented on the polite and respectful behavior of their children, they can say, "Thank you. I taught my children to be independent decision-makers who act upon personal knowledge of the importance of family relationships and family cohesion," rather than, "I taught them the Japanese value of obligation to the family and ethnic community."

Civil Rights and Ethnic Identity

During the 1960's, many of the Sansei in this study were young adults, working or in college. Ethnic Studies departments were being established in some universities, including the University of Wisconsin-Madison where an Afro-American Studies program was taking shape. Thirty years would pass before an Asian American Studies program would be instituted on this campus. But it was during the sixties and seventies that participants remember being asked if they were "foreign" students. While attending college in the midwest, some Sansei felt isolated as individual ethnics, but they didn't feel a sense of group membership as Japanese Americans. Having been reared to assimilate, many had not considered ethnicity as part of their self-identity. The more they thought about their roots, the more they began to wonder what they had missed, but there were few with whom they could share their questions. Some were indignant that they had been mistaken for being foreign since obviously they didn't speak with an accent, while others gravitated to international clubs or the few organizations that acknowledged diversity. A few of the Sansei (and later the Yonsei) chose to become politically active joining national Asian American movements.

Some simply ignored the movement for civil rights, assuming that they had not been denied their rights as citizens. Historically, the Issei and Nisei had to fight for their rights from the time of restricted immigration to the internment of both alien and citizen Japanese Americans. But since most of the midwestern Sansei saw themselves more as individual citizens, many did not join organizations like the JACL, the Japanese American Citizen's League, until later in life when they were working professionals. Allen Hida, former Midwestern Governor of the JACL, describes midwestern participation in the redress movement as limited to a few spokes-persons who gave testimonies at the public hearing held in Chicago, and to financial contributors to the political movement. Another Nisei organization that developed in the midwest was the Nisei Ambassadors Drum and Bugle Corps. Study participants like Lani and Kikuye, who were corps members, saw the organization as having a social and cultural purpose, rather than a political agenda. The youth corps reinforced the value of individual hard work for the collective benefit.

Some of the Nisei warned their children not to participate in political, civil rights marches because they were a visible minority. The legacy of having to be the model citizen shaped the college bound Nisei youth who left camp for the midwest. Those that followed, whether they attended college or not, were held to the same expectations and naturally passed them on to their Sansei children. The post war expectation to assimilate paved the way for a detachment from ethnic identification to a low-key profile and attempt to become somewhat invisible. One could act White and conceivably fit in by adopting the behavior of dominant society, even though one could not escape identification by race. Some Sansei who rebelled against the Japanese American norm (not sticking out) did so in a more social than political way. For example, several Sansei and Yonsei participants spoke of sabotaging or resisting their own educational development by not becoming "good students", or by putting peer socialization and extra curricular activities as a priority over study and high grades. In contrast to the Nisei quiet invisibility, some of the Sansei and Yonsei chose to become active and extroverted participants in social events and activities like cheerleading, sports and drama. This high visibility was regarded as a measure of acceptance, equality and membership in a dominant color-blind society.

Gender Roles and Cultural Transformation

It has been said that women often are the transmitters (or transformers) of culture. Japanese American women have done so by playing multiple roles, primarily as mothers inculcating values and expectations and nurturing growth and development of *ninjen*, and sometimes as workers or professionals outside the home. There have been a multitude of cultural influences, Japanese and European American, that have shaped the way in which midwestern Japanese American women have lived and reared their children. These will be discussed in terms of four historical contexts, the period of Japanese immigration, the internment period, the postwar period of adjustment, and the period of the civil rights and women's movement, which influenced each generation group in different ways.

In contrasting the emigration of Chinese and Japanese women to America and their differing perspectives on family and gender roles, Ronald Takaki (1993) points out that far more Japanese women came to join husbands, start households and rear children than Chinese women. The reasons for this discrepancy were cultural and structural. Takaki writes:

> Seeking to avoid the problems of prostitution, gambling, and drunkenness that reportedly plagued the predominantly male

> Chinese community in the United States, the Japanese government promoted female emigration. The 1882 Chinese Exclusion Act prohibited the entry of "laborers," both men and women, but militarily strong Japan was able to negotiate the 1908 Gentlemen's Agreement. While this treaty prohibited the entry of Japanese "laborers," it allowed Japanese women to emigrate to the United States as family members. (1993, p. 248)

As a result, sixty thousand Japanese women came as picture brides, including Issei mothers, grandmothers, and great-grandmothers of women in the current study. While Chinese women in the early 1900's were restricted to the farm and home, Japanese women were in the work force (60% of the industrial laborers were women). As experienced laborers more liberated than their Chinese counterparts, Japanese women were also receptive to the idea of traveling. Takaki (1993) describes it in the following way:

> Emperor Meiji himself promoted female education. Japanese boys as well as girls, he declared, should learn about foreign countries and become enlightened about the world. Female education included reading and writing skills as well as general knowledge. Japanese women, unlike their Chinese counterparts, were more likely to be liberated. . . Under the reorganization of the school system in 1876, English was adopted as a major subject in middle school. This education exposed Japanese women to the outside world. (p. 249)

Japanese views on gender and marriage also influenced emigration. The primogeniture inheritance system meant that the first son inherited all property and was obligated to be responsible for parents. Other sons were generally free to emigrate as were daughters since once they marry, they become members of their husband's families, treating his parents as her own. If a Japanese husband chose to emigrate, his wife was obligated to join him. Marriages were traditionally agreed upon by families rather than by individuals with "go-betweens" who made arrangements sometimes through initial exchanges of photographs if the families lived far apart. This tradition lent itself well to immigrants; thus, even if a son was in America, his family could arrange a marriage with a picture bride. Unfortunately, sometimes the pictures did not match the person arriving as one study participant humorously explained.

In camp, the Issei, who were not citizens, were not allowed to work, so often it was the Nisei men and women who brought in any family income. Some Nisei women in the current study worked as secretaries or in various offices across camp for relatively low wages while others were still in high school. Some, like M. Kana and Mona, chose to leave camp for employment or to enter college (or a technical school) which was allowed if it were outside the militarized zone. Although women were not always encouraged to leave by protective parents, camp authorities found that relocating women was easier than relocating men because they were perceived as less of a threat by receiving communities (James, 1987). Once settled in the midwest, most of the study participants continued to work by necessity, especially if their husbands were attending college and if their mother-in-laws or other relatives were available to assist with childcare. Some of the Nisei women even returned to secure their own college education after their children were grown, or at least school aged.

The post World War II years in America brought GI's home, sent women laborers home from the factories, created a new suburban culture, and flooded the popular airwaves with happy homemaker television commercials. It also introduced the social phenomenon of returning American soldiers with their Asian warbrides, which perpetuated the submissive Asian woman stereotype throughout and after the Korean and Vietnamese war years. And as Japan rebuilt itself to world power status with western influence and domination, information about it's contemporary culture permeated the American press. Starting in the late 1960's, a vision of the work-a-holic Japanese father and the *kyōiku mama*, who dedicated her life to the education of her children (particularly sons), created new stereotypes of the Japanese. All of these divergent images surrounding Nisei and Sansei between the late 1940's to the late 1960's made it difficult to assimilate. Images of foreign identity were being imposed on Japanese Americans, even though some midwesterners, who had not experienced direct racism, had come to adopt a color-blind perspective.

It is important to point out that the historical context and the receptivity of Japanese American women into educational institutions and the work force provided and prevented opportunities for these women. Schooling for some of the Nisei women was restricted during and after World War II for various reasons. Due to economic constraints, most of these women needed to work during the postwar years. In fact, many of the Sansei recall that their mothers worked at least part of the time while they were growing up. A sense of personal liberation for the Nisei women was emerging and would be passed on to their Sansei daughters, who have advanced beyond their mother's dreams. Mei Nakano (1990) describes this Nisei metamorphosis:

> Now that their children were in school, Nisei women had joined the work force by the thousands, primarily to finance their children's college expenses, but also to put their own training and talents to use. An unprecedented range of occupations had opened up to them since the civil-rights movement. Women found work as stenographers, bookkeepers, teachers, social workers, department store clerks, dental hygienists, and in all manner of employment that had been previously denied them. This exposure to the workplace, the locus which had driven the struggle for women's rights in many ways, energized the women's search for an ever more satisfying sense of selfhood, a desire to exploit their talents and to explore their inner selves. (Nakano, 1990, p. 198)

The civil rights and women's movements of the 1960's and 1970's brought new awareness and controversy for Japanese American women. Racial and ethnic identities were issues that remained undiscussed and underplayed in their households. "One should not call attention to oneself and must be careful not to become too political," had been the pervasive message. This emphasis seemed to contrast with the burgeoning Asian American political movements on the west coast. Although midwestern chapters of the JACL were involved with the redress movement (to secure a governmental apology and monetary compensation for interned Japanese Americans), they did so through a few affiliated centers in cities like Chicago, Illinois, Milwaukee, Wisconsin, Minneapolis, Minnesota and Dayton, Ohio. But for the most part, Nisei and Sansei women (and certainly most of those in this study) were not actively involved with the civil rights or Women's movements.

Issues of feminism emerged when some of the Sansei and Yonsei women spoke about discrimination in the workplace. It was felt by a few participants that they might have been denied equal access due to their gender rather than their race. This perception was interesting in that the feelings were quite strong and that the women were in scientific fields of medicine and computer science. Others who described themselves as being a "token minority" in their jobs were in the social sciences. Several women in each of the generational groups mentioned having been socialized to be less assertive both within the family and in the work place. Some Sansei felt that they had received mixed messages about their roles as females. Overall, Sansei and Yonsei participants thought their beliefs would be shared by feminists, but few actively participated in the Feminist movement.

Most of the Nisei in the current study had adopted western standards for marriage and several of the Sansei participants had intermarried with European Americans, which lead to what some refer to as structural assimilation (see Fugita and O'Brien, 1991). If indeed there was an acceptance of Japanese Americans into mainstream culture, there was also a renewal of ethnic identity as the Yonsei generation began to mature into adulthood. But after learning about arranged marriages, and in some cases of their own grandmothers as picture brides, Yonsei were not eager to repeat ethnic history. Sansei mothers began to examine their child-rearing philosophies and discovered that their Nisei mothers had relied upon Dr. Spock as well as advise from Issei grandmothers and aunts. They became as dedicated and committed to the role of motherhood as their mothers and grandmothers. They also found themselves supporting their children's education in unexpected ways, like speaking to a classroom of schoolchildren about Japanese food, or teaching *origami* during cultural arts festivals.

Sansei Anna shared a wonderful story that illustrates the kind of cultural transformation that has occurred across the generations. When she was asked to participate in a program about Japanese culture at her son's elementary school, she was delighted to discover that she was not responsible for the program content. Another mother, who was European American, who had lived in Japan, and was fluent in Japanese, would do the presentation. Anna would act as an assistant and a demonstrator. Later in the day, a foreign student from Japan would also visit the class. This combination of participants made explicit to the children the lesson that Japanese culture could come from one's heritage, from one's experiences, and from one's nationality.

In summary, as one glances across the three generations: the Nisei were bilingual and bicultural, acculturating before World War II then assimilating when they settled in the midwest; the English speaking Sansei were reared to assimilate but began to transform cultural concepts as their ethnic awareness began to develop and as they began to rear their own children; and finally, the Yonsei, including those who are biracial, began to construct their own sense of ethnic identity by transforming cultural concepts learned from family history and through study of contemporary Japan and of the Japanese American experience in the United States.

The Construction of Theory: American-ness

Throughout the study, I focused my inquiries on the construction of "Japaneseness" (ethnic identity) while many of my participants were actually communicating their conception of American-ness through the eyes of midwestern women of Japanese heritage. I was seeking to uncover their ethnicity while they were conveying their identities, inclusive of gender, class, race and ethnicity. They told me about their concept of self as being racially Asian, ethnically Japanese, and culturally and lingusitically mainstream European American. They shared their interpretations of the Japanese cultural concepts *amae* and *gambare* and their beliefs about child rearing and education. In order to put their responses into perspective, I will discuss the factors that I believe contribute to the transformation of ethnic minority culture. I use the term ethnic *minority* (Simpson & Yinger, 1985) to denote racial and cultural groups that have historically experienced social, economic, and political subordination in the dominant society.

The manner in which cultural concepts become transformed depends upon three elements affecting ethnics as a group at a given time (generational group) and place (geographical location): 1) the interpretation of the immigrant culture, 2) the shared historical legacy of the ethnic group and, 3) the salience of ethnic and racial identities to individuals within the group. I see all three as interrelated and capable of influencing the interpretation of ethnic culture and the self identification of individual ethnics, in this case, Japanese Americans.

Feelings of affiliation may be shared by members across and within generational groups, and active ethnic group participation positively increases the sense of ethnic group membership, but it is the individual who constructs "truth," or reality, through personal interpretation of life experiences. I found that there were multiple constructions or truths about race, ethnicity, gender, child rearing and education dependent upon the varying perspectives of these midwestern Japanese American women. How individuals responded, which identities they selected for themselves, influenced how they transformed the Japanese culture of their ancestors.

Interpretation of Immigrant Culture

When the cultural and linguistic contexts of an immigrant culture are unknown to later generations, traditions and cultural content becomes subject to decontextualized interpretations. For example, the Japanese tea ceremony becomes a meaningless performance, though elegant to observe, without an understanding of Japanese gender roles and the symbolism of interpersonal relations implicit in the ceremony. As a result, new meanings become attached to traditions and are perpetuated without consideration for the original intent. The concept of *enryo*, (not wanting to inconvenience others) is reciprocal behavior in

Japan where such consideration is expected and appreciated, but it became interpreted as reticence and inability to be assertive when applied in a western social context. Thus Sansei and Yonsei, who recognized their parents and grandparents *enryo* behavior, interpreted it negatively just as *amae* was interpreted negatively as spoiling when, in Japanese society, it is a positive interdependence. There are probably many other examples, including the Japanese song about cherry blossoms, *Sakura*, that illustrate how interpretations become altered by changing contexts, individual perceptions and ignorance of cultural knowledge.

The Shared Historical Legacy

When individual ethnics lack cognizance of the historical events that classify and define their ethnic group, they find little reason to bond with "fellow ethnics." Internment was one of those significant events that ascribed identity to an ethnic group based on racial characteristics and political events. After the war, Nisei, arriving in cities like Chicago, connected with other Japanese Americans by sharing camp experiences and stories of family resettlement. But Sansei and Yonsei, who may have been unaware of the social and psychological impact of internment or the heroism of the 442nd Regimental Combat Unit, did not reflect a sense of outrage for the removal of citizens' civil rights, or a sense of pride for those Japanese American servicemen. Their shared historical legacy had been kept silent as families focused on the American-ness of future generations. Bonding with fellow ethnics was discouraged by some midwestern Nisei parents and assimilation into mainstream culture was encouraged. As a result, individual ethnics readily began to adopt a color-blind perspective, which ignored their Japanese heritage and their minority status in American society.

The openly expressed discrimination against *Japs* on the west coast was perceived to be less severe in the midwest but the sense of shame and humiliation of incarceration was not easily forgotten. As Nisei began meeting fellow Japanese Americans, the shared victimization of internment, the need to find ethnic connections for their Issei parents, and the willingness to share information and insights about their new environment became points of reference that brought strangers together. "What camp are you from?" became familiar words as fellow Nisei became acquainted and settled. Amy Iwasaki Mass (1986) describes the elements of political awareness and psychological response felt by some Japanese Americans that may have contributed to a silent bonding too powerful to articulate:

> The truth was that the government we trusted had betrayed us. Acknowledging such a reality was so difficult that our natural feelings of rage, fear and helplessness were turned inward and buried. . . We used psychological defense mechanisms such as repression, denial, rationalization, and identification with the aggressor to defend ourselves against the devastating reality of what was being done to us. (Mass, 1986, p. 160)

But as Mei Nakano (1990) illustrates, this common attitude did not inhibit their sense of optimism for future generations:

> Although the Nisei woman would deny it then, her experience in exile had been devastating to her sense of self. She refused to discuss it, to dwell on it, wanting above all to get on with her life. This attitude became even more resolute when children began to arrive. (Nakano, 1990, p. 188)

As the non-interned Sansei, Yonsei and even Gosei generations learn the facts about their ethnic history in America, they will begin to understand the impact on their parents and grandparents and recognize the rationale for rapid assimilation during the postwar years. Although there are no personal experiences with internment or identification with the associated shame for them, there will always be a shared historical legacy that may become even more apparent as internment is included in American history books (The Japanese American Citizen's League produced a curriculum on the internment experience which can be purchased by public schools). As reparations have been paid, and apologies by the government given, the personal memories will fade as the Nisei generation ages. But as an historical legacy, the internment of Japanese Americans, as an example of governmental oppression of the civil rights of its citizens, should not be forgotten.

In my own experience as a midwestern Sansei, I have met a variety of responses to my ethnic heritage, ranging from well educated adults who are unaware of internment to those who are chagrined to discover that my family had been incarcerated. Hundreds of books have been written about the internment both documenting governmental and military perspectives and those offering sociological and political critiques. But most of the study participants have not read many of them. They chose to move beyond that part of history, claiming perhaps that it wasn't relevant to their daily lives, yet they know the effects on their family members. Reflecting upon her family and community, one Sansei participant noted, "Japanese Americans are a really repressed people." The legacy of internment, no doubt, caused this understandably human response, which may not be perpetuated across the generations.

The Salience of Race and Ethnicity

As the study progressed, I found some interesting divergences in views on the salience of race and ethnicity. Participants who moved to California or who had traveled abroad, particularly in Asian countries, tended to be more involved with Japanese American issues, ethnic community activities and Japanese cultural and philosophical orientations. At the other end of the spectrum there were a few who staunchly believed in the color-blind perspective and regarded race and ethnicity as not central to their identity formation or cultural orientation. Since ethnicity had not been reinforced in the upbringing of many midwestern Sansei, it was not salient unless individuals made it relevant to their lives by studying Japanese culture and language, investigating family heritage, or by participating in ethnic group activities.

The concept of emergent ethnicity proposed by Fugita and O'Brien (1991) states that reasons for the continuation of ethnic affiliation change over time. It is my belief that the civil rights and women's movements provided catalysts for Japanese women to redefine their racial and ethnic identities rather than perpetuate the approach of their parents and grandparents or to accept the identity that was ascribed to them through common stereotypes. But this did not evolve quickly or easily. Racial awareness of the interned Nisei was acute and negative so that when they resettled in the midwest they adopted a low profile, not readily congregating or promoting any Japanese culture. During the 1950's and early 60's many Sansei children continued the same approach, occasionally encountering indirect and covert racism. This changed for some of the women when the civil rights and women's movements placed racial, ethnic and gender identities into the sociopolitical limelight. But it was the younger Sansei and Yonsei women, as adolescents and young adults in high school, college or beginning professions, who were most influenced by these political events. Sansei and Yonsei women began to privately express renewed interest in Japanese culture though most were not politically active in terms of ethnic minority rights. A few Yonsei expressed strong views on racism and have become activists through their participation in college ethnic movements and through their writing and art. They have come to focus on the larger Asian movement while maintaining interest in their ethnic culture.

The degree of racial and ethnic awareness varied among study participants. Some even mentioned that this research project came fortuitously at a time when their ethnic awareness was being awakened by personal interest, queries from their young children or direct experience with racist attitudes. But direct participation in the civil rights and women's movements were rare for any of the women in the study for several reasons (a few attended marches and one became active).

First, I believe that the Sansei generally felt that they possessed their civil rights as native born citizens, and although many felt compassion for African Americans, they did not consider the movement as "their" cause. Nisei parents, who had been stripped of their civil rights during the war, worked incessantly to make certain that their children maintained theirs. Secondly, Sansei were socialized by their parents not to be negatively conspicuous in public so that overt action was generally not undertaken. Third, gender expectations for Japanese American women at the time was that of quiet compliance and even when Nisei mothers supported their daughters' independence, they did so in a relatively covert manner. And the fourth reason was that direct discrimination was infrequent for midwestern Sansei and Yonsei or sometimes went unrecognized. For example, during the seventies and eighties when Sansei were generally in the work force, several study participants reported being perceived as the token minority, although they did not consider this to be an unbearable negative because it provided opportunity to improve themselves.

Japanese Americans still face racism and ethnic stereotyping in American society today. Third, fourth and fifth generations of Japanese Americans are still mistaken for or even subconsciously considered foreign, and can face having their nationality and citizenship challenged anytime, anywhere in the United States. As the year 2000 approaches and we come to acknowledge our nation as a truly multicultural society, we are faced with the debate to end affirmative action while images of Japanese stereotypes (i.e. reference to the atomic bomb in Henry Beard's O.J.'s Legal Pad and Senator D'Amato's linguistic mockery of Judge Lance Ito) don't seem to fade over time. In light of the Oklahoma City bombing and the proliferation of para-military organizations, American racial and ethnic minorities have cause for concern.

One response of individual ethnics is to take these racist attacks personally and use them as catalysts for political action, becoming activists for eradicating public racism. Another response, common for those who have professionally and socially assimilated into mainstream workplaces and neighborhoods, is to separate personal accountability from group identity. Yes, Judge Ito is Japanese American, but the intense scrutiny and criticism of him was due to his individual performance rather than a reflection of his ethnic culture. What this color-blind viewpoint does not consider is that his judicial approach is a product of his personality, beliefs, experiences, upbringing and cultural background. There is one other response, which is perhaps more deeply embedded in Japanese culture. It is that of enduring (*gaman*) and even passing off racism as "their" problem, the perpetrator's problem so that the victim holds no responsibility. Embodied in the term *shikata-ga-nai* (it can't be helped; therefore, one should *gaman* or endure), like their Issei ancestors, some Sansei and Yonsei choose not to focus on racism.

In my own cultural upbringing, the latter approach seemed to dominate. My grandmother used the term *shikata-ga-nai* in different contexts but with the imperative that we move on and get over it. Taking negative things personally, for her, was generally a waste of time, and she had too much pride to let others assess her. She learned that being an Issei picture bride in California. My parents also often explained that hateful acts were the work of ignorant persons so that their racism reflected only upon the perpetrators, not the victims. This was their most effective means for instilling a strong self concept into their children. "Why should you believe those idiots?" was a phrase I remember hearing while growing up. It was expected that I would construct my own sense of identity as an individual ethnic.

The Individual Ethnic and Cultural Transformation

American-ness, as interpreted by study participants, includes the construction of ethnic identity (among other identities) in the absence of significant ethnic affiliation or community. Japanese cultural concepts appear to have been transformed with regard to the following variables: 1) the degree of personal interest in topics of race and ethnicity and it's relevance to their daily lives, 2) the nature and frequency of contact with nuclear, extended and other Japanese ethnic families, 3) the personal feelings of membership as a Japanese American in a dominant European American society, and 4) the knowledge of and appreciation for the culture of one's ancestors. These variables, in concert with the three elements affecting Japanese Americans as a group, historical legacy, immigrant culture, and the salience of race and ethnicity, have, I believe, contributed to individual cultural transformation.

In this study, the degree of personal interest in topics of race and ethnicity ranged from high involvement and access to information of JACL members to low interest and the belief that race and ethnicity "should not matter." Some participants, who considered themselves highly assimilated, still maintained some degree of interest, primarily in terms of Japanese food or traditions and especially during the holidays when they had more contact with family. The higher the degree of interest, the more likely the participants undertook the following kinds of activities: took courses in Asian American ethnic studies or Japanese language, investigated family immigration history, studied American race relations, attended Japanese ethnic events and celebrated (especially Japanese New Years) with Japanese foods. It is also important to note that interest in one's ethnicity may come at different times within a life span. For example, some participants indicated that they weren't interested in their Japaneseness until they went to college, or they began to rear their own children.

Several Sansei who found their Japanese American Identity highly relevant to their daily lives generally relocated to the west coast and/or had regular contact with a Japanese American community and organizations like the Japanese American Citizen's League. Two of the Sansei participants who were members of the Nisei Drum and Bugle Corps during their high school years in Chicago were immersed with the collective mentality promoted and nurtured within this organization. The likelihood of Sansei like these two women transforming Japanese culture is probably greater than Sansei who interacted with few or no other Japanese Americans in their schools, workplaces or neighborhoods.

Since family plays a relatively significant role for Japanese Americans, the nature of the contact with parents and siblings contributes to the transformation of culture. Within every family there are multiple interpretations of events, beliefs and motives for behavior. For example, two Sansei or Yonsei might attend an ethnic picnic in which there are hundreds of Japanese Americans; one might feel shocked and overwhelmed seeing so many Asian faces, while the other might feel a profound sense of belonging even though most of the people are complete strangers. Two Nisei may also have divergent responses to the hypothetical scene, one in which fond memories of community gatherings are recalled, another of ambivalence remembering when so many Issei and Nisei were forced to live together and build a sense of community for survival. One represents an attraction to Japaneseness, the other signifies a need or desire to escape from the identity. Both reactions were felt by different participants in the current study, both reactions might become catalysts for further study of Japanese Americans and of family history.

Extended family and quasi-kin played significant roles in the development of a sense of belonging for some midwestern Sansei and Yonsei. As an example, in some families like Nisei Mariko's, regular weekly and sometimes daily contact between siblings, grandparents, aunts and uncles provided the opportunity for children to learn about Japanese culture. Of Mariko's four children, surprisingly, two became actively involved in Japanese American organizations, while two appeared less interested (One learned privately through a close relationship with his grandmother). Most of the Sansei and Yonsei participants who did not live in the same city as their parents or extended family made regular visits, often so that grandchildren could spend time with grandparents. This desire for maintaining family connections even occurred via weekly phone conversations or during summer vacations when the entire family might move in with grandparents on the west coast. Quasi-kin connections were sometimes maintained as friends of the parents became surrogate "aunts" and "uncles" in name, but usually had no part in disciplining or decision-making regarding the children. These connections were often remnants of the original families that settled together and supported each other during the postwar years. They were part of a rich family history of informal ethnic community building.

Developing a sense of identification with one's heritage often begins with an understanding of the ethnic group's history, as well as culture. Very few of the families in the current study discussed immigration, early years of settlement, internment or redress. A few brought photographs of family Issei taken at the turn of the century to the group interviews. But generally, only when school term papers were being written by Sansei and Yonsei did the subject of internment even come up in most families. Thus there was little knowledge of the political and historical contexts in which the Issei and Nisei lived during the early 1900's through even the 1930's. For many of the midwestern Sansei and Yonsei, the source of their knowledge about internment came from a few scant paragraphs in their high school American history books, or perhaps a course on Asian American history in college. Two participants recalled feeling very self-conscious sitting in class when their teachers discussed Pearl Harbor, although their peers didn't ridicule them. I recall being an adult before I ever interacted with anyone about my family internment history. They all occurred in educational settings; once as a classroom teacher in Colorado when one of my colleagues had worked for a short period of time in a camp, once when working on a calligraphy project in North Carolina when a retired teacher wanted to know more about my family and couldn't believe they had been interned, and finally as a college professor in Wisconsin when a few of my fellow colleagues wanted to learn more about the topic from my parents who were to visit my multicultural education class.

Gaining knowledge of one's historical legacy, or roots in American history, is merely the beginning task. Knowledge of how these events affected the interpretation of culture is perhaps more significant because these interpretations are the building blocks for the transformation of culture. If the interpretation is that Japanese culture was essentially destroyed by camp life, and that life outside camp required assimilation for survival, then traditions and beliefs brought from Meiji culture might be purposefully ignored and replaced by "All American" mainstream ideas. In fact, a pervasive message of school curriculum in camp was that of Americanization (James, 1987). But if a strong sense of self as a person of Japanese character was inculcated, then assimilation might be regarded as merely a means for survival and Meiji culture might become transformed rather than buried for future generations. The legacy of victimization, of patriotic sacrifice, of the lack of minority group empowerment and of ultimate personal perseverance were rarely communicated on a personal level. As a result, the legacy of internment can be interpreted as a badge of courage promoting a proud sense of belonging or as a sense of shame that lead to psychological problems and dysfunctional families. Both perspectives were expressed by study participants.

Finally, as a means of understanding and appreciating the culture of one's heritage, some participants attempted to embrace Japanese culture. They have taken the interest and time to learn about contemporary Japan, have visited Japan, learned to speak Japanese, and have reached out to the many Japanese visitors to the United States. Several report that they are indeed different from the Japanese "nationals" and that Japan is a foreign yet vaguely familiar country to them. Racially they feel a connection, but culturally, they feel less connection, just as many African Americans have often expressed more cultural connections with those whose families originated in America as slaves than with those still living in Africa. But as African Americans have gained insight and enrichment from their contacts with people from Cameroon, Nigeria, Senegal and South Africa, Japanese Americans can gain perspective about their own families from those who live in Japan. According to this study, few have studied the Meiji culture and philosophies that the Issei immigrants brought with them as a means for understanding the origin of the worldviews their grandparents and parents developed over the generations.

Family portrait, 1991

Appendices

Appendix A : Study Design

Pilot Study

I conducted an ethnographic pilot study of seven midwestern Japanese American women (3 Nisei, 3 Sansei and 1 Yonsei), which was published in *A Gathering of Voices on the Asian American Experience* (1994). Findings of the pilot study indicated that there was a strong sense of family commitment, an expectation for working hard and "Doing your best," and an assimilationist perspective in terms of ethnic identity. Being Japanese American was regarded as a private or family matter, while contact in society required accepting a "color-blind" perspective. Ethnicity was generally considered irrelevant to daily life, although that did not mean that the women were not proud of their heritage. Most of the participants were not part of an active Japanese American community. Good public behavior and success in school were family expectations but were not explicitly described as Japanese American values or beliefs.

Research Questions

The two fundamental questions that frame the inquiry of this study are:

1. How do racial and ethnic identities of midwestern Japanese American women influence their perspectives on child rearing and education?

2. Have Japanese cultural beliefs about child rearing and education been transformed or reconstructed by midwestern Japanese American mothers across generations?

These questions were analyzed from the Nisei, the Sansei and the Yonsei women's perspective. In order to provide a context in which these women were formulating their racial and ethnic identities and their perspectives on child rearing and education, I attempted to uncover their interpretations of three socio-political and historical events; the

Internment of Japanese Americans during World War II, the Women's Movement and the Civil Rights Movement.

I selected these three events as focal points because they were not merely historical periods or life experiences during which these women developed their views and identities, but they were historical events in which American society clearly defined these women by their racial and ethnic groups. The internment provided the context of racial segregation and disenfranchisement of U.S. citizenship. The Women's movement and Civil Rights movement together created the context in which Asian women were disempowered and assumed to have a secondary status.

The women in the study indicated that they were influenced by these three historical events in decidedly different ways. For example, the internment experience for Nisei women contributed to their desire to make their children more independent and assimilated. The Sansei and Yonsei, on the other hand, knew very little about the camp experiences of their mothers and grandmothers, and they became more cognizant of their American historical roots when the movement for reparations began. (See the Redress Bill or the Civil Liberties Act of 1988 in Nakano, 1990, pp. 202-207). Internment was rarely a subject discussed at home.

Two of the women in the pilot study, who were well educated professionals, felt more in tune with the Women's Movement than the Civil Rights Movement, interpreting any discrimination as a result of gender bias rather than racism. They had grown up removed from ethnic communities where issues of racial discrimination were shared and political action reinforced. The Nisei women, however, faced overt racism in most societal contacts on the west coast and were grateful to have jobs during the postwar years in the more accepting midwest.

Theoretical Base

This study draws from a combination of Postmodern, Interpretivist and Feminist theories. Feminist interview methods of open-ended, interactive questioning (Oakley, 1981), the inductive approach to data gathering and analysis (Guba, 1990) and the construction of "grounded theory" (Lather, 1986) were used in this study. Guba concludes that interpretivist research is "relativist" in that there are multiple realities, "subjective" since data is created through an interactive process between inquirer and inquired and "dialectical" because constructions are derived through mutual consensus. The notion of the acceptance of multiple realities, rather than "one truth" is consistent with recent postmodern theoretical perspectives. Susan Hekman (1990) explains that a postmodern feminism would "take the position that there is not one (masculine) truth but, rather, many truths, none of which is privileged along gendered lines" (p. 9).

The women in this study and I jointly probed issues of child rearing, family, education, race, ethnicity and gender. My job as researcher was to interpret reality through their eyes. Therefore, this study reflects both the researcher's and the participants' words.

Study Participants

Participants for this study were recruited through state and national JACL (Japanese American Citizen's League) newsletters, WOAA (Wisconsin Association of Asian Americans) and Asian American Studies and Student Association meetings and through "word-of-mouth,"or informal networking. Personal networking proved to be the best source, although that method contributed to a highly educated participant group. Once potential participants were identified, an introductory letter, outlining the research questions, the mode of participation, and a data sheet were sent inviting midwestern Nisei, Sansei or Yonsei women to join the research project.

All of the 34 women (8 Nisei, 17 Sansei and 9 Yonsei) invited to participate in this study were either presently residing in the midwest, had grown up (childhood and/or adolescent years) in the midwest, or had lived in the midwest for at least ten years. Of the Nisei, I was particularly interested in women who were reared on the west coast, interned during World War II and relocated to the midwest after the war. This historical context is relevant to the development of their ethnic identity and to their conception of family.

In selecting participants, I was interested in including mother-daughter dyads and siblings groups. Two families in the study spanned three generations. Two families had Nisei mother and two Sansei daughters (actually three if I count myself as a participant with my mother and sister). Three mother-daughter dyads participated (two Nisei-Sansei, one Sansei-Yonsei).

The Nisei age range at the beginning of the study was 67 years to 80 years, the Sansei age range was 28 years to 73 years and the Yonsei age range was 17 years to 35 years. Being a mother was a preference but not a requirement for participation in the study. Of the thirty-four participants, eleven were grandmothers, ten more were mothers and thirteen had no children (6 Sansei and 7 Yonsei) (Table 8). All names used in this study are pseudonyms selected by each participant.

Table 8. Maternal Status and Residence of Participants, 1994.

Participant	Maternal Status	Children	Reared	Residence
Nisei				
Chiyo	Grandmother	3	California	Wisconsin
Mariko	Grandmother	4	California	Illinois
Mia	Grandmother	2	Washington	Wisconsin
Mona	Gr-Grmother	3	Washington	Wisconsin
Masako	Grandmother	3	California	Wisconsin
Chizu	Grandmother	3	California	California
M. Kana	Grandmother	2	Washington	Wisconsin
Mrs. K	Gr-Grmother	1	Ca & Japan	Illinois
Sansei				
Grapdelight	Mother	2	Ohio	Wisconsin
Obasan	Mother	3	Wi & Ks	Wisconsin
Anna	Mother	2	Wi & NY	Wisconsin
Shigeko	Grandmother	3	California	Wisconsin
Mimi	Mother	2	Wisconsin	California
Amelia Bedelia	Mother	2	Wisconsin	Minnesota
Akiko	Grandmother	2	Wisconsin	Wisconsin
Lesye	.	.	Minnesota	Pennsylvania
Kim	.	.	Wisconsin	Maine
Connie	Grandmother	3	Ca & Ill	Illinois
Imoto	.	.	Wisconsin	Wisconsin
Mariko	Mother	2	Wisconsin	Tennessee
Bonnie	Mother	2	Wisconsin	Wisconsin
Lani	.	.	Illinois	Illinois
Mitzi	.	.	Iowa	Wash. D.C.
Mika	Mother	2	Wisconsin	California
Kikuye	Mother	2	Illinois	California
Yonsei				
Leia	.	.	Ks & Pa & Wi	Wisconsin
Jasmine	.	.	Illinois	California
Shigeko	.	.	Ohio	California
Emily Akemi	.	.	Ca & Wi	Wisconsin
Yano	Mother	2	Illinois	Wisconsin
Jane	Mother	2	Illinois	Wash. D.C.
Erika	.	.	Wisconsin	California
Fusako	.	.	Illinois	Wisconsin
Alana	.	.	Wisconsin	California

Appendix B: Methodological Approach

Feminist Interview Methodology

This study views women through a variety of prisms, female, racially Asian and ethnically Japanese American. Treating women from the subject position, the study focuses on the women's self-reported interpretations of their own identities. The women both responded to my questions and were free to question me about my perspectives, thereby jointly constructing knowledge. By sharing my experiences, I encouraged them to reflect upon similar or divergent experiences of their own.

The research process itself and the nature of the topics researched provided the potential for consciousness-raising and empowerment. As each participant probed her own belief systems and uncovered her ethnic and racial identities, she was placing herself in both the historical and everyday contexts of the society in which she lives. By reflecting, articulating and sharing views with others she discovered the power of her own ability to rear children in a racist and sexist society.

Cook and Fonow (1986) raise a concern for the ethical implication of feminist research, specifically the exploitation of women as the object of knowledge. My concern was for the accurate representation of these women from their position as Asian Americans, as Japanese Americans and as mothers. The construction of who they are must come from themselves, from their own historical perspectives, told in their own voices with their own interpretations.

Fraser and Nicholson (1990) in their discussion of postmodern feminism write: "Theory here would be explicitly historical, attuned to the cultural specificity of different societies and periods and to that of different groups within societies and periods . . . when its focus became cross-cultural . . . its mode of attention would be comparativist rather than universalizing, attuned to changes and contrasts instead of to cover laws" (p. 34). Thus, this research does not attempt to speak for all midwestern Japanese American women but for a subset of individual Nisei, Sansei and Yonsei women.

The women shared their perceptions growing up as daughters with male and female siblings, and they articulated their views on parenting both male and female children. They were not specifically asked to differentiate between how they reared their sons compared to their daughters, but certain gender biases began to emerge in their conversations. The father figure or male role model was implicit in discussions of family life and child rearing, and would be considered present in a relational manner, even though the interpreting and reporting voice was that of a female. Only one Sansei and one Yonsei mother were single parent head-of-households, but their extended families provided regular contact with uncles and grandfathers for their daughters. The feminist perspective adopted in the current study would be considered gender inclusive, meaning that men were part of the social, familial context being studied. The omission of an explicitly male perspective does not necessarily bias a study according to postmodern feminist Susan Hekman (1990). Rather, it would take the position that there is not one (masculine) truth but many representations of truth, none of which is privileged along gendered lines (p. 9).

Ethnic Identity Survey

This study focuses on the self-reported ethnic identity of participants based upon their sense of belonging as De Vos & Romanucci-Ross (1975) might put it, or their subjectively appropriated identities as defined by Thornton (1992). Participants were asked to rate themselves on a scale of one (low) to ten (high) as to how they perceived their Japaneseness. They were also given room to comment about how they interpreted the term Japaneseness, and most did. Some gave long justifications for their rating, while others merely stated a few examples of their experiences with Japanese cultural events or artifacts.

A list, which was sent out to all participants with an introductory letter, included questions that reflect pertinent topics associated with child rearing, education and Japanese cultural norms. The style of presenting the questions reflects the feminist conversation methodology and were provided so that participants could formulate their answers and write responses at their convenience. Individual interviews were designed to continue this dialogue, seeking clarification on points made and allowing more in-depth probing of participants' views. See appendix C for the questions.

Some participants wrote extensively while others gave short answers to parts of questions. I felt that it was important to provide several options so that participants would feel free to comment at their own comfort level. Some chose not to answer on paper but preferred instead to cover the questions during an individual interview. This was also acceptable and perhaps reflects my sense of *enryo*, not wanting to inconvenience others, or to at least make it as easy as possible for the women to participate. I also gave long timelines for returning the questions so that those who were busy and hadn't put this research as a high priority could still participate. I received several phone calls from women in California who were incredibly busy but wanted to give feedback. Comments like "I hope you can still use this" or "I hope it isn't too late" were met with gracious acceptance.

Indepth Individual Interviews

Feminist interview methodology requires the use of semi-structured and unstructured (or open-ended) interviewing as the primary data-gathering technique. The open-ended nature of the questions allows the researcher to generate theory using an inductive approach, arriving at explanations for a given set of facts. "Open-ended interview research," writes Reinharz (1992), "produces nonstandard information that allows researchers to make full use of differences among people . . . (it) offers researchers access to people's ideas, thoughts, and memories in their own words rather than the words of the researcher" (pp. 18-19).

This study used an inductive approach, which allowed me to hear and respond to the voices of the women, giving them freedom to share their feelings seeing me as a friend rather than a "data-gatherer" (see Oakley, 1981; Belenky et al, 1986 and Gilligan, 1982). I built rapport and attempted to gain a reciprocity within the cultural context of respect for elders. Being trusted by my participants was of high priority perhaps because the Japanese (and Japanese American) code of conduct by which I was raised assumes that I would never do anything to embarrass or misrepresent those in my ethnic group. Developing harmonious relationships with my participants during the research process was also important since some of my participants were family friends and relatives. Thus, there were personal reasons as well as academic and scholarly criteria for maintaining the integrity of the data produced in this study.

Participants were interviewed once in depth on a one-to-one basis in their or my home (or a place of their choice). At the onset of the interview session I stressed and continued to reinforce the goal of joint meaning making. I reviewed the two general research questions which were presented in the initial letter of invitation to participate and asked if there was any need for clarification. Then I asked open-ended questions about their upbringing, their perspectives on child rearing, and their education. Some women were concerned about whether they had given me the information I was seeking. Others expressed a strong desire to be helpful. I assured them that I had no preconceived ideas or expectations to be fulfilled. This feminist interview methodology allowed me to expose my sensitivity to issues, to be empathetic and to learn actively from the women I interviewed. The research process proved to be empowering for both myself and my participants.

Interviews were audio taped and transcribed with participants having the opportunity to read and revise the transcriptions. Only five women expressed interest in reading their transcripts. This didn't seem unusual since I considered the reading of transcripts to be somewhat burdensome and potentially embarrassing to the participants (some Nisei women felt that they couldn't express themselves well). I continued to encourage participants to share this aspect of my research through phone calls and personal contact.

Group Conversation Interviews

During individual interviews, some women expressed curiosity about other participants' views on the topics we discussed. There was a sense of wanting to know if their personal thoughts were particularly unique or if they were shared by other Japanese American women. Comments such as, "You need to talk with my sister about that . . .," "Mrs. ___ might not agree with me about this, but . . . ," "My mother and I might interpret that differently . . . ," and "I think others would agree with me on . . . " began to emerge. This gave me the opportunity to lay some foundation for participation in the group sessions.

Group interview sessions were designed to serve two major purposes. First, they provided a setting where participants were free to share their viewpoints with those who, it might be assumed, understood *where they were coming from*, and to create a place where a group identity and sense of affiliation could emerge. For some of the women, especially the Nisei, speaking about intensely personal experiences is difficult and usually not done (Kikumura, 1981). Japanese cultural restraints dictate that one does not readily stand up and announce "this is what I've done" or "this is how I feel." In addition, there were generational as well as cultural differences in interactional styles that needed to be considered when establishing group sessions. For some more "Americanized" Sansei and Yonsei women, speaking about personal viewpoints and feelings proved to be liberating. As one participant put it, "No one ever asked about my ethnicity before." Following this comment she spoke openly and at length about her *Japaneseness*. For some, especially some Nisei women, listening and experiencing the youthful enthusiasm of the Sansei and Yonsei proved to be enlightening and enjoyable.

Second, by bringing these women of different generations together for the purpose of sharing their perspectives, I created an opportunity for the participants to engage in consciousness-raising. The group conversations provided a forum where Nisei women could reflect upon the constraints on their lives while rearing children during the postwar years. Sansei and Yonsei could share the dilemma they face looking Asian but speaking and acting "American" in a midwestern society which adheres to a color-blind orientation preferring to ignore their racial difference. Dialogue among the women of three generations helped them understand why action against both discrimination and patriarchy was difficult if not impossible due to historical and political circumstances impacting each of the three generational groups.

Four inter-generational group sessions were held; two in Madison, Wisconsin, one in Milwaukee, Wisconsin, and one in Glencoe, Illinois (a suburb of Chicago). The first session, held in Madison at my home, had the largest and most diverse group present. Those in attendance included three Nisei (Chiyo, Mona and M. Kana), three Sansei (Shigeko, Bonnie and Imoto) and one Yonsei (Yano). Imoto's sister was visiting and also joined the group. I was fortunate to have an assistant, a fellow graduate student, who happened to be Japanese American (from Utah), to take notes, run the tape recorder, and display the photos.

The second session, held in Milwaukee at Anna's home consisted of three Sansei (Anna, Obasan and Akiko) and two Yonsei (Fusako and Erika). It included one mother-daughter dyad (Akiko and Erika). The third and fourth groups were smaller with four participants each. In Chicago, Connie, a Sansei, opened her home to the group which included her mother, Mrs. C., Nisei Mariko, and Sansei Lani. And finally, in Madison once again, Yonsei Leia hosted the fourth group which included Emily Akemi, another Yonsei, and two Nisei women, Chiyo and Mia. Sansei Grapdelight had originally consented to participate, as she was a friend of Leia's, but felt constrained by the group setting, and chose not to attend. She later indicated her reluctance stating that she felt uncomfortable discussing private family matters and personal beliefs.

Participants at the group interviews were asked to bring photos of their families to share, as a way of stimulating conversation and building rapport. These were displayed so that the women could view them informally during the lunch or dessert period. Each participant was asked to answer two questions at the beginning of the session: 1. "How has participation in this research project so far influenced your feelings of being Japanese American?" and 2. "How do you feel about coming to this group interview today?" Then, the purpose of the group sessions was introduced: to interact and discuss issues gathered from individual interviews and to develop feelings of affiliation, support and empowerment. Photos were shared, and then five topics generated from the individual interviews were introduced. These included: Japaneseness, family support, group consciousness, communication style, and work ethic. Conversations generally flowed freely as participants shared and asked questions of each other. The goals of the group interviews were to create a mutually constructed cross generational conversation, to personally empower each participant and to raise gender and ethnic consciousness.

Photographs that were shared included: family holidays and celebration, pictures that depicted Japanese American culture (I have one of my sister and me dressed in our kimonos), children and grandchildren, inter-generational family portraits, and families during different historical periods. They acted as a catalyst for sharing stories and perspectives on the life experiences of these women and as a concrete means of acknowledging shared membership into this group of Japanese American women. The concept of using the photos was adopted from the research of Richard Chalfen (1987) who used the photo collections of two Japanese American families as data representing their ethnicity and as symbolic forms communicating the families' cultural beliefs. Family albums, according to Chalfen, symbolically define and order the world and are pictorial evidence of how people see themselves in the process of change.

At the end of the daytime sessions, lunch was provided, and dessert was shared after the evening sessions. Informal conversations and reconnecting of women who had not seen each other for a while occurred. Of the 20 women who participated, only nine did not know others in the group they attended. The others knew at least one of the other participants. Some of the Yonsei had not met the family friends of their mothers but knew of them. It is unclear what immediate impact the group sessions had on the participants, although a few appreciative comments were written and shared. The feelings of connectedness could extend through a lifetime.

Responses to Literature

A small selection of literature written by Japanese American women was used as a data source and as a catalyst for evoking memories, developing viewpoints, and sharing experiences. Each woman in the study was given a compilation of stories, essays, and poetry selected for its ethnic content and relevancy to the lives of Japanese American women. I am not certain if any of the authors grew up or lived in the midwest, nor do I know of which generational groups the authors were members. Participants were invited to respond to a set of questions regarding the literature. All of the selections represented different authors' perspectives, which might be easily understood by and appeal to one generation, while being novel and informative to another generation. For example, Tina Koyama's story of the family dinner could be interpreted by Nisei and Sansei women in different ways as they reflect upon their own family experiences empathizing with the memorable story characters. Nisei women might come to understand their own Issei mothers when reading *Through Harsh Winters*, by

Akemi Kikumura, while Sansei and Yonsei women might not relate to the cultural context of an Issei woman's life.

Participants were also encouraged to recommend other pieces of literature written by Japanese American women which they find personally meaningful. I also included two of my poems as a way of sharing my perspectives and the significance of literature to my own ethnic identity. Each piece of literature was analyzed using an informal method of abstracting cultural themes from the text. Selected pieces reflected the author's interpretation of Japanese American culture and met one or more of the following themes: 1. It exposed ethnic awareness or ethnic pride, 2. It described experiences of racism or discrimination, 3. It provided a contrast between generational or cultural viewpoints and/or, 4. It focused on relationships within the family context (especially mother-child or extended family relationships).

To facilitate responses I printed out five sets of open-ended questions (see appendix C) with an empty sheet for responses for each question set. The questions were designed to investigate personal reactions both to reading literature and to the cultural content presented in the selections; not to critique the literature. I expected to find differing degrees of empathy or identification with Japanese culture and the Japanese American experience which would reflect a sense of belonging (ethnic identity) or personal empowerment. The responses would also illustrate diversity within one ethnic group. Responses were coded in a similar manner as the individual interviews and supplemented those emergent themes. The written responses also could verify the verbal responses given in interviews thereby serving the purpose of triangulation of data sources. The questions addressed the following topics: personal reactions and interpretations of the literature, examples of similar experiences, relationships among family members, ethnic identity ratings at the end of the study, and roles of Japanese American mothers.

Participation in Study Components

Participation in any component of the study was voluntary. The chart on the next page is a composite overview of the women's participation. Only six of the thirty-four women were able to participate in all five of the study components. But thirty-two of the women rated themselves on the Ethnic Identity Scale. Of those, twenty participants completed the Survey, and twenty-two were individually interviewed. And nineteen of the women were able to meet in one of the Group Conversation Interviews. I was pleased with the commitment to the research and the warmth by which it was received.

Table 9 Participants and Study Components.

Participant	Pilot Study	Ethnic Identity Scale	Survey Questions	Individual Interview	Group Conversation Interview	Literature Response
Nisei						
Chiyo	X	X	X	X	X	X
Mariko	.	X	X	X	X	.
Mia	X	X	X	X	X	X
Mona	X	X	X	X	X	.
Masako	.	X	X	.	.	X
Chizu	.	X	.	X	.	X
M. Kana	.	.	.	X	X	X
Mrs. K	.	.	.	X	X	.
Sansei						
Grapdelight	.	X	.	X	.	X
Obasan	.	X	.	.	X	X
Anna	X	X	X	X	X	X
Shigeko	.	X	X	X	X	.
Mimi	X	X	X	X	.	X
Amelia B.	.	X	.	X	.	X
Akiko	.	X	.	X	X	.
Lesye	.	X	X	.	.	.
Kim	.	X	.	X	.	.
Connie	.	X	X	X	X	X
Imoto	.	X	X	X	X	X
Mariko	.	X	X	.	.	X
Bonnie	X	X	.	X	X	.
Lani	.	X	X	.	X	X
Mitzi	.	X	X	.	.	.
Mika	.	X	X	.	.	X
Kikuye	.	X	X	.	.	.
Yonsei						
Leia	.	X	.	X	X	.
Jasmine	.	X	.	.	.	.
Shigeko	.	X	.	.	.	.
Emily A	.	X	.	X	X	.
Yano	X	X	X	X	X	X
Jane	.	X	.	X	.	.
Erika	.	X	X	.	X	X
Fusako	.	X	X	X	X	.
Alana	.	X	X	.	.	X

Data Analysis and Trustworthiness

In this study, I sought to identify emergent *categories* and to *code* the interview transcripts from each participant. The categories that were used in analysis included: ethnic identity, racial identity, stereotypes, gender, child-rearing beliefs, schooling, support for education, Japanese culture, Japanese language, Japanese interactional style, assimilation, family relationships, parent-child interactions, internment, work ethic and role expectations.

In searching for beliefs and perspectives, care was given to identifying both explicit statements and implicit indications of the viewpoint of individuals. The following statement by Gehrie (1976) about his research is relevant to my study: "This study represents an example of basic research into the experience of a small group of individuals, and does not attempt to formulate conclusions to the wider group or to groups in general" (p. 356). Therefore, the categories or themes that emerged from these data are not necessarily representative of the beliefs of all midwestern Japanese American women.

Using an inductive approach (Rudestam and Newton, 1992: Goetz and LeCompte, 1984: Erickson, 1986), I examined the data in each of these categories for *emergent themes*. As themes were identified, the data were compared across the three generational groups, Nisei, Sansei and Yonsei. The following list of themes emerged from the individual interviews:

1. Working hard and doing your best were seen as important personal attributes.

2. Supportive family relationships were considered important.

3. Assimilation was a goal (or a given) even though recognition of oneself as a visible minority was evident.

4. Education (including a college degree) was highly valued.

5. Parent-child communication tended to be indirect and somewhat non-verbal.

6. Children and child rearing was a high priority, although it did not preclude a career or an education.

7. Both independence and conformity were seen as positive attributes.

8. The range of ethnic identity or feelings of Japaneseness was very broad.

9. Gender roles were clearly defined for Nisei women but less restrictive for Sansei and Yonsei women.

In order to assure trustworthiness, this study utilized methodological triangulation and participant verification (a combination of member checks and face validity). Data was gathered from the individual interviews, questionnaires, and responses to literature in order to identify emergent themes. These themes, in turn, became topics for the group interviews which created new data, sometimes supporting viewpoints expressed in individual interviews. Finally, as feedback was gathered from interview transcripts and responses to the vignettes, participant verification was secured and a new layer of interpretation was created.

Development of Vignettes

The group sessions produced multiple data sources, such as the photographs shared by participants, the audio tape of the group conversation, the initial questionnaire and informal field notes made by the author or research assistant. After each group session, I made journal entries about my observations and impressions and listened to each tape, outlining the events and occurrences. For the first group session, I asked to keep the photographs and made a descriptive list of them, by participant. I did not continue this procedure since the groups became smaller and some participants did not bring pictures. Others brought albums or collages which did not represent a selectiveness on their part. As a result, the photos served as a catalyst for communication and sharing more than a consistent data source for information about the participants.

I then recreated my version of each group session and reported it in a vignette form: "The moment-to-moment style of description in a narrative vignette gives the reader *a sense of being there* in the scene," writes Erickson (1986, p. 150). Using my field notes and the group session agenda, I reconstructed the conversations including interactive responses among participants and non-verbal communication. A relaxed comfort level for each group session was easily attained so that participants began to freely communicate with each other, asking questions and sharing thoughts. For example, some of the Nisei women were interested in the family backgrounds of the Sansei and Yonsei women, asking where their grandparents originally came from in Japan and asking where their parents lived before internment. The vignettes were designed to capture and report the nature of the respectful yet, informal interactions across the generations that I observed.

Erickson (1986) asserts that in the research report, the vignette "has functions that are rhetorical, analytic, and evidentiary" (p. 150). It is analytic in that certain features of social action and meaning are highlighted while others are not. It grounds abstract analytical concepts in concrete particulars by reporting specific actions taken by specific people together. To reiterate the value of this research technique, Erickson explains: "It is the combination of richness (in detail) and interpretive perspective that makes the account valid. Such a valid account is not simply a description; it is an analysis" (p. 150). These vignettes were shared with some of the participants and informal feedback of their impressions were gathered. They were used as a data source like the individual interviews.

Study Bias

I have included information about family members who have *not* participated in order to emphasize that the perspectives presented are unique to the women in the study and should not be generalized to represent all midwestern Japanese American women. In some ways, I would have liked to know the reasons why they chose not to participate as it may broaden the scope of perceived ethnic identity. It may also reflect a level of awareness and interest in Japanese American culture as well as it's priority in daily life. For example, Connie mentioned that her other daughter, Jane's sister, had just begun a high powered job as a bank vice president and simply did not have the time to give to the study. Without speaking directly with her, I do not know whether her interest in her own ethnic identity is low and that along with her busy schedule caused her not to participate. I am also reluctant to call and pursue her reasons, perhaps in part due to my own feelings of *enryo*, not wanting to impose on her. It would put her into a position of having to explain, which may be potentially embarrassing since her mother, sister, and grandmother are all part of the current study.

Others declined to participate (or selected particular parts of the study in which to participate) because they were not mothers and felt that they had little to contribute to a study on child rearing. This was both articulated to me directly as well as shared by participants who recommended other friends. Sixty-four letters of invitation were sent out. Two Nisei women declined due to poor health. One Yonsei woman from Minneapolis was very interested, but then called me from Denver indicating that she would be living in Japan for the next year and that the timing was not good for her participation. Of the participants' relatives, eleven declined to participate. There were twenty-one non-respondents: two Nisei, twelve Sansei, and seven Yonsei.

Of the final 34 participants, most were well educated, working, or retired women. The high level of education and professionalism may have been a function of the networking procedure used to identify participants. Often women who do not have connections with college-educated peers and family have less access to and/or even interest in research projects. There was no specific effort to seek out women in this category. Therefore, the final cohort may have reflected the core group of pilot study women originating in Madison, Wisconsin, a university town with a relatively large number of foreign students and a reputation for being progressive.

The current study intentionally did not include the participation of men, which proved to open some new insights about gender expectations in Japanese American families. One interesting indication of this was the suggestion by a few Nisei women that I speak with their husbands (when they originally thought the subject was about Japanese Americans and either internment or political history). They did not perceive themselves as having the knowledge or background for offering insight or information. This may also have been a function of the roles passed down from Issei parents where women dominated the household, often making decisions about children and family concerns, while the men dealt with the outside or European American world. Even when I explained that I was interested in their personal opinions, some were reluctant to participate, perhaps partly because it was a feminist study. I wonder if more Nisei women would have participated if husbands were included in the study. I also recognize the liberating effect that the in-depth interviews had for some of the women. They freely discussed gender differences and even complaints about their husbands and fathers. For the Sansei and Yonsei women, there was little concern about a study exclusively on and about women.

It is important to note once again that participants were invited to join any and all aspects of the study. This variability has contributed to the strength and development of each portion in differing ways. For example, thirty-two women gave Ethnic Identity ratings initially while only seven did so at the end of the study. Women who lived in locations where group sessions were easily accessible readily participated, while others could not. I would have liked to supplement with more telephone follow-up interviews but found that to be difficult. This choice, for example, may have prevented me from doing more indepth data collection from participants who had relocated to the west coast and could have provided a stronger multicultural perspective.

Appendix C: Forms

Participant Data Sheet

Pseudonym _____
Name _____
Maiden _____
Address _____ Phone_____
Place of Birth _____
Age at the beginning of this research project _____
Is your ancestry 100% Japanese? _____
Nisei____ Sansei____ Yonsei____
If not, what is your ethnic background? _____
Parents Names   Place of Birth   Are they living?
_____
_____

Siblings and their ages:
   Brothers_____
   Sisters _____
Name of Spouse _____
Is your spouse Japanese American? _____ If not, what is his ethnic background? _____
Names, sex and ages of children and grandchildren:
_____
_____

With which Japanese relatives do you have regular contact? How often?
_____
How many Japanese Americans are among your friends? _____
How often do you socialize? _____
Have you been to Japan? _____
When and for how long? _____
_____
Do you speak or understand Japanese? _____
Did you attend Japanese school while growing up? _____
How long?_____
What is your highest level of educational achievement? _____
Degrees earned: _____
Universities attended:
_____
Other post high school education:
_____

What did you study?
_____
What percent of the students in your schools were Japanese American?
High school_____
Junior/middle school _____
Elementary _____
What were your religious affiliations while growing up? Did you attend churches with a large Japanese American (or Asian American) membership? Please explain.
_____

How frequently, within the last year, have you attended Japanese American (or Asian American) cultural events? Please explain.
_____

On a scale from 1 (low) to 10 (high) where would you place yourself in terms of your "Japaneseness" (ethnic identity)?

1------2------3------4------5------6------7------8------9------10

Please explain
_____

Ethnic Identity Survey

Information for participants

Each number has a series of questions that relate to and expand upon a given topic. You may answer each question directly or provide your general perspectives on the topic. Please indicate the number to which you are responding. I would appreciate having the data sheets returned immediately, but you may take your time answering these questions. I will contact you by phone after December 1st to begin picking up finished questions and to set up individual interviews. Postage for feedback returned by mail will be reimbursed. Feel free to call me at (608) 244-0625 if you have any questions. Thank you.

    1. Sometimes I feel "all American" and don't think about my ethnicity. It was when I first became a teacher and again after I became a mother, that I began to look back at my Japanese roots. Have you thought about your "Japaneseness"? Can you

describe times when you recognize yourself as being Japanese American? What indication do you get from others that they notice your ethnic heritage?

2. I don't recall my parents specifically talking with us about our heritage but we always knew we were Japanese American. While growing up, did your parents ever talk with you about being Japanese or Japanese American? When and under what circumstances did this occur? What kind of approach to discussing family heritage have you taken with your children?

3. There are two Japanese terms *amae*, relating to the mother-child relationship and *gambare*, relating to personal characteristics. How would you define these words? Were the words or concepts behind the words part of your child rearing? How were they communicated?

4. How would you characterize your early childhood (preschool, kindergarten, elementary) schooling experiences? Describe your classmates, teachers and schoolwork. Were your parents involved with your education? How did they support your learning?

5. What kind of expectations for achievement did your parents have of you during junior high (or middle school) and high school? What strategies did your parents use to communicate their expectations? What happened if you did not meet them?

6. Paint a picture of yourself as a student. How would you characterize yourself? How do you feel about that image? Did you face any of the stereotypical images of Asians as "smart" or "high achievers"? How did your classmates and teachers perceive you as a student?

7. While growing up, what kinds of messages were given to you by your parents and other family members about your social behavior? Were there any special expectations because you were a girl? Describe how these messages were communicated. As a mother, what kind of messages have you passed on to your children regarding their behavior?

8. Japanese American women face two common stereotypes: the Model Minority and the Exotic Oriental woman. What do you

think about these? Have they affected your life in any way? Provide any examples of times you felt stereotyped.

9. Becoming a mother changed my life in many ways. I'm sure it does for all women, but some people are more prepared for this role than others. How would you describe your role as a mother? How and from whom did you learn child-rearing skills? For participants who are grandmothers: How would you compare your role as a mother with that of your daughters or daughter-in-laws? How has the role of motherhood changed through the generations (Issei, Nisei, Sansei and Yonsei)?

10. I would like to talk a little about child rearing during camp with participants who were interned. Are you comfortable with this topic? Can you recall how mothers cared for their young children in the relocation centers? Once children were in camp schools, how were parents involved with their children's education?

11. How would you characterize your relationships with each of your children when they were young? Was it similar to the relationship you had with your mother? Why, or why not? Was it different for sons and for daughters?

12. It was our family custom for the maternal grandmother to buy her grandsons a traditional samurai doll. My mother had to go to California to get a doll for my son and returned with three for all of her grandsons. Are there any Japanese customs passed down in your family? Can you describe any beliefs or customs having their roots in Japanese culture that are meaningful to you today? What are you doing to maintain these traditions?

13. Have you heard about the contemporary Japanese *kyōiku mama* (or education mothers)? What do you think of their roles in Japanese society? Do you see any elements of their behavior or goals in the way you were reared or the way you rear your children?

14. Are there any values that you feel strongly about and work to instill in your children? Which values relate to the education of your children?

Thank you for your time and effort. I *truly* appreciate it. Individual interviews will expand upon some of the issues you have discussed here. If there are any related topics that you have pondered about race, ethnicity, child rearing, education, or academic achievement please feel free to share them with me. As I said before, this research is designed as a collaborative effort so your input on the direction of the study is welcome.

Group Interview Agenda

(6:30) Arrival, name tags, informal introductions
Group convenes

1. Short acknowledgment of each participant by Susan.

2. Participants fill in 2 questions, label each of their photos and place them in an envelope for passing around.

3. Collect questions and share photos by passing envelopes in a circle. Encourage conversation. Place the pictures on tag board under each participant's name so they are displayed together.

4. Go over the *purpose* of this session.

    To interact and discuss issues gathered from individual interviews. To develop feelings of affiliation, support and empowerment.

5. Comment about the microphone and tape recording of the session. It records multiple voices and will be used as data in a similar fashion as the individual interviews.

Participants should feel free to jump in and offer their viewpoints, stories, and personal experiences. The intent is that this become a conversation so they should feel free to respond to each other and ask questions of each other. I will be introducing the topics as we go along.

(7:00)   TOPICS to discuss

Japaneseness: How did you interpret this word? Being Japanese American, ethnic identity, Japanese culture,

Japanese language, race, attitudes, values? Difference between Japanese and Japanese-American?

Family support: How is this done in your family? Who assumes the responsibility for maintaining family cohesiveness?

Group consciousness: How important is this in child rearing? Discuss how significant each of the following items are to you: "I want my children to be . . . " independent, a team player, sensitive to others, competitive, cooperative, self sufficient.

Communication style: What kind of approach do you generally use to communicate your desires to your children? Direct, indirect, authoritative, quiet, conditional. How do you deal with confrontation?

Work ethic: Values listed from the survey sheets included:
    Try (Do) your best
    Work hard
    Have a strong will to succeed
    Try to achieve the ultimate in whatever you do or become

Give some examples of how any of these apply to you or in rearing your children.

8:30   Final comments and thank-yous

1. Express appreciation for their open sharing. Thank hostess for the use of her home for the session.

2. Invite parting comments about the session. Have a sheet of paper at door (on the desk) with pens for any comments.

Invitation to coffee & dessert
Group Interview Feedback

How has participation in this research project so far influenced your feelings of being Japanese American?

How do you feel about coming to this group interview today?

Literature Selections by Japanese American Women Authors

1. *Through Harsh Winters:The Life of a Japanese Immigrant Woman* (1981) by Akemi Kikumura

2. *Beyond Manzanar:Views of Asian-American Womanhood* (1985) by Jeanne Wakatsuki Houston

3. *Camp Notes and other Poems* (1986 3rd ed.) by Mitsuye Yamada Mirror Mirror

4. *Desert Run:Poems and Stories* (1988) by Mitsuye Yamada
    Masks of Woman
    A Mother's Touch

5. *Home to Stay: Asian American Women's Fiction* (1990) eds. Sylvia Watanabe and Carol Bruchac
    Family Dinner by Tina Koyama

6. *The Loom and Other Stories* (1991) by R.A. Sasaki

7. *The Forbidden Stitch: An Asian American Women's Anthology* (1989) edited by Shirley Geok-lin Lim, Mayumi Tsutakawa and Margarita Donnelly

    Eleven A.M. on my Day Off, My Sister Phones Desperate for a Babysitter by Sharon Hashimoto
    Proud Upon an Alien Shore by Rose Furuya Hawkins

8 *Come Spring: Journey of a Sansei* (1992) by Hariko Okano

9. *I am Sansei* and *Maternal Tsunami* by Susan Matoba Adler

I am Sansei (1981)
Susan Matoba Adler

I am Sansei
I am the fruit of my parents' suffering.
I reflect the strength by which they endured.
They were humiliated and relocated.
Torn between two cultures, they reassured
Themselves, silently, of their identity.

The Nisei dilemma: heredity versus culture.
The government said, "Make a choice.
Affirm one at the expense of the other.
Are you Japanese or are you American?
We demand to hear your voice."
Silently, they fractured their identity.

I am Sansei.
I am growing ripe in a loquacious era.
I harvest material comfort and security
From my parents' determination to succeed.
From my grandparents' stolen dignity,
I recapture my cultural heritage.

Maternal Tsunami (1981)
Susan Matoba Adler

Maternal tsunami
Of anticipation,
Silently surges within me.

Cascading hopes
Of parenthood yearning,
Engulfs my ship of serenity.

Cresting white caps
Of responsibility,
With tacit changes to endure.

Thundering cry
On the beach of reality,
Our precious baby to nurture.

Feedback Questions:

1. What is your personal reaction to or interpretation of these literary selections? Which were your favorites? Please describe why.

2. Do you have any personal experiences similar to the ones presented in the literature? Please describe them.

3. Some of the selections cross generations or present relationships among family members. From your experience, how have specific family members influenced your views on child rearing and education?

4. Some selections presented various views on self-identity. At the beginning of the study, I asked you to rate yourself in terms of your *ethnic identity*. Now, at the end of the study, on a scale of 1 (low) to 10 (high) how would you rate yourself? Please comment on your interpretation of ethnic identity in relationship to some of this literature.

5. The concept of the Japanese or Japanese American mother was presented in various pieces of literature. How would you compare yourself to these characterizations and to your own role models?

Bibliography

Adler, S. M. (1993). I am sansei. In A. F. Ada, V. J. Harris, & L. B. Hopkins (Eds.), *A chorus of cultures: Developing literacy through multicultural poetry* (p. 189). Carmel, CA: Hampton-Brown Books.

Adler, S. M. (1994). A pilot study of midwestern Japanese American women: Perspectives on child rearing and education. In A. White-Parks, D. Buffton, U. Chiu, C. Currier, C. Manrique & M. Piehl (Eds.), *A gathering of voices on the Asian American experience* (pp. 27-35). Ft. Atkinson, WI: Highsmith Press.

Albert, M. D. (1980). *Japanese American Communities in Chicago and the Twin Cities*. Unpublished doctoral dissertation, University of Minnesota.

Angelou, M. (1993). *Wouldn't take nothing for my journey now*. New York: Bantam Books.

Armor, J., & Wright, P. (1988). *Manzanar*. New York: Random House, Inc.

Barratt, M. S. (1993). Early child rearing in Japan: Cross-cultural and intra-cultural perspectives. *Early Development and Parenting, 2*(1), 3-6.

Barratt, M. S., Negayama, K., & Minami, T. (1993). The social environments of early infancy in Japan and the United States. *Early Development and Parenting, 2*(1), 51-64.

Barringer, H. R., Gardner, R. W., & Levin, M. J. (1993). *Asians and pacific islanders in the United States*. (1980 Census) New York: Russell Sage Foundation.

Befu, H. (1986). The social and cultural background of child development in Japan and the United States. In H. W. Stevenson, H. Azuma, & K. Hakuta (Eds.), *Child development and education in Japan* (pp. 13-27). New York: W. H. Freeman Co.

Belenky, M. F., Clinchy, B. M., Goldberg, N. R., & Tarule, J. M. (1986). *Women's ways of knowing: The development of self, voice, and mind*. Basic Books, Inc.: Harper Collins Publishers.

Bourdieu, P. (1986). The forms of capital. In J. G. Richardson (Ed.), *Handbook of theory and research for the sociology of education*. New York: Greenwood Press.

Caudill, W. P. (1952). Personality and Acculturation. *Genetic Psychology Monographs, 45*, 3-102.

Caudill, W. P., & De Vos, G. (1956). Achievement, culture and personality: The case of the Japanese Americans. *American Anthropologist, 58*, 1102-1127.Caudill, W. P., & Frost, L. (1974). A comparison of maternal care and infant behavior in Japanese-American, American and Japanese families. In W. P. Lebra (Ed.), *Youth, socialization and mental health: Vol*

3. *Mental health research in Asia and the Pacific* (pp. 3-15). Honolulu: The University Press of Hawaii.

Caudill, W. P., & Plath, D. W. (1974). Who sleeps by whom? Parent-child involvement in urban Japanese families. In T. S. Lebra, & W. P. Lebra (Eds.), *Japanese culture and behavior: selected readings* (pp. 277-312). Honolululu: The University Press of Hawaii.

Caudill, W. P., & Weinstein, H. (1974). Maternal care and infant behavior in Japan and America. In T. S. Lebra, & W. P Lebra (Eds.), *Japanese culture and behavior: Selected readings* (pp. 255-276). Honolulu: The University Press of Hawaii.

Chalfen, R. (1987). *Turning leaves: The photograph collections of two Japanese American families.* Albuquerque, University of New Mexico Press.

Cheung, K. (1993). *Articulate silences: Hisaye Yamamoto, Maxine Hong Kingston, Joy Kogawa.* Ithaca, NY: Cornell University Press.

Connor, J. W. (1974). Acculturation and family continuities in three generations of Japanese Americans. *Journal of Marriage and the Family, 36*, 159-165.

_____ (1977). *Tradition and change in three generations of Japanese Americans.* Chicago: Nelson-Hall.

Cook, J. A., & Fonow, M. M. (1986). Knowledge and women's interests: Issues of epistemology and methodology in feminist sociological research. *Sociological Inquiry, 56*, 2-29.

Daniels, R., & Kitano, H. L. (1970) *American racism: Exploration of the nature of prejudice.* Englewood Cliffs, NJ: Prentice-Hall Inc.

Daniels, R., Taylor, S. C., & Kitano, H. L. (1991). *Japanese Americans: From relocation to redress.* Seattle: University of Washington Press.

De Vos, G., & Romanucci-Ross, L. (1975). *Ethnic identity: Cultural continuities and change.* Palo Alto, CA: Mayfield Publishing Company.

De Vos, G., & Wagatsuma, H. (1973). *Socialization for achievement: Essays on the cultural psychology of the Japanese.* Berkeley: University of California Press.

Doi, T. (1974). Amae: A key concept for understanding Japanese personality structure. In T. S. Lebra, & W. P. Lebra (Eds.), *Japanese culture and behavior: Selected readings* (pp. 145-154). Honolulu: The University Press of Hawaii. (originally 1962)

_____ (1991). Giving and receiving. In B. Finkelstein, A. Imamura, & J. J. Tobin (Eds.), *Transcending stereotypes: Discovering Japanese culture and education* (pp. 9-11). Yarmouth, ME: Intercultural Press, Inc.

Erickson, F. (1986). Qualitative methods in research on teaching. In M. C. Wittrock (Ed.), *Handbook of research on teaching.* New York: Macmillan.

Espiritu, Y. (1992). *Asian American panethnicity: Bridging institutions and identities.* Philadelphia: Temple University Press.

Bibliography

Fraser, N., & Nicholson, L. J. (1990). Social criticism without philosophy: An encounter between feminism and postmodernism. In L. J. Nicholson (Ed.), *Feminism/ Postmodernism*. New York: Routledge.

Frost, L. (1970). Child raising techniques as related to acculturation among Japanese Americans. Masters thesis, California State University, Sacramento.

Fugita, S. S., & O'Brien, D. J. (1991). *Japanese American ethnicity: The persistence of community*. Seattle: University of Washington Press.

Gehrie, M. J. (1976). Childhood and community: On the experience of young Japanese Americans in Chicago. *Ethos, 4*, 353-383.

Geertz, C. (1973). *The interpretation of cultures*. New York: Basic Books.

Gilligan, C. (1982). *In a different voice: Psychological theory and women's development*. Cambridge: Harvard University Press.

Goetz, J. P., & LeCompte, M. D. (1984). *Ethnography and qualitative design in educational research*. Orlando, FL: Academic Press.

Gordon, M. (1964). *Assimilation in American life: The role of race, religion, and national origins*. New York: Oxford University Press.

Guba, E. G. (1990). *The paradigm dialog*. Newbury Park, CA: Sage Publications.

Hashimoto, S. (1989). Eleven a.m. on a day off, my sister phones desperate for a babysitter. In S. G. Lim, M. Tsutakawa, & M. Donnelly (Eds.), *The forbidden stitch: An Asian American women's anthology* (p. 199). Corvallis, OR: Calyx Books.

Hawkins, R. F. (1989). Excerpts from proud upon an alien shore. In S. G. Lim, M. Tsutakawa, & M. Donnelly (Eds.), *The forbidden stitch: An Asian American women's anthology* (pp. 21-24). Corvallis, OR: Calyx Books.

Hekman, S. J. (1990). *Gender and knowledge: Elements of a postmodern feminism*. Cambridge, MA: Polity Press.

Hendry, J. (1986). *Becoming Japanese: The World of the Pre-school Child*. Honolulu: University of Hawaii Press.

Hess, R. D., Kashiwagi, K., Azuma, H., Price, G. G., & Dickson, W. P. (1980). Maternal expectations for mastery of developmental tasks in Japan and the United States. *International Journal of Psychology, 15*, 259-271.

Hess, R. D., Azuma, H., Kashiwagi, K., Dickson, W. P., Nagano, S., Holloway, S., Miyake, K., Price, G. G., Hatano, G., & McDevitt, T. (1986). Family influences on school readiness and achievement in Japan and the United States: An overview of a longitudinal study. In H. Stevenson, H. Azuma & K. Hakuta (Eds.), *Child development and education in Japan*. New York: W. H. Freeman & Co.

Higa, M. (1974). A comparative study of three groups of "Japanese" mothers: Attitudes toward child rearing. In W. P. Lebra (Ed.), *Youth, socialization and mental health: Vol. 3. Mental health research in Asia and the Pacific*. Honolulu: The University Press of Hawaii.

Holloway, S. D. (1988). Concepts of ability and effort in Japan and the United States. *Review of Educational Research, 58*(3), 327-345.

Holloway, S. D., Kashiwagi, K., Hess, R. D., & Azuma, H. (1986). Causal attributions by Japanese and American mothers and children about performance in mathematics. *International Journal of Psychology, 21*, 269-286.

Hosokawa, B. (1969). *Nisei: The quiet Americans.* New York: William Morrow & Co.

Houston, J. (1985). *Beyond Manzanar: Views of Asian-American womanhood.* Santa Barbara, CA: Capra Press.

Howe, K., & Eisenhart, M. (1990). Standards for qualitative (and quantitative) research: A prolegomenon. *Educational Researcher, 19*(4), 2-9.

Imamura, A. E. (1991) Introduction: Families as mirrors of society. In B. Finkelstein, A. E. Imamura, & J. J. Tobin (Eds.), *Transcending stereotypes: Discovering Japanese culture and education* (pp. 43-47). Yarmouth, ME: Intercultural Press, Inc.

James, T. (1987). *Exile within: The schooling of Japanese Americans 1942-1945.* Cambridge: Harvard University Press.

Johnson, C. L. (1976). The principle of generation among the Japanese In Honolulu. *Ethnic Groups, 1*, 18-35.

Kendis, K. O. (1989). *A matter of comfort: Ethnic maintenance and ethnic style among third-generation Japanese Americans.* New York: AMS Press, Inc.

Kiefer, C. W. (1974). The psychological interdependence of family, school and bureaucracy in Japan. In T. S. Lebra, & W. P. Lebra (Eds.), *Japanese culture and behavior: Selected readings* (pp. 342-356). Honolulu: The University Press of Hawaii.

Kikumura, H. (1981). *Through harsh winters: The life of a Japanese immigrant woman.* Novato, CA: Chandler & Sharp Publishers, Inc.

Kitano, H. L. (1961). Differential child rearing attitudes between first and second generation Japanese in the United States. *Journal of Social Psychology, 53*, 13-19.

_____ (1969). Japanese-American Mental Illness. In S. Plog, & R. Edgerton (Eds.), *Changing Perspectives on Mental Illness* (pp. 256-284). New York: Holt, Rinehart & Winston.

_____ (1976). *Japanese Americans: Evolution of a subculture.* (2nd ed.). Englewood Cliffs, NJ: Prentice-Hall.

Kitano, H. L., & Daniels, B. (1988). *Asian Americans: Emerging Minorities.* Englewood Cliffs, NJ: Prentice-Hall.

Kitano, H. L., & Kikumura, A. (1973). Interracial marriage: A picture of the Japanese American. *Journal of Social Issues, 29*, 66-81.

Kondo, D. K. (1990). *Crafting selves: Power, gender, and discourses of identity in a Japanese workplace.* Chicago: The University of Chicago Press.

Koyama, T. (1990). Family dinner. In. S. Watanabe, & C. Bruchac (Eds.) *Home to stay: Asian American women's fiction* (pp. 80-85). Greenfield Center, NY: The Greenfield Review Press.

Lather, P. (1986). Research as praxis. *Harvard Educational Review, 56*(3), 257-277.

Lebra, T. S. (1974). Reciprocity and the asymmetric principle: An analytical reappraisal of the Japanese concept of on. In T. S. Lebra, & W. P. Lebra (Eds.), *Japanese culture and behavior: Selected readings* (pp. 192-207). Honolulu: The University Press of Hawaii.

Lee, S. J. (1996). *Unraveling the "model minority" stereotype: Listening to Asian American youth.* New York: Teachers College Press.

Levine, G., & Rhodes, C. (1981). *The Japanese American Community: A Three-Generation Study.* New York: Praeger Publishers.

Le Vine, R. A., & White, M. (1986). *Human conditions: The cultural basis of educational development.* Boston: Rutledge & Kegan Paul.

Lewis, C. C. (1988). Japanese first-grade classrooms: Implications for U.S. theory and research. *Comparative Education Review, 32*(2), 159-172.

Lowe, L. (1991). Heterogeneity, hybridity, multiplicity: Marking Asian American differences. *Diaspora, 1,* 24-44.

Lyman, S. M. (1994). *Color, culture, civilization: Race and minority Issues in American society.* Urbana: University of Illinois.

Mannari, H., & Befu, H. (1991). Inside and outside. In B. Finklestein, A. E. Imamura, & J. J. Tobin (Eds.), *Transcending stereotypes: Discovering Japanese culture and education* (pp. 32-39). Yarmouth, ME: Intercultural Press, Inc.

Marcus, G. E., & Fischer, M. (1986). *Anthropology as cultural critique: An experimental moment in the human sciences.* Chicago: The University of Chicago Press.

Mass, A. I. (1986). *Amae: Indulgence and nurturance in Japanese American families.* Unpublished doctoral dissertation, University of California, Los Angeles.

Masuda, M., Matsumoto, G. H., & Meredith, G. M. (1970). Ethnic identity in three generations of Japanese Americans. *The Journal of Social Psychology, 81,* 199-207.

Matsumoto, G. M., Meredith, G. M., & Masuda, M. (1973). Ethnic identity: Honolulu and Seattle Japanese-Americans. In S. Sue, & N. Wagner (Eds.), *Asian Americans: Psychological perspectives* (pp. 65-74). Palo Alto, CA: Science and Behavior Books, Inc.

Maykovich, M. K. (1972). *Japanese American identity dilemma.* Tokyo: Waseda University Press.

Meredith, G. M. (1966). Amae and acculturation among Japanese-American college students in Hawaii. *Journal of Social Psychology, 70*, 171-180.

Minister, K. (1991). A feminist frame for the oral history interview. In S. B. Gluck, & D. Patai (Eds.), *Women's words: The feminist practice of oral history* (pp. 27-42). New York: Routledge.

Mizokawa, D. T., & Ryckman, D. B. (1990). Attributions of academic success and failure: A comparison of six Asian-American ethnic groups. *Journal of Cross-Cultural Psychology, 21*(4), 434-451.

Montero, D. (1980). *Japanese Americans: Changing patterns of ethnic affiliation over three generations.* Boulder CO: Westview Press.

Mura, D. (1991). *Turning Japanese: Memoirs of a sansei.* New York: The Atlantic Monthly Press.

Nakane, C. (1972). *Japanese Society.* Berkeley: University of California Press.

Nakano, M. T. (1990). *Japanese American women: Three generations 1890-1990.* Berkeley: Mina Press Publishing.

Narayan, K. (1993). How native is a "native" anthropologist? *American Anthropologist, 95*, 671-686.

Nieto, S. (1992). *Affirming diversity: The sociopolitical context of multicultural education.* White Plains, NY: Longman Publishing Group.

Oakley, A. (1981). Interviewing women: a contradiction in terms. In H. Roberts (Ed.), *Doing feminist research.* Boston: Routledge.

O'Brien, R. W. (1978). *The college nisei.* New York: Arno Press.

O'Brien, D. J., & Fugita, S. S. (1991). *The Japanese American experience.* Bloomington: Indiana University Press.

Ogawa, D. (1971). *From Japs to Japanese: The evolution of Japanese-American stereotypes.* Berkeley: McCutchan.

Okano, H. (1992). *Come spring: Journey of a sansei.* Vancouver, Canada: Gallerie Publications.

Omi, M., & Winant, H. (1986). *Racial formation in the United States from the 1960's to the 1980's.* New York: Routledge.

Osajima, K. (1987). Asian Americans as the model minority: An analysis of the popular press image in the 1960s and 1980s. In G. Y. Okihiro (Ed.), *Reflections on shattered windows: Promises and prospects for Asian American studies* (pp. 165-174). Pullman, WA: Washington State University Press.

Ovando, C. J., & Collier, V. (1985). *Bilingual and ESL classrooms: Teaching in multicultural contexts.* New York: McGraw-Hill.

Peak, L. (1991). *Learning to go to school in Japan: The transition from home to preschool life.* Berkeley: University of California Press.

Peshkin, A. (1988). In search of subjectivity-one's own. *Educational Researcher*, October 1988, 17-22.

Powers, S., Choroszy, M., & Douglas, P. (1987). Attributions for success and failure of Japanese-American and Anglo-American university students. *Psychology, A Quarterly Journal of Human Behavior, 24*(3), 17-23.

Reinharz, S. (1992). *Feminist methods in social research.* New York: Oxford University Press.

Root, M. P. (1992). Loyalty, rootedness and belonging: The quest for defining Asian American identity. In L. C. Lee (Ed.), *Asian Americans: Collages of identities* (pp. 175-183). Ithaca, NY: Asian American Studies Program, Cornell University Press.

_____ (1992). *Racially mixed people in America.* Newbury Park, CA: Sage Publications.

Sasaki, R. A. (1991). *The loom and other stories.* St. Paul, MN: Graywolf Press.

Sata, L. (1973). Musings of a hyphenated American. In S. Sue, & N. Wagner (Eds.), *Asian Americans: Psychological perspectives* (pp. 150-158). Palo Alto, CA: Science and Behavior Books, Inc.

Sato, N., & McLaughlin, M. W. (1992, January). Context matters: Teaching in Japan and in the United States. *Phi Delta Kappan,* pp 359-366.

Simons, C. (1987). They get by with a lot of help from their *kyōiku mama. The Smithsonian,* March 1987, 44-53.

Simpson, G., & Yinger, J. (1985) *Racial and cultural minorities.* New York: Plenum.

Sing, B. (1989). *Asian pacific Americans: A handbook on how to cover and portray our nation's fastest growing minority group.* Los Angeles: The National Conference of Christians and Jews.

Singleton, J. (1991). The spirit of "Gambaru". In B. Finklestein, A. Imamura, and J. Tobin (Eds.), *Transcending stereotypes: Discovering Japanese culture and education* (pp. 119-125). Yarmouth ME: Intercultural Press, Inc.

Slaughter-Defoe, D. K., Nakagawa, K., Takanishi, R., & Johnson, D. J. (1990). Toward cultural/ecological perspectives on schooling and achievement in African- and Asian-American children. *Child Development, 61,* 363-383.

Stephan, C. W. (1992). Mixed heritage individuals: Ethnic identity and trait characteristics. In M. Root (Ed.), *Racially mixed people in America* (pp. 50-63). Newbury Park, CA: Sage Publications.

Stevenson, H. W. (1992). Learning from Asian schools. *Scientific American,* December 1992, 70-76.

Stevenson, H. W., Chen, C., & Lee, S. (1993). Mathematics achievement of Chinese, Japanese, and American children: Ten years later. *Science, 259,* 53-58.

Sue, S. (1973). Ethnic identity: The impact of two cultures on the psychological development of Asian Americans. In S. Sue, & N. Wagner (Eds.), *Asian*

Americans psychological perspectives (pp. 140-149). Palo Alto, CA: Science and Behavior Books, Inc.

Sue, S., & Kitano, H. L. (1973). Stereotypes as a measure of success. *Journal of Social Issues, 29,* 83-98.

Sue, S., & Okazaki, S. (1990). Asian-American educational achievements: A phenomenon in search of an explanation. *American Psychologist, 45,* 913-920.

Sue, S., & Sue, D. W. (1975). Chinese-American personality and mental health. *Amerasia Journal, 2,* 158-202.

Suzuki, B. H. (1977). Education and socialization of Asian Americans: A revisionist analysis of the "model minority" thesis. *Amerasia Journal, 4,* 23-52.

_____ (1980). The Asian American family. In M. D. Fantini, & R. Cardenas (Eds.), *Parenting in a multicultural society* (pp. 74-102). New York: Longman.

_____ (1989). Asian Americans as the "model minority" outdoing whites? or media hype. *Change,* November/December 1989, 13-19.

Tabachnick, B. R., & Bloch, M. (1995). Learning in and out of school: Critical perspectives on the theory of cultural compatibility. In B. B. Swadener, & S. Lubeck (Eds.), *Children and families "at promise": Deconstructing the discourse of risk* (pp. 187-209). Albany: State University of New York Press.

Tachiki, A. (1971). Identity. In A. Tachiki, C. Wong, & F. Odo (Eds.), *Roots: An Asian American reader* (pp. 1-5). Berkeley: UCLA Asian American Studies Center.

Takaki, R. (1989). *Strangers from a different shore: A history of Asian Americans.* Boston: Little, Brown & Co.

_____ (1993). *A different mirror: A history of multicultural America.* Boston: Little, Brown & Co.

Thornton, M. (1992). Finding a way home: Race, nation and sex in Asian American identity. In L. C. Lee (Ed.), *Asian Americans: Collages of identities* (pp. 165-174). Ithaca, NY: Asian American Studies Program, Cornell University Press.

Tobin, J. (1991). Images of Japan and the Japanese. In B. Finklestein, A. Imamura, & J. Tobin (Eds.), *Transcending stereotypes: Discovering Japanese culture and education* (pp. 7-9). Yarmouth, ME: Intercultural Press, Inc.

Tobin, J., Wu, D., & Davidson, D. (1989). *Preschool in three cultures: Japan, China, and United States.* New Haven, CT: Yale University Press.

Trueba, H. T., Chen, L. L., & Ima, K. (1993). *Myth or reality: Adaptive strategies of Asian Americans in California.* Washington DC: The Falmer Press.

Tsukamoto, M., & Pinkerton, E. (1988). *We the people: A story of internment in America*. Elk Grove, CA: Laguna Publishers.

Uchida, Y. (1982). *Desert exile: The uprooting of a Japanese American family*. Seattle: University of Washington Press.

Weglyn, M. (1976). *Years of infamy: The untold story of America's concentration camps*. New York: Morrow Quill Paperbacks.

White, M. (1987). *The Japanese educational challenge: A commitment to children*. New York: Kodansha International.

Yamada, M. (1983). Invisibility is an unnatural disaster: Reflections of an Asian American woman. In C. Moraga, & G. Anzaldua (Eds.), *This bridge called my back: Writings by radical women of color*. Latham, NY: Kitchen Table Women of Color Press.

_____ (1986). *Camp notes and other poems*. Berkeley: Shameless Hussy Press.

_____ (1988). *Desert run: Poems and stories*. Latham, NY: Kitchen Table Woman of Color Press.

Yamamoto, J. (1968). Japanese American identity crisis. In E. Brody (Ed.), *Minority group adolescents in the United States*. Baltimore: Williams & Wilkins, Co.

Yamamura, Y. (1986). The child in Japanese society. In H. Stevenson, H. Azuma, & K. Hakuta (Eds.), *Child development and education in Japan* (pp. 28-38). New York: W. H. Freeman & Co.

Yanagisako, S. J. (1985). *Transforming the past: Tradition and kinship among Japanese Americans*. Stanford, CA: Stanford University Press.

Yoshimura, E. (1971). G. I.'s and Asian Women. In A. Tachiki, E. Wong, & F. Odo (Eds.), *Roots: An Asian American reader* (pp. 27-29). Berkeley: UCLA Asian American Studies Center.

Index

442nd Regimental Combat Unit, 156

Adler, 22, 108
akarui, 114
Albert, 27, 33, 45, 99
amae, viii, 4, 22, 42, 58, 114, 156
amaeru, 42, 58, 115
amayakasu, 43
Amerasian, 3
American-ness, 4, 139
Angelou, 131
Armor & Wright, 100
Asian, 3
Asian American, vii, 3

Barringer, Gardner, & Levin, 117, 119
Befu, 23, 117, 128
Bourdieu, 105

call girl, 4
Caudill, 83
Caudill & De Vos, 67
Caudill & Frost, 47
Caudill & Plath, 42
Caudill & Weinstein, 41, 47
Chalfen, 174
chu, 21
Connor, 25, 47, 83
Cook & Fonow, 169

Daniels & Kitano, 100
De Vos & Romanucci-Ross, 65, 170
De Vos & Wagatsuma, 67
Doi, 22, 42, 61
doryoku, 24

Dragon Lady, vii

emergent ethnicity, 137, 158
enryo, 9, 21, 143
enryo syndrome, 21, 61
Erickson, 179
Espiritu, 65, 69, 73
ethnic identity, 3, 4, 154

Fraser & Nicholson, 169
Frost, 47, 84
Fugita & O'Brien, 32, 57, 137, 154, 158

gaman, viii, 4
gaman suru, 115
gambare, viii, 4, 24, 107
Geertz, 11
Gehrie, 10, 30, 177
giri, 20, 144
Goetz & LeCompte, 177
Gordon, 77
Gosei, 17
Guba, 166

Ha zu ka shi, 129
haji, 8, 61, 129
hakihaki, 115
hakushi, 41
hana, 2
hansei suru, 115
happa, 1
Hashimoto, 188
Hawkins, 188
Ha-zu-ka-shi, 21, 61
Hekman, 166, 170
Hendry, 41, 42, 43, 107
Hess et al, 110
Hess et al., 110

Hida, 149
Higa, 48
Hi-ge, 21, 61, 129
Holloway, 111
Honne, 22
Hosokawa, 18
Houston, 24, 97, 128, 188
Howe & Eisenhart, 6

ie, 23, 44
Imamura, 113
inter-marriage, 5
Issei, vii
isshokemmei, 24

JACL, 5, 149
James, 144, 145, 152, 163
Japanese American Citizen's League, 3, 5
Japaneseness, viii, 4, 140
Japs, vii
Johnson, 44, 80

Kendis, 83, 84, 85
ki, 24
Kibei, 17
Kiefer, 19, 20, 23, 31, 45, 77
Kikumura, 8, 172, 175, 188
Kitano, 10, 21, 46, 61, 63, 129, 140, 148
Kitano & Daniels, 29, 33, 37, 73, 136
Kitano and Daniels, 29
koden, 50, 144
Kodomo no tame ni, vii
kokoro, 24
Kondo, 7, 11
Koyama, 174, 188
kuro, 24
Kusuda, 146
kyōiku mama, vii, 113
kyoiku mamas, 152

Lather, 166

Le Vine & White, 109
Lebra, 78
Lee, 98, 112
Levine, 47
Levine & Rhodes, 136
Lewis, 115
Lowe, 69
Lyman, 17, 27, 33

Madam Butterfly, vii
Manjiro, 18
Manzanar, 3
Marcus & Fischer, 11, 135
Mass, 43, 61, 143, 156
Masuda et al., 83
Matsumoto, Meredith & Masuda, 83
Matsuri, 12
Meiji school curriculum, 107
Meredith, 42
Minyo, 12
Mitsuye Yamada, 4
Mizokawa & Rychman, 119
model minority, vii, 3, 65
Montero, 27, 37, 77, 136
Mordkowitz & Ginsburg, 117
Mura, 72

Nakane, 19
Nakano, 28, 30, 44, 105, 117, 152
Narayan, 11
National Japanese American Student Relocation Council, 146
Nieto, 135
Nikkei, ix, 15
ningen, xiv, 114
ningen-rashii, xiv, 114
ninjo, 21, 116
Ninomiya Sontoku, 107
Nisei, vii
Nisei Drum and Bugle Corps, 161

Index

O'Brien & Fugita, 20, 30, 76, 107
O'Brien, R. W., 122
Oakley, 166
Ogawa, 98, 99
Ojigi, 21
Okano, 188
Omi & Winant, 33, 37
omiyage, 50, 144
omote, 22
on, 21
origami, 154
oriko, 115
Osajima, 37, 98
otonashii, 114
Ovando & Collier, 142

Particularism, 23
Peak, 116
Peshkin, 5, 7
picture bride, 14
postmodern feminism, 166
Powers et al., 118
Price and Hatano, 108

racial identity, 4
Redress Bill, 30
redress movement, 153
Reinharz, 8, 171
rikai, 115
Root, 3, 5, 32

Sansei, vii
Sasaki, 188
Sata, 78
Sato & McLaughlin, 113
Schneider & Lee, 118
sensei, 107
shikata-ga-nai, 160
Shitsuke, 41
Simon, 109
Simons, vii, 113
Simpson & Yinger, 155

Sing, 99, 100
Singleton, 107
Slaughter-Defoe et al., 109, 112
soto, 22
Stephan, 32
Stevenson, 111, 117, 131
Stevenson et al., 111
subjectivity audit, 7
Sue, 45, 79, 99, 148
Sue & Kitano, 116, 117
Sue & Okazaki, 69, 98, 116
Sue & Sue, 80, 87, 99
sunao, 114
Suzuki, 19, 29, 37, 44, 67, 69, 98, 109, 116, 140
Suzy Wong, vii

Tabachnick & Bloch, 67
Tachiki, 99
Tachiki et al., 68
taiko, 12
Takaki, 27, 150
Tatemae, 22
Thornton, 3, 5, 103, 170
Tobin, 22
Tobin et al., 44, 112, 115
token minority, 153, 159
Trueba, Cheng & Ima, 109

uchi, 22
Uchida, 28
ura, 22

wakaraseru, 115
war bride, 4
War Relocation Authority, 27, 145
Weglyn, 85, 104
White, 43, 107, 114, 117
WRA, 27, 145

Yamada, 96, 136, 188
Yamamoto, 20, 120
Yamamura, 41

Yanagisako, 5, 18, 39, 53, 73, 105, 137
yellow peril, vii, 3

Yonsei, vii
Yoshimura, 98, 100